A STOLEN CHILDHOOD

A STOLEN CHILDHOOD

The Life and Times of David Earl Moyer: 1895-1987

For: Sr. Nora,
Many thanks for
all the years of
friendship & support.
Enjoy!
Love
Ruth

Ruthann D. Moyer

Proceeds of this book will benefit ProjectSTEP, Boston, Massachusetts
http://www.projectSTEP.org

Library of Congress Control Number:		2008904196
ISBN:	Hardcover	978-1-4363-4178-3
	Softcover	978-1-4363-4177-6

This book was printed in the United States of America.

To order additional copies of this book, contact:
Xlibris Corporation
1-888-795-4274
www.Xlibris.com
Orders@Xlibris.com
42302

CONTENTS

In memory of my parents, Charles "Skinny" and Anastasia Power Moyer and my paternal grandparents, Vincent Cassel and Ellcora Aldred Moyer: the earliest influences in my life

and
to the future:

my grandchildren: MJ, Sean, Andrew J, PJ, Steffi, and Kaylee Carr

A Bequest of Music
penultimately and beyond—

Warmth, love, sense and charm,
forever a need.
So too renewal,
change, gift and giving,
doubt, uncertainty,
humor, pranks and fun,
these too so noted.
DM and students,
thereby so quoted!

And so too—Ruthann,
who here shares their fun,
spirit, need and charm,
forward then backward,
with such loving warmth!

Bless the author for the tireless work she has undertaken, years on end—
interviewing librarians; researching locations, residences, schools, family and city
records; speaking and writing to friends, colleagues, former students; traveling to
Vinalhaven Island plus other parts of this country, also to Europe where David
Moyer fought during World War I and to Berlin, where he studied as a child
and a young man; even walking the streets where he walked! Seemingly she left
nothing untouched.

Ruthann knows more about my own family and our lifetimes than do I.

What a story she tells!

William Moyer
Wayland, Massachusetts
February 2008

Trombonist, later Orchestra Personnel Manager
Boston Symphony Orchestra, 1952-1987

Acknowledgments

Special thanks to the following individuals and organizations who contributed archival material, memories, and assistance in the preparation of this book: descendants of David and Jessie Moyer including William Cassel Moyer, Betsy Green Moyer, Frederick Moyer, David and Jeffrey Moyer, Judy Moyer Shreiner, and Gayna Uransky. Also I would like to thank Mrs. Anna Selfridge of the Allen County Historical Society, Lima, Ohio, Jeanne Porreca, researcher of Lima, Ohio, Beatrice Ateya for her German translations, Suzanne Moulton Greig, Dr. Bernadette B. Flanagan, Michael J. Carr, Muriel Moyer Geiger Lewis, Cynthia Reber Smith, George F. Moyer, Joyce Arnold, the late Trudy Paddock, Carl and Margaret Englehart, the late Bertha Winslow, Larry Biond, John McCandless, graphic artist and Helen Doherty Morrison, reader, both of Derry, Eire, for all of their assistance in the preparation of this book.

The Stolen Child

by

W.B. Yeats, 1886

Where dips the rocky highland
Of Sleuth Wood in the lake,
There lies a leafy island
Where flapping herons wake
The drowsy water-rats;
There we've hid out faery vats,
Full of berries
And the reddest stolen cherries.
Come away, O human child!
To the waters and the wild
With a faery hand in hand,
For the world's more full of weeping than you can understand.

INTRODUCTION

David Earl Moyer is my great-uncle. He was my paternal grandfather's youngest brother. Uncle Earl, as we knew him, had an unusual childhood, even for a musical prodigy of the age in which he lived. Uncle Earl and Aunt Jessie would visit my widowed grandmother in suburban Philadelphia whenever they would make the journey from Ohio. For me, these occasions were always a mix of great excitement and anxiety. I was the one chosen by my family to be a pianist, and whenever they would visit, I had to perform for them. They were polite, gracious, and encouraging after the little performance. However, in my mind and memory, he was always the most fascinating relative I knew. He was my very own family icon, and he would have been embarrassed if he were ever made aware of that fact. This humble, charming man was so much more than what he appeared to be. My knowledge of him was simply that he was a musician and a teacher, but I never knew that in addition, he was a performing classical pianist from the age of six, a cabinet maker, a marvelous conversationalist about almost anything, and more importantly, a modest man who loved music so much that he spent his life sharing it with anyone who would listen.

Every life tells a story. Included in all life stories are, of course, the many characters that interact with the individual; these characters have the power to make or break the individual and, therefore, play a decisive role in their successes or failures. This is especially true for the child prodigy.

What is a prodigy? The standard definition is a child who achieves adult mastery by or before the age of ten.[1] That age-old definition can be more clearly stated in more modern terms: a prodigy is one who is extremely gifted within a particular domain. There have been negatives associated with the term "prodigy," but now, hopefully, they are long discarded. Prodigies, in David's day, were received publicly with great and not so great acclaim. They were seen as freaks, anomalous humans, *wunderzicklein*, and in David's case, the marvelous midget. Maestro Lorin Maazel, conductor of the New York Philharmonic Orchestra, a former musical prodigy himself, in an interview with Janos Starker, also a former child prodigy, stated that one of the problems surrounding the early prodigy was that prodigies in general were exploited by their teachers, and in some cases, their parents, by being carted around the world as a circus attraction—not going to school, not interacting with their peers and not being allowed to feel that they have a normal life."[2] This quoted statement does reflect, in our minds, the reality of David's young life, but for him, his experience of prodigy was completely normal as he never questioned or belittled it.

Educational psychologist Ellen Winner has written extensively on the subject of extraordinarily gifted children or prodigies. "A prodigy is simply a more extreme version of a gifted child, a child so gifted that he or she performs in some domain at an adult level."[3] There are three main characteristics that, according to Winner, are present in all truly gifted children: precocity, insistence on marching to their own drummer, and the ever-present "rage to master." The prodigy, accordingly, is a more extremely gifted child than the simply gifted child.[4]

There is no documentary evidence that David's parents had ever suspected, before the arrival of a potential boarder, Mary Halter Walsh, that David possessed any hidden talent for music. However, it is possible that David's parents did recognize something different or distinctive about their youngest boy without being able to identify or put their finger on just exactly what it was. Mary Walsh's involvement or intervention was absolutely critical in bringing David's potential to light at such a young age. His ability to replay what Mary had just performed at the piano gave his parents their first evidence of David's natural musical ability. Mary's delight in this phenomenon and her interpretation of its significance in terms of what she could do with it and what it could do for her must have been exciting. The revelation that they could witness must have been a cause of great joy for his parents. His distinctive difference was now clear, and they understood and appreciated for the first time when his gift lay open before them. The big question then arises. What led them to freely surrender David's childhood and development to this woman, newly arrived in their lives?

Some of the answer must surely lie in Ida and Joseph Moyer's mind-set formed from their own experiences and rooted in the deep biblical faith from their childhood communities. To them, David's talent, ultimately, was God's gift, and a gift, in their Christian belief system, was to be fostered for the service of God and the community. Making music was also an integral and central element in much Christian worship. The Moyers must have felt some religious imperative to help David advance his learning and his gift. Mary had, in the minds of Joseph and Ida, uncovered his vocation, and in the estimation of the Moyers, certainly with Mary's enthusiasm and encouragement, they judged that she possessed the skills and the know-how to guide David's musical development. To the Moyers, she must have seemed the agent sent as a guide at the proper moment in the appropriate context.

Mary Halter Walsh was a much more complex and paradoxical person than the Moyers could have ever known at the time of their decision. However, the combination of Mary's personal ambitions and her impressive skills of salesmanship and organization, together with the Moyers' simple but sincere conservative religious and subcultural background, go a long way in setting the early direction of David's fascinating formative years. It is also very important to recognize that David was happy with his newfound talent and with his mentor.

Another instance of the Moyers' strict adherence to the social/cultural/religious precepts learned in their communities of origin can be seen in the fact that they never owned any of the five homes in Philadelphia, where they lived.[5] In order to purchase a home, they more than likely would have had to borrow money that bore with it interest to be paid to the lender. This was forbidden by the Mennonites and Bible-based texts such as Deuteronomy 23:19, "You shall not charge interest to your countrymen: interest on money, food, or anything that may be loaned at interest" and Psalm 15:5, "He does not put out his money at interest, nor does he take a bribe against the innocent. He who does these things will never be shaken." Also, the Schwenkfelders believed in the separateness of male and female roles in the marriage. "The handling of money, clearly beyond the common activities of Schwenkfelder women, required male authority."[6] The borrowing of money other than for the purpose of actual survival and only from members of their own communities was, therefore, verboten!

The Moyers probably should have investigated other ways that David could have progressed with his music and continued to live in their own home under their parenting influence, but they did not. Joseph and Ida were obviously taken in by Mary and her mentoring relationship with their son, and from then on, they followed her lead, and basically, they surrendered their parenting role of David to someone who was little more than a very talented lodger. Mary took not only David but added two boys from an orphanage in the Bowery of New York to complete her dream known only to her. Two more childhoods were then lost as well.

David's early life as a prodigy was unique. In *Musical Prodigies: Perilous Journeys, Remarkable Lives*, Claude Kenneson traces the lives of thirty-six prodigies and their families from Mozart to Bejun Mehta. In his study, there were no prodigies that were sent off on their own at less than age six to study with a teacher or mentor without the family moving with them. For some families, this caused financial hardship, but in spite of that, they still managed to move house and home to gain the expertise necessary for their prodigy to succeed, however always under their daily supervision.

Artur Rubinstein left his family home in Lodz, Poland, at age ten with his mother for the final audition with Maestro Joseph Joachim in Berlin, Germany. He was accepted for study with Joachim and with some of the other greats in Berlin at that time. Young Artur stayed in Berlin for six years without his mother!

However, he did have a sister that resided in the same city during his early years in Berlin. Lodz was accessible to him and his parents by train. This was very different from David's situation where many times, there were thousands of miles between him and his family. Prior to Artur's acceptance by Joachim, the Rubinstein's had made direct contact with the musical masters of the day in both Warsaw and Berlin to investigate the best possibilities for musical education for their child. They did not rely on advice from willy-nilly strangers where they lost both contact and influence with their child and his young life. In addition, there were two conditions made by Joachim if he was to take responsibility for their son's musical education: they had to promise not to exploit his prodigious talents publicly and to ensure that Artur received a full education until he was artistically mature. According to Rubinstein, they complied fully with the conditions Joachim laid out for them, and Artur was always grateful for his parents' compliance.[7]

The challenge to any biographer is to keep constantly before one's mind the whole life of the subject in tandem with the many events that compose that life. While the parts come together to make up the whole, the whole, in its own way, illuminates the significance of the many different events in a developing life. David Moyer's life is no exception to this requirement.

From his humble beginnings in Philadelphia, Pennsylvania, to the world stage as a performing child prodigy, David Earl Moyer's commitment to excellence in everything he basically put his hands to—whether it was his own study of music in his youth, his service in World War I, model airplane building, cabinet making or performing for heads of state, teaching about music to just about anyone who was interested, as well as being the most dedicated of students himself—it is the man he became that was so endearing to all who knew him.

David, the fourth child and fourth son of Ida Cassel Moyer and Joseph Allebach Moyer, was born April 29, 1895, in Philadelphia. David's very early life began the same way as all of us began. Nothing remarkable is noted about his origins. Born at home to his parents and three older brothers, life was simple: family, hearth, home, and God Almighty were the well-established values in the Moyer household. David's story is astonishing, not only for his early talent, but as the story develops he travels far and wide to perform, he studies in Germany, begins a college teaching career, serves in World War I and eventually becomes a full professor of pianoforte at the very well respected Oberlin Conservatory of Music in Ohio. In retrospect, it becomes clear that the original decision of his parents to leave the Pennsylvania Mennonite farming community of Lower Salford, Montgomery County, Pennsylvania, on the day of their marriage in 1885 set the stage for experiences and opportunities that may never have been possible had they stayed on that farm within the bosom of the Mennonite/Schwenkfelder family. It was the first of several unconventional decisions they would make for themselves and their children.

CHAPTER I

Beginnings and Connections

David's ancestry is one that reflects two religious traditions: the Mennonites and the Schwenkfelders. The first of David's maternal ancestors to arrive in America was Johannes Kassel or Cassel, a Mennonite, in 1686.[8] Johannes was born and raised in Kriegsheim in the Palatinate (Palatinate of the Rhine, a state of the Holy Roman Empire) of Germany. The history of the Palatinate reflects a land area and a population that rarely had any continuity, political or religious. In the sixteenth century alone, the region and its people had to change their religion five times because the ruler of the area changed. The age-old concept of *cuius regio, ejus religio* prevailed, i.e., the regional ruler determined the regional religion. In 1544, the elector Louis V was in full support of Catholic doctrine; 1556-1559 Lutheran beliefs were instituted under Frederick II and Otto Henry; the Reform movement became the state religion under Frederick II in 1576 and reverted back to Lutheranism under Louis VI in 1583; and once again, the Reform movement was reinstituted under ruler John Kasimer in 1592.

This erratic shifting of politics and religion provided the platform for the Anabaptist movement to gain a rather solid foothold and continued to develop among the populous regardless of the strength of the resistance of the various rulers who tried to safeguard against it. Anabaptism, literally meaning "rebaptism," does not fully characterize the belief system of these people. They vehemently rejected the practice of infant baptism, but celebrated adult baptism as the central experience of faith in God and Jesus Christ. Coupled with this commitment, they interpreted the gospel in a stringent, literal fashion reflected in an unadorned, simple, and somewhat self-contained and self-sufficient way of life. It was their biblical ethical way of living community life that marked their distinctiveness and defined them as a separately identifiable Christian movement.

The Mennonites, influenced by Menno Simmons and his teachings in Holland, completely rejected the traditional Catholic ideal that the sacrament of baptism could be validly administered to infants and children. He drew on the precepts of the Swiss Baptists that silent prayer by adults and the individual and evangelical preaching to the community were the keys to the grace necessary for salvation. Although he wasn't the founder of this Anabaptist movement, his name became so associated with it that a separate sect established itself and the followers referred to themselves as Mennonites. This sect of the Anabaptist tradition lived simply and dressed plainly and without affectation. They were good farmers and prospered while in the Palatinate but faced persecution by the various rulers because of their religious ideals and the obvious violation of the civil law of the time that dictated that all persons must follow the established church of the region.

In 1671, the English/Dutch Quaker, William Penn, began traveling and preaching as a layman throughout Europe.[9] His basic theme was freedom for all men from state control over religious matters and matters of conscience. He became very popular as a preacher and made subsequent trips to the Palatinate since he was well aware of how the Anabaptists and Quakers suffered under present rule. He arrived in Kriesheim August 23, 1681, and had all intentions of preaching to a very interested group. His intentions were thwarted by a Calvinist minister and enforced by the local bailiff's deputy residing in Kriesheim.[10] In response to this government ban, a "silent meeting" was held six miles away in Worms where many of the original groups traveled to hear him. A silent meeting is a "traditional Quaker form of worship, and is designed to facilitate the direct inspiration of the Inner Light . . . one in which the people meet in silence and only speak when they feel the Spirit of God is actually motivating them to speak."[11] The following Sunday, August 26, William Penn once again appealed to the ruler, Count Karl Ludwig, for permission to preach, and this time, it was granted. Penn was at last able to speak to the people of Kriesheim, and he preached in a local barn to those interested people.[12] In attendance at this meeting were Yellis Cassel and his two sons, Johannes and Heinrich Cassel, and other members of the Mennonite community who became even more inspired by hearing Penn in person and continued the dialogue with him after the preaching. It appears from the literature available that it was at this meeting that Penn informed the Cassels and others in attendance that "he had a large tract of land in America where the conscientiously scrupulous could settle and enjoy their religious opinions without restraint."[13]

A few years later, in March 1686, Johannes Cassel, accompanied by his wife and his five children along with other Mennonites, left the Palatinate and sailed to Philadelphia. The journey took the usual seven months, and when they arrived on November 20, 1686, they settled in what was then known as the Borough of

Germantown, a borough of Philadelphia.[14] Johannes was a weaver by trade and became involved in the civic affairs of his new community. There was already established in Germantown a Mennonite Community, and Johannes joined them immediately. He was known for his participation in civic affairs as one of the first signatories on the application for a charter for the borough and served as a committee member of the First Council of Germantown. Johannes died in 1691 in Germantown at the age of fifty-two.[15]

In a taped conversation, David, in his later years, at the dinner table one night in January 1975, had his own way of explaining to his son and grandchildren, in the most affectionate way, how his ancestral family came to America:

> The Moyer family along with many other families had been brought over from Europe by William Penn who had interviewed the people along the Rhine, people who were rather religious but were dissatisfied with the government there. They were somewhat like Quakers but a little different strain. So it was William Penn in the late 1600's who went along the Rhine telling those people, "Come to America. We've got exactly the same kind of country you have here in the Rhineland." And it was absolutely—rolling hills just like the Rhineland. And beautiful farmland, a reddish clay soil. William Penn dickered with the Indians to buy the land and of course cheated the devil out of them. He'd give them a string of beads and buy a hundred acres.[16]

While David related the story of his ancestral migration in this rather colorful streamlined way, it probably represents the way he learned family history through oral tradition as a young child. His own maternal grandfather, David Metz Cassel, on his visits to the Cassel farm probably couched the tradition in a very vivid, concretely detailed, and picturesque fashion to grip the attention and to fascinate the ears of his grandchildren. The practice of embellishing the essence of the story by using some non-historical facts or altering or adding details indelibly fixes the core of the tradition in young receptive minds. Possibly in the grandfather's own childhood, these details had already been incorporated into the stream of the family story. On the Cassel side of David's family, he is listed as the 449th descendant of the original Cassel family in America.[17]

The other side of David's maternal ancestry is the Kriebel (Kribel) family. At the time of the Kriebel family immigration, Silesia was under the control of Austria. We believe the progenitor of this family, Caspar Kriebel, was born in Deutmansdorf, Lower Silesia, around 1650. Later, the family moved to Hapersdorf where he met and married Anna Borman with whom he had five children. The two youngest sons, Melchior, born 1680, and Christoph, born 1688, as well as their older sister, Susanna, immigrated in 1734 to Pennsylvania and settled in

Map of Montgomery County, Pennsylvania, 1884

Towamencin, Montgomery County. The first land grant in Towamencin Township was from William Penn's commissioners to Benjamin Furley on June 8, 1703.[18] Local history of the area suggests that the name Towamencin, American Indian in origin, actually means "Poplar Tree."[19] However, legend also suggests that when Heinrich Fry bought his land near the creek, there was an Indian village nearby, and when the local chief observed two white men clearing trees near the creek, he supposedly said "Towha-men-seen,"[20] meaning "two white men seen." This explanation appears to be widely accepted by local historians, and it's probably as good any.

The map of Montgomery County, Pennsylvania, of 1884 shows that Towamencin is located almost exactly in the center of the county. This fertile, rich land was ideal for the farming immigrants from Europe, who sought new lives in peace and freedom of religion. What makes the Kriebels unique to this area is that in 1734 they were among the first group of Schwenkfelder immigrants to arrive in Pennsylvania.

The Schwenkfelders, founded by Caspar Schwenkfeld, a reformer and nobleman (1489-1561), "attracted both the rich and poor in his personal campaign for the true expression of the apostolic Word."[21] Schwenkfeld's main emphasis was on the biblical texts that brought him a new understanding of the real purpose of religion which he taught to others. He was an ordained Roman Catholic priest but decided that there was a better way to achieve salvation than adhering to theories and dogmas. He realized early that there was a sociology involved in the practice of religion, and he brought attention to the poor living conditions of the peasants and paved the way for some social improvements.[22] His views were different from other reform-minded attitudes of his era. A clear understanding of the sacraments and spiritual renewal were necessary for every individual. He became involved in many of the theological controversies of his day; however, he never became involved in disparaging or vilifying his adversaries personally. He believed that the Christian lifestyle emanated in every aspect of the individual's life as a Christian and not just as external behavior put on or adopted for temporary special occasions.[23] Baptism, whether as an infant or an adult, was still an area of controversy among reformers and traditionalists of the time. In this way, Schwenkfeld was in sympathy with the other Anabaptist groups, but he did not believe there was a need for a physical rebaptism. He was convinced that the idea of inner conviction toward Christian living was more essential, and he himself was never re-baptized as an adult. Schwenkfeld taught his followers that if others desired this rebaptism, then they should be permitted this ceremonial action. More important was his conviction that the power of change in the individual rested entirely on his or her personal commitment to Jesus Christ.[24] Schwenkfeld by his rather radical views alienated most of the other reformers of his time as well as the Church of Rome. His flocks of followers were forced to flee the persecutions they were enduring for the sake of their beliefs. They found themselves a scattered people in Silesia, Bohemia, Moravia, Swabia, Switzerland, Italy, and Holland. By 1700, most followers of Schwenkfeld were found only in the Gorlitz and Liegnitz sections of Silesia. In 1720, the emperor Charles VI, through a Jesuit mission formed solely for the purpose of ridding the area of these rebellious peoples, decided on total extermination for this rather small group of one thousand five hundred that remained in the already-mentioned areas of Silesia. These long-suffering peoples were not permitted to sell their goods, their lands, to emigrate or to have a Christian burial once they had been hunted down and killed.[25] Many of the Schwenkfelders fled to Saxony for a short time where they found refuge at Berthelsdorf. After approximately a year, they were ordered to leave and were determined to go to America where they believed they would be certain of religious freedom. It is interesting to note that like the Amish, it was the entire religious group that moved on to Pennsylvania; in other words, none was left behind to further face the extermination attempts of the established churches and the civil princes. These once-hunted people (all two hundred of them representing forty families) from Silesia then traveled to Rotterdam, Holland, and boarded a ship that left the port of Rotterdam on the evening of June 28, 1734. Some sympathetic Christians in Holland provided their passage at the time.

Douglas Wiegner in his *Journey to the New World* quotes from his own ancestor Christopher Wiegner's diary describing this rather treacherous crossing. "There was the horrible reality of summer winds, storms, sea sickness suffered by the daring travelers; frightening meetings with other ships and the death of seven people out of approximately 200 who set sail from Rotterdam."[26] During this journey, they spent eleven days on board the ship while docked at Plymouth, England. It was in Plymouth that Christopher Wiegner mentioned "going to the town to refresh our bodies," and two days after arrival there, a woman gave them some money.[27] By September 24, 1734, the small band of settlers arrived in Philadelphia. Ever since that date of arrival the Schwenkfelders have celebrated that day as *Gedachtniss Tag*[28] or *Remembrance Day* as their personal thanksgiving to God Himself for surviving the journey from their beloved Silesia and a celebration of the freedom to practice their religion in safety in the New World. Upon arrival, the Schwenkfelders were assisted by the Dutch or Holland Mennonites with financial support and gradually began to establish their small community as farmers.

Once in safe surroundings, different family members began the process of recording their family histories and gathering their religious literature, and by 1753, they developed a regular system of religious meetings in private homes. There was no such thing as a ministry officer or minister, so the heads of the families conducted religious services in one another's houses. These people had such a long-suffering history of being hunted that they appeared to hide for their first fifty years in Pennsylvania. They built no meetinghouses or churches although they did set up schools for their children. It wasn't until 1762 that they published their first hymnal and catechism. Their hymn book was printed for them by Christopher Sauer, a printer in Germantown, and in it were a number of hymns composed by Caspar Schwenkfeld as well as a few borrowed from the Brethren, another Anabaptist movement and from the Moravians. It took until 1782 for this sect to establish itself as a separate church. Originally a people of peace and simplicity, they lived out what they interpreted the Gospel message of the Christian life to be. The Schwenkfelders were good neighbors to others outside of their own communities and allowed burial of non-Schwenkfelders in their graveyards. One prohibition, however, was the intermarriage of Schwenkfelders and Roman Catholics. This prohibition would create a crisis of immense proportions in the lives of David's family. Although pacifist in their orientation, over time they did involve themselves in wars fighting for their new country. These plain and simple people, like many of the Moravians, Quakers, and Mennonites, eventually assimilated into American culture. Their plain and simple attitudes can be found among those who still live on the lands their ancestors founded. David Moyer was the 661st descendant of this line.[29]

Concerning David's paternal ancestry, the first to immigrate to the new land of America was Christian Allebach in 1719. Christian, son of Peter Allebach, was born in Baden-Württemberg, Germany, about 1680. He immigrated to the Philadelphia area from Crefield near the Dutch border in 1719 with his first wife Maria Ann Friedt Grater and their four children. According to the Pennsylvania Archives, it was other colonists that requested that he come and establish a cloth-making business as he was an expert weaver.[30] The well-recorded genealogy of the Stauffer family informs us that "the name of Allebach is common in Montgomery County, Pennsylvania"; however, it was not common in terms of other immigrants from 1727 until 1775 from the Germanic regions in the new colonies.[31] It appears from the data available that all Allebachs are descendants of the same Christian Allebach.

By 1730, Christian Allebach was a well-established landowner and was involved in the local Mennonite community. There are records available that he signed a petition to the then governor of Pennsylvania dated May 20, 1728, asking that the residents of Skippack receive some Commonwealth protection from feared Indian attacks.[32] Christian's first wife, Maria, died in 1745, and he married Elizabeth Godshall the following year. Shortly after their marriage, at age sixty-six, Christian succumbed to death himself. In his will, in addition to providing for his wife Elizabeth and his eight children, he left provision for his "child yet to be born."[33] The Allebach line that David Moyer descends is from

Christian's third child, David, who was born about 1717 in Skippack, Montgomery County, Pennsylvania. David was the 115th descendant of this line.[34]

David's other paternal family line, the one that gave to him his surname, all hailed from the village of Bern in Switzerland. The Reverend Peter Moar (Swiss spelling)—Meyer and Moyer (both German spellings for the same family)—immigrated to the new colonies in 1741.[35] Peter was the second child of five born to his parents. The most accurate information dates the year of his birth as 1723. Peter, at age eighteen, was already a minister of the Mennonite Church and experienced the sufferings imposed on him and his flock of brethren by the Calvinists of the state-sponsored reformed church. Around 1740, Peter led his widowed mother (name unknown) older sister (no name recorded, b. 1720) and three younger brothers, William b. 1725, Jacob b. 1728, and Henry b. 1733, across Switzerland to the Palatinate of Germany and remained with friends in the general vicinity of Kerbach for approximately a year before setting sail to America.[36] He must have been a very capable young man to set out with his family on this journey to a new land that offered religious freedom for all. We have no supporting documentation as to the ship on which they traveled or port of arrival, but it has been surmised that they landed in Philadelphia and made their way to an already-established Mennonite community in Springfield Township, Bucks County, Pennsylvania. Reverend Meyer (Moar/Moyer) continued his preaching and farming in Bucks County, married, and fathered fourteen children, three of whom died very young.[37] Peter died at his farm in Springfield Township, Bucks County, Pennsylvania in 1800.[38]

It is from Rev. Peter Meyer's son, Johannes (John), born November 2, 1757, that David Earl is descendant.[39] Johannes married Elizabeth Detweiler, and after their marriage, they took over the old Detweiler homestead in the adjoining county of Montgomery where they lived in an old log cabin that had been used as a Mennonite meetinghouse before the Franconia Meetinghouse was built.[40] Johannes owned three hundred acres of land, which he divided into three farms for three of his sons, one of whom was Jacob Detweiler Meyer, great-grandfather of David Earl. Jacob's profession is listed as tailor, and not farmer.[41] The use of either Meyer or Moyer is not known, but all of Johannes's children are listed as Moyer, and not Meyer.[42]

It is at this time in the family lineage that the maiden name of the mother (Landis in this case) appeared as the second name of every child born. All seven of Jacob's children, both male and female, have the second name of Landis.[43] Jacob's second son, William Landis Moyer, born April 8, 1820, was to become the father of Joseph Allebach Moyer, the father of David Earl and his three older brothers.[44] The occupation of this branch of the Moyer family was predominantly that of farmer while several served as preachers in addition to farming. The Mennonites had large families, and all members of the household had their assigned duties reflecting the Mennonite tradition. The women and girls worked in the fields next to the men during harvest time while still being responsible for preparing the meals and keeping the home in spotless condition. Both Mennonites and Schwenkfelders insisted that the girls of the home also be taught sewing and other domestic work. Schooling for all the children only ran for a five-month term to allow necessary time for the children to help with the planting and harvesting in the respective seasons of the year. Education of the children was paramount for the Mennonites. The school building was generally erected before the church building, and when the church was built, it was usually attached to the Mennonite school building or, at least, erected nearby. Many times, the church building style resembled that of a large barn more than a traditional church-style building. One reason for this architectural choice was that more members of the community could attend services at one time in this type of building than could be accommodated in a more traditional-style church. The schoolmaster was selected from the local community and was paid accordingly for his services.[45]

This brief overview of David's ancestry reflects the deep ethos of a people who endured bitter persecution in Europe. They had the courage and confidence to undertake a treacherous journey to a strange land with a strange language, and they valiantly turned the danger of extinction into a life of faith and dignity. In the case of the Schwenkfelders, they saw in William Penn a prophet of a new future, and they placed their trust in his ideals and invitation to a new life.[46] David's ancestors, once in America, lived a secluded life in reasonably small isolated communities, not really striving for economic wealth or fame or fortune. They were happy to be in a place where they could raise their families in peace among their neighbors whom they trusted and who shared their religious ideals and values. Yes, they can be well described as simple folk without pretense or affect; they were gentle people, albeit firm, about what they wanted for themselves and their children.

CHAPTER II

The Philadelphia History

Joseph Moyer and Ida Cassel, prior to the marriage, had decided to leave the farming community of Towamencin and settle in the city of Philadelphia. They both hailed from farming families and were well aware that there really wasn't enough land for them to have a successful family farm. Farmland was passed from parents to several children; therefore, the farming land available to each family member became smaller and smaller over the years. According to David, "They didn't want to farm anymore. "The farm had run down somewhat."[47] Joseph and Ida were married in the tradition of the Schwenkfelders at the Cassel farm in Lower Salford, Montgomery County, Pennsylvania, on Thanksgiving Day, November 26, 1885. After the wedding ceremony, attended by the bride and groom, two witnesses from the community, and the minister, a large reception was held by the two families and the larger congregation. Substantial refreshments were served to the guests who attended in the barn as it was the only place large enough for the community to gather. For these very large celebrations, the bride's family prepared the food, and the guests ate in shifts since few families would have had enough dishes and utensils to feed everyone at once.[48] The happy wedded couple began their journey to Philadelphia where Joseph had already rented a house at 3532 Warren Street.[49]

The Blockley area of Philadelphia (Powelton Village in the modern era), where Joseph and Ida resided, has had an interesting and unique history. In our present time, the name Powelton Village is used to describe this area, which is part and parcel of Philadelphia's University City where the two large universities Drexel University and the University of Pennsylvania are located.[50] Their house was large, more than adequate for the new bride and groom and their future children—mansard roofed and stone structured three stories, six bedrooms, two living rooms, dining room, kitchen, and no indoor bathroom.

Blockley was a modernized residential and industrial area in the latter 1800s compared to its early origins as a ferry port for the Schuylkill River that bounded the area on the east side. The noted local popular historian, Leon Rosenthal, in 1963 referred to Powelton as "the town that never was."[51] In 1682, William Penn, the founder of Pennsylvania, gave his permission for the development of a ferry service across the Schuylkill River at Market Street (originally known as High Street) so residents of Blockley could have access to goods on the other side of the river. The original owner of this ferry service, a Mr. England, rarely kept to any set schedule and wasn't at all impressed that his duty as a ferry operator was for the convenience of his passengers and not just a wealth increaser for himself. Others tried unsuccessfully to compete with England in operating ferry services to no avail.[52] However, about 1700, one of England's competitors, a Mr. Powel, finally gained the necessary permission to run his ferry across the Schuylkill River and also built a fine large tavern with overnight accommodation for the drovers and others taking their animals and farm goods to the abattoirs and markets on the other side of the river. The Powel family amassed a great sum of money from this ferry business and from running the tavern. They were later to be considered one of the wealthier families in the area surrounding Philadelphia.

As time went on, ownership of the ferry business and tavern moved on from the Powel family, and several other families owned and operated the ferry and tried their hands at building various makeshift bridges across the Schuylkill. The Commonwealth of Pennsylvania's legislature ordered that a more permanent covered bridge be erected, and the architect Lewis Wernwag was commissioned to carry out this endeavor in 1812-13.[53] The bridge, made originally of wood by Wernwag, lasted only a few years, and in the end, it is believed that a deliberately set fire caused its final destruction in 1838.[54] An attempt in 1842 was made by Charles Ellet to erect a wire suspension bridge at the request of the local commissioners of the district now known as Spring Garden.[55] Over time, even this wire suspension bridge deteriorated, and traffic across the Schuylkill was again interrupted. By 1875 a new bridge, (double decked) and constructed of stone, was completed and given the name "Spring Garden Street Bridge." This same bridge is still in operation today.[56]

A descendent of the original Powel family, J. Hare Powel, had erected a stately mansion on land that had once belonged to the English banking family known as Baring. As stated by Rosenthal (1963): "The imposing front of the mansion was adorned with massive granite columns and its lawn extended down to the river."[57] The Powel family and other successful families built estates in this area as summer retreats to escape the heat and filth of Philadelphia during this time. As the eighteenth century progressed, more and more developers bought land in this area and built houses of different sizes and styles, but most were large homes for large families built in the Italianate style. The Powel family by 1852 had sold most of their lands to the Pennsylvania Railroad, and the remainder was sold off to developers where many houses were built, most probably between 1869 and 1890. [58] The majority of residents in this area, at the time Joseph and Ida took up residency, were of German heritage, so Joseph's and Ida's German-accented English was more than likely acceptable and understandable by many they encountered.

The area was busy as most urban neighborhoods were at this time when Joseph and Ida set about organizing their new home. Joseph worked for a produce company and drove a delivery wagon. In time, he would come to own his own produce business supplying fresh grown items purchased from the farmers where he and Ida had been raised and selling them to shops in the city. Ida busied herself with household chores, renting some of the bedrooms to lodgers while engaging in dressmaking for clients as well as caring for her expanding family.[59] Ida's younger sister Elizabeth moved in with Joseph and Ida before their first child arrived so she could learn the dressmaking trade from her older sister. For Joseph and Ida, this arrangement was acceptable even though they were just newly married. Family relationships were paramount to these people. Together, Joseph and Ida made ends meet and lived a simple life, continuing the tradition of their respective communities of origin. Ida was the eldest of her parents' children, seven born in all, so she was well experienced in housekeeping and childrearing. After Ida and Joseph married, her parents, David and Amanda Kriebel Cassel, had two more children born in 1886 and 1889.

Within two years of their marriage, the first child, a boy, arrived. Vincent Cassel Moyer was born October 2, 1887; thirteen months later, a second son, Wilmer Cassel Moyer, was born November 5, 1888; two years and five months later, number 3 son, Townsend Cassel Moyer, arrived April 30, 1891; and David Earl Moyer, the youngest son, was born April 29, 1895, and the Moyer household was completed.

The houses here are similar to the house where David Moyer was born.
Photo: Courtesy of Larry Biond

Ida returned to her parents' home to birth the first three children as did many married women in those days. David, however, was born in Philadelphia, not in Montgomery County as his brothers had been. The Mennonite tradition of giving the children the mother's maiden name as the child's second name or middle name is important to Mennonite genealogy. Families, multiple groups of Moyers, Cassels, Schwenks, Kriebels, Oberholtzers, Hartranfts, Yeakels, Schultzs, and Dreshers needed to be aware of their blood relations so that marriages would not take place among those related too closely. David's name was different: he never was given the middle name of Cassel. David remedied this situation with his own family by giving his youngest son, William, the middle name of Cassel. According to his memoirs recorded and transcribed in January, 1975, by his son and daughter-in-law (William Cassel Moyer and Betsy Green Moyer), David, then aged eighty, gives a reasonable explanation for this departure in the name chosen for him:

> Ma felt very bad about that (lack of Cassel as a middle name) because they gave me the name of Earl since my older brothers liked that name. A silly reason, but anyway that was it.[60]

Within the immediate Moyer family circle, David was always referred to and called Earl, not David. This changed with the arrival of Mrs. Mary Walsh to the Moyer household. It wasn't until years later that his extended family found out that his name was actually David, and not Earl. To bear this out, a letter has survived from his first cousin Edward Reber written to David, May 13, 1984, to inform David that their aunt Ms. Emma Cassel, aged ninety-five, had passed away. The letter begins "Dear Earl."[61]

David Earl Moyer about 1900, Philadelphia, Pa.
Photo: Courtesy of Moyer Family Archives

CHAPTER III

Mary Walsh

According to David's own description of his early life, his family's circumstances changed drastically, though subtly, in 1900 when he

> was about five when a woman came to our door—a total stranger. She said to my folks, "Through the window . . . while I was walking by I saw a nice piano in your living room."[62]

David's mother, Ida, used to play the piano, "a bit-hymns" while his father, Joseph's, hobby was also church music. Joseph knew nothing about music, according to David, but he did sing in a church choir; "maybe through instinct, he could read a part. He must have taught himself . . . he wasn't bad . . . singing baritone or almost bass."[63] The Mennonite community did not have musical accompaniment with their hymns. They were all sung a cappella by the congregation.

> I'm going to start a studio in this neighborhood, and I'm looking for a place to live, a piano, and children who might be interested in taking music lessons, [64]

announced this woman, Mrs. Mary Walsh, through the open window of the Moyer house where she stood. David's parents thought this was a good idea for their boys to learn music, and the fact that they had such a large four-story house, they had rooms to rent to this woman and said, "Yes."[65]

Until the arrival of Mrs. Walsh to the Moyer home, there is no evidence that David or his brothers were anything but conventional, happy, active children. David's three brothers did attend the local elementary school and played sports in the summer's warm weather. According to David, he only attended school for six months.[66] However, David's life began to change and his future to unfold as he demonstrated a propensity for the piano in response to Mrs. Walsh's teaching. His three older brothers also took music lessons from this woman but didn't seem to progress too far because they were involved in sports, according to David. However, his oldest brother, Vincent, progressed at least to the point where his parents invested in a rather beautiful well-crafted violin that is still in the possession of his eldest granddaughter, Muriel Moyer Geiger Lewis.

Mrs. Mary Walsh was the woman's name (or so the Moyer family was told), and she was from Lima, Ohio. According to her, "her family was in the oil business and they were fairly well to do people."[67]

Mary was a fluent speaker of the German language and so were Joseph and Ida Moyer. In both the Mennonite and Schwenkfelder traditions, the speaking of German was significant in keeping their cultural heritage alive, and it was the women who had the major responsibility for maintaining German in their lives. The men were not held as responsible for preservation of culture as the women were since their work as farmers required contacts outside the community, causing them to speak as much English as was necessary for economic success.[68]

> At that time, she was just Mrs. Walsh. After a year or two in our home, she had become almost not an American but an international person. She spoke German, French, Italian, of course English, and with the greatest of ease—she was one of those individuals who could pick up languages quickly. She had lived quite a while in Europe.

> We got to know her quite well. There was oil at one time in Ohio—now gas. Their family name was Walsh. When she was a young girl her parents had sent her to Europe for an education. She studied with Hans Barth—he was the Director of the Hochschule in Berlin and was the teacher of Artur Rubinstein. She knew Joachim and all those famous, famous people. She even met Brahms at that time.[69] [A lapsus linguae or perhaps a transcription error: it was actually Heinrich Barth about whom David was speaking.]

According to photographic records of the period, Mary Walsh only spent about nine months or less in the Moyer household. At almost age eighty, David can be forgiven for a few inaccuracies. Mary Walsh may have known of a few of the musical geniuses of her time, but it is highly unlikely that she in fact "knew" these people as David stated. Research into this woman and her background reveals a somewhat different person than the one she presented to the Moyer family. First, her family name was not Walsh. She was born Mary Belinda (Linn)

Halter to Johannes Andrew Halter and Mary Baker Giessey in Southampton, Cumberland County, Pennsylvania, in 1858. Thorough searches of passenger and immigration lists state that the first time this woman entered the United States from anywhere in the world was in August 1903 when she arrived in the United States aboard the *Phoenicia 2* from Cuxhaven, Germany. The passenger record states her name as Mary Halter; "Ethnicity" is listed as American German; "Last Place of Residence": New York; her "Age at Arrival" is forty-three years, and her marital status is listed as (M) for married. The fact that she listed herself as two years younger than she actually was is forgivable since many women of that period didn't want to admit to any particular age. It is unreasonable to assume that she was truthful to the Moyers regarding her own training in Europe. Travel records in and out of New York City, whether going to or returning from Europe for the period when she would have studied do not show her being listed, and her family's lack of finances lead to one conclusion. These statements by Mary were nothing more than pure fantasy. David's parents were not sophisticated, cosmopolitan people. They were from simple farming stock. They may have taken up residence in the city, but at heart, they were still simple farming people. More than likely, they had never heard of Joachim and Barth or the Hochschule für Musik in Berlin, Germany.

Mary's ancestry was combined German and Swiss with a bit of English Puritan added to the mix. Her ancestors appear to have been honest, hard-working people, all from immigrant stock much like David's ancestry. The ancestral line from her maternal grandmother, Elizabeth Mary Cable (Kobel), has been recorded with a continuous lineage dating from 1385 with the birth of Albrecht Kobel in Wenger, Switzerland. The first ancestor of this Cable (Kobel) family to immigrate to the United States appears to be Philip Kobell (Kobel), born in Switzerland c. 1700. We do not have evidence of the exact year of his immigration; however, his first five children were all born in Switzerland while his sixth child, named Saloma, was born in Pennsylvania.[70]

According to U.S. Census records, Mary's father, Johannes Andrew Halter (called Andrew), was born in 1824 to a family of Pennsylvania farmers in Southampton.[71] There are at least five Southamptons in Pennsylvania; the one referred to here is in Cumberland County, approximately a hundred miles south of Harrisburg, Pennsylvania, in the south central area of the state. Andrew Halter busied himself with his trade of saddlery in addition to working his small farm. From census records of that time, it appears there was little money in the family. Andrew died in 1859 in Mansfield, Ohio,[72] and left his wife with four small children to care for on her own in Pennsylvania: Virtue Amelia, born 1850; Ellen, born 1852; John, born 1853; and Mary Belinda, born 1858. There are no records to show why Andrew was in Ohio at the time of his death. He may have been working at his trade as a saddler when he was stricken with the dreaded typhoid fever that took his life. In an unpublished biography by local Lima author Mary Belle Linnell about Mrs. Virtue Amelia Halter Davis, Mary's eldest sister, Virtue Amelia, informs us that the Halter family arrived in Lima in 1863 when she was twelve years old. [73] The Federal Census for Cumberland County, Pennsylvania, for 1860 lists Andrew's farm as worth $70.00.[74] However, in 1873 Mrs. Mary Halter, widow of Andrew, filed final legal papers with the courthouse in Lima accounting for the amount of $270.76 from her husband's estate and demonstrated to the court how she had spent that money to raise her children.[75] The spending power of the $270.76 in 1860 would represent a spending power of $ 6,324.36 in 2005.[76] Andrew was thirty-five years of age, and his young wife, Mary, was thirty-two when he died. Mrs. Mary Baker Giessey Halter seems to have settled into life in Lima quite easily with her young growing family. We have no information regarding relatives already in Lima that may have assisted her. Census records for Southampton, Cumberland County, Pennsylvania for 1860 do not list her and her children as living there. Maybe, they moved in with other family members in Cumberland County at the time, or the farm was missed entirely in the federal census that year.

Halter Homestead, Lima, Ohio, 1868
Photo: Courtesy of Allen County Historical Museum

This small group of five Halters first appears in the census of 1870 in Lima, Ohio, where the third daughter, Mary Belinda, is listed as being twelve years old and at school. It appears from the photo above that the Halters lived in a large wooden house in Lima in October 1863. The American nation was at war at this time. The Civil War was well underway and travel must have been dangerous. It is likely that they traveled by train from nearby Somerset, Pennsylvania, as there was a large B & O Railway station there in 1863. In 1853, there were trains served by eleven railroads running from Chicago to the East and back, and in 1860, there were a hundred trains a day.[77] Train travel for this small group was probably the only feasible way to get to where they wanted to go.

Mrs. Mary Halter successfully managed to own and run a large boardinghouse in Lima for most of her life after 1870.[78] It is not feasible that a widow with four young children whose deceased husband had a total of $270.76 (including the value of his real estate) at the time of his death in 1859 would be able to move her family and their belongings the distance from Southampton to Lima, Ohio, and once there, establish herself. Be that as it may, Mary Baker Halter did just that! The 1860 census for Lima, reveals no families with the name of Halter, Giessey, Cable, or other ancestral names already resident when Mrs. Halter and her four young children arrived, nor is there any record in the Pennsylvania Census for the same year of a family by either name residing in that state.[79]

It is important to remember that whenever any one person or group migrates from one place to another, whether it is across an ocean, state lines, or even from urban to rural life or the reverse, there are many factors operative. The push-pull theory of migration as explained by E. S. Lee always applies.[80] Push-pull theory involves the push of forces, whether social or economic, pushing the person or persons from one location to another. Simultaneously, there are the pull factors that attract the person or persons to migrate to the new location. We will never know Mrs. Halter's reasons for this venture, but her decision to leave her home in Southampton and relocate in Lima, Ohio, impacted heavily on her and her children.

Mrs. Halter was one of her parents' ten children still living when she migrated. Her husband was one of seven. Their children, Virtue Amelia, Ellen, John, and Mary, would not continue to know their maternal or paternal grandparents as they had once known them. They were cut off from numerous aunts, uncles, cousins, and others in their extended family for all time. The question of why rears its head and is unanswerable through any documentary research. Perhaps, Mrs. Mary Halter simply had a yearning or a need to separate herself and her children from her own and her late husband's families of origin to create a new world for herself and her children? That is probably as acceptable an explanation as any because no other explanation can be verified.

There is little information regarding Mary Belinda's upbringing in Lima, Ohio. There, her mother, Mary Baker Giessey Halter, set herself up as a boardinghouse landlady and raised her four children as best as she could. In the previously mentioned unpublished manuscript by Linnell, the author states

> Very soon after the arrival of the family in Lima, (Virtue) Amelia became prominent in dramatic and musical circles, even though she was still a mere child. She joined the Thespian Dramatic Club and acted parts in plays such as "East Lynn" and "Still Waters Run Deep."

> But Amelia's future in dramatics came to an end with the closing of that season because her mother considered it altogether wrong to belong to church and to a theatrical group at the same time.[81]

It is worth noting that Virtue Amelia also played the piano and organ. Her brother John is mentioned in these manuscripts as singing bass in the choirs and choruses. Mary Belinda and Ellen are not mentioned. Andrew Halter, father of the family, had spent time in the Pennsylvania Militia Band prior to his death and won several awards as a bugler. From the documentation available in 1870, the Halter family occupied a large home and at times had eight men boarders plus her three unmarried children. Her eldest daughter, Amelia, was living there as well with her husband, Ebenezer Davis.[82] John Halter, the only son, at age seventeen was already working for a local marble cutter; Ellen, age 18, is listed as "at home" and Mary Belinda is listed as "at school." By 1880, there is evidence that Ellen Halter had gone into the dry goods business with a partner, Mrs. Harriet or "Hattie" Watson, wife of S. W. Watson of Lima. In the same year, there is evidence that Mary Belinda had already started her music teaching in Lima. An article from the *Allen County Democrat* dated November 11, 1880, reports the success of "Miss Mary Halter's music class rehearsal at the home of S. A. Smith on Union Street" in Lima. Eighteen selections were performed by sixteen students."[83] The news piece continues

> The performance throughout was a success and speaks well, both for the teacher and the pupils. The parlors were comfortably seated, there being more than sixty persons present, all of who [sic] were highly entertained.[84]

There is no way to ascertain whether this was the first public presentation in Mary Belinda's teaching career, a career that extended over sixty-one years till her death in 1941, but it is refreshing to know that she did in fact have this success at age twenty-two.

We have no definitive evidence to suggest where Mary Belinda received her musical training, but according to the "Reminiscences from Taped Family Conversations with David Moyer," she herself always said that she did study in Europe as a young adult. David often makes reference to famous musicians she introduced him to as a child when he played in New York and other American cities. David believed everything she told him.

But the question still remains: who was this Mary Belinda (Linn) Halter Walsh that appeared virtually out of nowhere at the Moyer family's front door in 1900?

The name Walsh is a misnomer. She never used that spelling for her name. She may well have been saying Welch or Welsh to David's family when she walked up to their home in Philadelphia and spoke through the window to David's mother, but regardless of her name, whether it be Walsh, Welch, Welsh, Berlino, or Halter, she was known forevermore to the Moyers and their descendants as Mrs. Walsh.

According to U.S. State Department documents where Mary herself gave the necessary information in order to obtain passports, she claimed to have been married to a William Welch in one document, and on another document, she claimed to have been married to a William Watson Welch and still another name of William Welch Berlino.[85] There is no proof that Mary ever married anyone by these names, either in Ohio or Europe. The *Lima Times Democrat* for May 10, 1919, stated that Mary Belinda was the widow of John H. Kunneke of Columbus Grove, Ohio, before she married the German Mr. Berlino.[86] Mary Belinda, in fact, did marry John H. Kunneke of Columbus Grove, Ohio, on September 20, 1882, at Immanuel Lutheran Church in Lima. However, there is no reason to believe she ever married anyone by the name of Berlino. She simply made up the name Madame Marie Berlino!

John Harmon Kunneke was born in Columbus Grove, Ohio, January 13, 1858, to Theodore Kunneke and Mary E. Featheringill. Theodore, John's father, immigrated to the United States at age seventeen. Prior to settling in Columbus Grove, he traveled around the United States working in various trades. Once in Columbus Grove, he worked as a merchandiser and then began a building and contracting business. Through his building business, he was responsible for most of the houses and business buildings in Columbus Grove. "Few men in Columbus Grove are better or more favorably known than Mr. Kunneke, and he is one of the well-do-do men of the township."[87] From this information, it appears that Mary married a man with potentially comfortable resources. There is a record of John's petition as plaintiff seeking a divorce to which Mary Belinda, the defendant, never responded. She was served with a summons by the Sheriff of Lima and again, no response. Although no decree of divorce is on file at the Putnam County Courthouse, a date on the cover of the petition states that a divorce judgment was rendered in November 1885.[88] She did not use the name Kunneke either before or after the divorce was decreed. John died in 1907 after being married two more times. The Lima press never referred to her by her married name in the many articles written about her. As "the girl with all the talent from Lima," she was never known as Mary Walsh, but as Linn, Lynn, or Lenna Halter.

Belinda Halter (Madame Berlino), Pittsburgh, c.1905
Photo: Courtesy of Allen County Historical Museum

This fact is borne out by evidence from old photos of her taken in Pittsburgh, Pennsylvania, in other venues in the States, as well as Berlin, Germany, where she (or someone) had written the name Belinda Halter with the name Madame Berlino added underneath in parentheses. She seemed to use her legal or Christian name of Mary on official documents prior to 1903; however, in all documentation after 1903, she consistently used her nom de plume of Madame Marie Berlino. Arrival documents as well as passport applications bear this out.

Amazing as it may seem, Mary Belinda Halter Berlino aged only twelve years during the nineteen years of traveling to and from Germany. This is not an unusual finding when researching various people. Many times, people deliberately make themselves a couple of years younger for convenience sake. However, there were many tall tales about her that have been recorded in the local press publications of Lima when it was either she herself or a family member who informed the press of her whereabouts and her accomplishments. Mary Belinda even changed her date of birth from January 28, 1858, to January 28, 1867.[89] Sadly, this untruth about her age is the preface to the "Mary Walsh" story.

David reported that Mrs. Walsh's family was in the oil business in Lima, Ohio, and they were very wealthy, but we now know this also to be untrue. Her mother, Mrs. Halter, probably did make a good living in the boardinghouse business prior to the discovery of oil in Lima in 1885 and perhaps a bit more during the heady "black gold Texas tea" years in Lima until the oil actually ran out around 1900. But even to imply that they were well off would be an overstatement. Comfortable maybe, but from the census records and Lima City Directory Records, Linn Halter's mother lived until 1912 running a boardinghouse. Hardly the occupation of someone deemed wealthy! A private researcher in Lima has provided some sad but truthful information regarding the Halters and the possibility of owning oil wells. Mary Belinda's brother, "John D. Halter went bankrupt in 1891 to the tune of more than $10,000.00 in debt, including two mortgages on his property amounting to $6,400.00 and another debt of over $3,500.00 for supplies for the Monument Company (that he owned) and miscellaneous debts. He was also in debt as a half owner of some oil well drilling equipment—his half of the bill being $261.00. However, he died unexpectedly, October 6, 1910, leaving no will or estate papers, even though he had continued to work at the monument company as a stone cutter up to the time of his death."[90] His poor wife, childless, was left destitute, and no one has been able to find any trace of her after his burial. Regrettably, when Mrs. Mary Baker Halter, mother of Mary Belinda, died March 18, 1912, of old age; her will was published in the local Lima newspaper. She made her will in 1893 and never changed it after that date. Mrs. Halter left her only son, John, $5.00, saying she had already given him a considerable amount of property. Furthermore, the only thing she owned was the house she lived in, and this was left to her single daughter, Ellen, the businesswoman. She also left Ellen all of the furniture and then divided the rest of her personal belongings, one-third each to her three daughters, Amelia, Ellen, and Mary Belinda.[91] When both Mary Belinda's brother and mother died, she was in Berlin, Germany. It appears a harsh act to publish someone's will in a newspaper, but this may have been a prudent way of alerting John's creditors that when his mother died, he inherited almost nothing.

When Mrs. Walsh entered the lives of the Moyer family in Philadelphia, they were convinced that she was a widowed woman and possessed a proven talent for music, especially a talent for teaching young children to play the piano. But why was she in Philadelphia in the summer of 1900? The *Lima News* for February 7, 1900, printed an article about a talent-show type of entertainment that was being organized to benefit the local hospital. The last paragraph of the article states

> This morning, Miss Halter, [Madame Berlino] left for New York, where she has accepted a position. During her five months stay in our city, she has received the attention of our best musicians who recognized her wonderful ability. All hope she will at some future time return to our city to remain permanently.[92]

Two more questions arise: Where was she prior to her last five months in Lima? What happened in New York City to her celebrated job? The answer to the first question comes from Federal Census Records for 1900. The records for Akron, Ohio, list a Mary B. Halter working in a hotel there as a waitress.[93] There is no certain answer as to why Mary left the New York City job. Certainly, her ability as a teacher of music was evidenced by the fact that David progressed rapidly in a very short time. By January 1901, Mary had approached David's parents and requested that they allow him to go to New York City with her for extended piano studies. David's parents were shocked by this request and initially responded, "No. He can't do that. He has to go to school."[94] Mary Walsh, as seemed to be her style, had an instant answer for them: "Oh, no. I'll get a tutor for him."[95] David's parents conceded to Mary's wish, and she set off with David in tow for the glories of New York City. David had not reached his sixth birthday.

What were his parents thinking at this time? Were they so enamored with this woman that they totally trusted her to take their little son safely to New York? Perhaps they felt that David's ability to play the piano so well was some kind of gift from God Himself! They certainly gave their permission for this venture for their youngest son. We will never know what motivated Ida and Joseph Moyer to agree to such a plan. We can only imagine the scene at the Pennsylvania Railroad Station located on Broad Street in Philadelphia when David Earl Moyer boarded that train to New York for the first time. His mother must have been very sad, and David must have been confused and frightened. It is one thing to have a music teacher share your home and teach you something new; however, it is an entirely different experience, both intellectually and emotionally, to board a train without your Ma and Pa and without your brothers and go away with someone who had been part of your family as you knew it but who now becomes your family. What did David's three older brothers think of this arrangement that took their little brother to a place where they had never been and only heard about in books?

Chapter IV

Brooklyn Days

Mary chose Brooklyn as the city where she and David would live: "Mrs. Walsh rented a big old house, 1200 Fulton Street . . . an old stone house in a great big yard on a large open square . . . there was a sign on the house that read, 'George Washington Slept Here.'"[96] Although David was impressed with the living arrangement, it wasn't a house at all, but a rather large apartment on the second floor of a business block. The store beneath, as well as many stores in the block, was a piano dealer. The house David is referring to as the one with the sign that stated, "George Washington Slept Here" was actually the Bloom Lefferts Homestead located at 1224 Fulton Street a few houses further up the block.[97]

Bloom Lefferts Homestead, Brooklyn, New York
Photo: Courtesy of Brian Merlis

There is no recorded evidence that George Washington ever actually slept at this residence, which belonged to Nicholas Bloom who in 1785 sold the house to Charles Turnbull, an officer of the British Army. In Historic *Homesteads of Kings County* by Charles Andrew Ditman, 1909, George Washington is never mentioned.[98]

David appears to have forgotten that his first residence was 85 Lafayette Avenue, Brooklyn, above a piano dealer. During David's time on Fulton Street, with the exception of the Bloom Lefferts Homestead, all buildings were ground-floor shops and apartments rising two-or-three stories. The living arrangement appears adequate from what David tells us, and Mary proceeded to take on as many students of piano as she could organize. At that time, David was playing Czerny as well as Mozart Sonatas. David explained in 1975 that he "used to walk up to the keyboard and play Czerny, Op. 298 . . . I would sizzle through that stuff like mad. The faster I played, the more I liked it." Her method of teaching, according to David was "marvelous":[99]

> She insisted on two pianos, side by side. Then we would learn something . . . Sometimes a four-hand number . . . I'd learn my part. Or a solo piece I wanted to play. She'd say. "Well, now, come on, you imitate exactly what I do" and then she'd play just fast enough to make me scratch to keep up. We would play it together. In no time I was playing the piece as well as she did.[100]

David had lessons on the piano almost every day and practiced about two hours a day both on his own and with Mrs. Walsh. He learned about forty of the eight hundred or so Czerny Etudes as well as learning chord progressions to enhance his ear training. "I really felt the harmony,"[101] said David. He was approximately six years old and could feel harmonic progressions. This statement of David's leads us to consider that he must have had some natural gift for music and his success at such a young age was not totally the work of Mary Walsh. However, it must be stated that Mary did provide the discipline and environment necessary for David to realize his talent. By all accounts, she was a very gifted music teacher of children. We have no evidence that she ever taught adults.

From reading David's "Reminiscences," we realize that very early on, one thing Mary Walsh could do was attract students and make a living doing just that: teaching music. She also excelled at convincing people to allow their children to study with her and, in David's case, even take him away from his own family in Philadelphia to New York City for further study. The tutors that Mary Walsh promised the Moyers that David would have never seemed to have materialized. She may have tutored him herself in reading and other subjects she felt appropriate, but it was the practice of music, the learning to read music, write music down on paper, and the harmonic ear development that seemed to take up David's time. In the context of the written word, David always admitted quite openly that he never learned to "speel" (spell), and his personal letters that survive and his World War I daily journal that he preserved demonstrate this fact. At the time, if David had stayed at home with his family, he would have been in school learning the rudiments of reading, writing, spelling, and arithmetic, but instead he was doing something that was much more exciting and rewarding to him personally. But he was not only missing out on the skills of regular education but he was also isolated from socialization with other children his own age.

We can only imagine how different his life would have been if he had remained at home with his older brothers and parents and attended the local elementary school. It's obvious that Mary Walsh had other ideas and goals for David as well as herself. David does recall how at various times he experienced loneliness and homesickness. David remembered that he was quite good at train travel. He would make the round-trip journey between Brooklyn and Philadelphia alone. Mary also adopted two dogs and a cat for David. Rexie and Beauty, the two small fox terriers, and the cat appear in all the early publicity photos with David alone and later show up with the two younger boys Mary Walsh eventually adopted. These lovely pets must have been very dear to David and provided some ease from the emotional loss he must have been experiencing.

> For some reason or other, she wanted a couple of more children. She had none of her own.[102]Shortly after she took me to Brooklyn she adopted the two boys.[103] (1903)

> Their name was Dougherty, Irish kids. They were brothers. And she adopted them through some agency. One was three and the other was four.[104]

> The parents were terrible, pure trash, poor as church mice, and, of course, the state came along and took the kids away from the parents because they lived in this horrible part of New York City. Those were the circumstances under which she adopted them from the welfare people.[105]

David seems harsh in his judgment of the parents of these two boys. However, he was only seven or eight years old when the two boys entered his life in Brooklyn. David's only information regarding the origins of these brothers and any opinion regarding their circumstances would have been simply repetition of what Mary chose to tell him. Recently, it has been discovered that their names were not Dougherty at all! It was, according to records, actually Haggerty, and they were only age three and two when they entered the household.[106]

It was the Bowery, according to David, where Mary found the two young brothers to adopt, thereby, expanding her own little family from two to four people. The history of the Bowery begins around 1651 when Peter Stuyvesant bought the land. The name itself comes from the Dutch word for farm (*bowerij*).[107] It was originally "a fine, prosperous farming community." However, by the time David lived in New York, the Bowery had earned a worldwide reputation as a place where people that had experienced hard luck, perhaps caused by drunkenness, lack of employment, or personal depression usually ended up. They had not the means to live in any other place. In short, the Bowery is viewed as a large "legendary slum."[108] The area also was inhabited by many of the recently immigrated, and they lived in tenement house buildings that were always overcrowded with sometimes ten or more people sharing one room.[109] Due to the harsh economics of the times, many families often were left without fathers because of accidental injury and death in unsafe working conditions, and this left the women and children to make a living as best they could. In addition, diseases spread rapidly in these overcrowded, worn-out areas, and the unsanitary conditions led to early deaths of adults and children. Orphanages were built throughout New York City to help care for the recently orphaned children and children of families who could not provide enough food to feed their growing families. Many times, children became wards of the court, and in the Bowery, this was rather commonplace in the early 1900s.

As early as 1853, Charles Lorring Brace and a group of businessmen formed the Children's Aid Society to help these unfortunate, desolate children.[110] In *Dangerous Classes and My Twenty Years of Work among Them*, Charles Brace describes the living conditions of the children he tried to care for. He and his business friends were able to "place out" over one hundred and fifty thousand children between 1854 and the early 1930s.[111] This placing out included the ever controversial Orphan Train system. Children, usually males, were placed on trains for the West, and people there were organized and would take the children and raise them and teach and give them a chance at knowing a different life and, perhaps, adapting to it and becoming good citizens. The children were expected to work on the farms and do what any other child would do growing up on the plains. The Orphan Train system would appear harsh to us today, but it was a way of giving children a chance. Many times, the particulars of family relationships among the children were not considered by their prospective caretaker families or adopting families. Brothers were separated, sadly.[112] For Paul and Arthur Haggerty, their story was a bit different. It was Mary Halter Walsh, now using her nom de plume of Madame Marie Berlino, who went to the Children's Aid Society in the Bowery and adopted the two boys. Paul was born in 1899, and Arthur approximately two years later. The boys were the sons of John Joseph Haggerty and Ellen Monkhorn.[113] Mary must have wanted two children, and the fact that these brothers were available for adoption was obviously an acceptable arrangement.

New York Law, Chapter 830, passed June 25, 1875[114], states that:

> Adoption, as provided for in this act, is the legal act whereby an adult person takes a minor into the relation of child, and thereby acquires the rights and incurs the responsibilities of parent in respect to such minor. (Section 1)[115]

The laws of New York allowed a person of good character to be examined in court by a judge who could then make the order directing that the child shall henceforth be regarded and treated, in all respects, as the child of the person adopting."[116] Mary, at age forty-five, who had David in her care for the purpose of musical education approved by his family, was probably testament enough that she was of good character and the children she was adopting would have the opportunity to develop and even have a lifestyle superior to the life they were living in the orphanage or with their parents. We do know that Ellen Monkhorn was still living at the time of her sons' adoptions and that they were placed in the care of the Children's Aid Society for their own benefit. She also had a daughter, Gertrude, born during the interim between the birth of these two sons, and she did not place her with the society. New York adoption law did not state during this era that there were waiting periods and socioeconomic assessments as are a part of the adoption process of today. The main responsibility of the Children's Aid Society was to find good homes for the children placed in their care as expeditiously as possible. The Haggerty boys became the Berlino brothers overnight!

This seemingly kind act of Mary's must have caused some emotional consternation with David at the time. Although he never goes into great detail about his reaction to this event or, for that matter, any of his life events, we can only attempt to take on the mind of an eight-year-old already apart from his family of origin and living in what to him must have seemed a very different environment with the two younger boys sharing his space, Mary, the cat, and his two beloved fox terriers. David never refers to those he lived with as his family or the Berlino boys as his brothers. He knew all too well that his family lived in Philadelphia, and he was always aware he was away from them. But he never really complained or said much other than this was the way young musicians lived during the period.

Mary would have had her work cut out for her with Arthur and Paul at only two and four years old. She decided to change Paul's name to Robert and Arthur's name to Clarence after the adoption. When Mary met David, he was in his own home in Philadelphia, a well-ordered, nurturing environment. David was two months away from his sixth birthday when he boarded that train in Philadelphia to travel to New York City with Mary the first time in 1901. He was washed, starched, pressed, polished, well mannered, and ready to enter the New York phase of his study with his mentor without needing intense behavioral discipline. The situation of Robert and Clarence must have been very different for Mary as she more than likely had to start from scratch in teaching them good discipline, manners and acceptable behavior as well as the basics of music, and whatever else they needed to learn. Mary was up for the tasks at hand. It is apparent from the documentation that her intention in adopting these two young boys was to teach them music and to add them to the already-successful prodigious programming of David. He quotes Mary saying, "Oh, talent, it's 90% hard work, and 10% talent."[117] The two little boys did progress in their musical education. Mary bought a "quarter fiddle for one and a quarter cello, the cutest little thing you ever saw, for the other. And she taught them how to play. All the while, I was playing piano, of course,"[118] recalled David. In addition to her familial responsibilities to the three boys, Mary also had to take in music students to help support her little troupe as well as herself. She was a busy woman and somehow managed to keep things going. It is interesting to note that in press releases available prior to 1904, no mention is ever made of the two boys living with David and Mary.

The first newspaper article that we have about David was written in a New York City newspaper and probably before 1903 when he made his first public appearance. The article is brief but does show a photograph of David with one of his beloved fox terriers (we don't know which one) with the headline, "Boy of Eight Aspires to Display Musical Talent to the Public: David Earle Meyer, Boy Pianist."

"David Earle Moyer is said to be Master of the Classics on the Piano."
Photo: Courtesy of Moyer Family Archives

David Earle Moyer is only eight years old, but he is already recognized as a musician of very unusual talents. His extreme youth has so far prevented him from appearing in public. At his house, No. 85 Lafayette Avenue, Brooklyn, David today said: "I think I must have played the piano when I was a baby, for I can't remember when I did not love music. I lived in Philadelphia then and would have remained there if Mme. Bertini had not visited our house and heard me play. Mme. Bertini is from London and now teaches me every day.

I practice five hours each day and do not get tired even then. My favorites are Chopin, Bach, Mozart, Czney [Czerny], Schumann, and all the old masters. I like popular music, but Madame won't let me play anything but the masters. I guess she knows what's good for me for Madame plays the piano a great deal better than I do. But I don't play the piano all the time. I have great fun with Beauty and Rexie, my two fox terriers, and yesterday I built a top automobile. I hope it won't be long until I can play in public. I want to show what Madame has taught me."[119]

The two misspellings of David's name and the misspelling of Madame's name in the above-mentioned article could simply be typesetter's errors or a journalistic lack of precision. The "five hours per day of piano practice" as stated in this article does conflict, however, with David's own words in his "Reminiscences" regarding his early days in Brooklyn, "I practiced about two hours a day both alone and with her."[120] This discrepancy may or may not be significant although it perhaps is more indicative of the fact of simply having more time on his hands because Mary had less time for David in order to give extra time to her recently adopted sons and also adequate time to devote to her paying students.

It is interesting that David never mentions any schooling tutors in this article. One would think he would have mentioned them as an additional important part of his life or at least a part of his world. Schooling tutors are not mentioned because there may not have been any. From the above newspaper article, we can get a sense of the isolated life David was living compared to the life he had with his Ma and Pa and three older brothers in Philadelphia. This article leads us to believe that there was no one else in his life other than Mary and his pets. We know that is not the case.

In the above photo, we can see David's walleye. Walleye, medically known as strabismus is defined as a condition of the eye muscles "when the two eyes don't line up or move together properly."[121] It appears that strabismus is caused by some lack of strength in the particular eye muscle that is weaker than the other eye. This condition, if left untreated, can cause some vision loss, but not total. David had this eye condition all of his life, and it appears more obvious in full-frontal photographs of him than in profile pictures.

Harvard professor of neurobiology, Margaret Livingstone, has studied this condition in four self-portrait paintings by Rembrandt. In addition, she has examined the self-portraits of Marc Chagall, Gustav Klimt, Edward Hopper, Andrew Wyeth, Joseph Stella, Alexander Calder, Man Ray, and Pablo Picasso.[122] "The eyes of the great 17th Century Rembrandt are crooked. The eye on the right side of the painting looks straight at the viewer, but the other eye looks off to the side. Rembrandt painted these self portraits by looking in a mirror, so his left eye would be the one looking off to the side."[123] Livingstone's conclusion is that Rembrandt and the other artists were "stereo blind," that is, they could not see three dimensions fully; therefore, their visual world was basically flat. Dr. Livingstone concludes that this eye condition in artists may actually be an advantage rather than a disability: "Stereovision is an important cue for depth perception, yet it can be a hindrance to an artist trying to depict a three-dimensional scene on a flat surface . . . Art teachers often instruct students to close one eye in order to flatten what they see. Stereo blind artists can simply paint what they see. Therefore the condition might be an asset instead of a handicap."[124] Additionally, "other researchers have reported that talented art students show a higher than usual rate of dyslexia"[125] understood to be a reading deficit. Poor stereovision and dyslexia often occur together. Does this study of Dr. Livingstone suggest that maybe part of the reason that David never learned to spell was because he couldn't because of his walleye? It is very possible. Regarding David, his visual problem never really seemed to bother him. It certainly did not interfere with his ability to sight-read music at an early age or to progress and enjoy his marvelous stage career. Later in David's life, he did wear glasses, and according to his daughter-in-law, Betsy Moyer: "He felt he could see well enough with glasses."[126] David's youngest son, Bill, stated that he never heard his father mention how he came by his walleye.[127]

Mary did experiment with David's name as evidenced by her writing his name differently on the back one of the two photographs taken on February 12, 1901. The cover photograph may look a bit ridiculous to us, but male children, especially those categorized as a prodigy during the waning of the Victorian Era, did in fact wear these costumes for performances, etc., particularly, if they were under age five.[128] The expression on David's face in this photo shows his discomfort being dressed in this fashion. On the back of the second photo, Mary had written the date as February 12, 1901[129]. On the back of this same photo, Mary had written Earlitta Moyer. One can only imagine what significance Mary intended in writing that feminine form of his name. It seems strange that someone would deliberately write a female name on the back of a photograph of a male child. Did she not consider the fact that this photograph might survive after the taking of the photo and in later years cause David some distress? In fact, there are two copies of this same photo in the collection. It is very possible that David expressed his objection to her at the time of the photographic sitting, and she simply kept the photos with her written remarks just as an expression of her sense of humor. The following photograph was also taken and was probably much more to David's satisfaction.

David Earl Moyer, February 12, 1901
Photo: Courtesy of Moyer Family Archives

Mary's handwriting on the back of this photo simply states "David Earl Moyer and (Moyer) Pianist."[130]

The above photograph and the photograph on the cover of this book were more than likely taken by a photographer contracted by the Henry Hazelton Piano Manufacturers of New York at the piano company's sales rooms or warerooms as they were called. Piano manufacturers of this era did not shift their pianos from one photographic studio to another for a few promotional pictures. To avoid this, the photographers accessed decals depicting the name of the particular manufacturer and simply changed the decals on the pianos as required. These photos also allow us to observe that David must have been a very obedient child.

The fact that he was the son of a Mennonite/Schwenkfelder family, he would have had to have been a very obedient child as this was an important imperative in these families to establish obedience as a major value. Victorian-era society was extremely intolerant of children that were not well behaved: this was the era of children being seen, and not heard. There were children of that era, just as in today's world, who were not obedient and were referred to as street urchins, etc., and if sparing the rod and spoiling the child did occur, the family suffered the results of this behavior and the ensuing social ostracism. David's willingness to don a dress for a photo can be interpreted as his willingness to obey and, therefore, to please Madame.

The same styles of costumes were used for the two boys that Mary adopted. The photo below taken in 1903 is the first photo we have of the three boys together. Baby Clarence is in a dress.

David Moyer, Robert and Clarence Berlino, 1903
Photo: Courtesy of Moyer Family Archives

David may not have been performing in public as we would understand "public," defined as a formal concert in a place where anyone with the means to pay the admission fee can attend, but he does tell us in his reminiscences that he played in wealthy people's homes as the entertainment, most probably after fine formal dinners:

> Sometimes I would play for a little group somewhere. I never played in Carnegie Hall or any place quite like that, but I used to play for people. Somehow she would find her way to wealthy homes. I can't remember the names of some of those people, but I can remember going into their homes. It didn't mean anything to me, you know, just a great big living room with a lot of people there and then, "Come on, David, go over there, and play something, will you." I can remember the pieces—Bach Inventions—I had a lot of them under my fingers. Mendelssohn's Rondo Capriccioso was one of my favorites. Perpetual Motion by Weber. I was about seven or eight.[131]

At this phase in young David's life, Mary Walsh became more than a musical instructor or guardian to David; she in fact assumed the role of formal performance agent as well. Whether she had established a price for these at-home type performances or she merely took what was offered by the host and hostess is unclear, but it is clear that she needed to make money to further support herself and the three boys in New York City. This was, of course, in addition to what she earned as a private music instructor, and quite possibly, she received a regular income from David's parents to pay his personal expenses. The Moyers would have been very aware that it cost something to house and feed a child, buy those fancy suits, and pay for the photographers. With such a plethora of photos that have survived, the photographic costs must have been somewhat expensive and were probably not all complimentary from the piano manufacturers. More than likely, the Moyers did contribute to David's support during these early New York City years. It is even conceivable that they were billed for those daily lessons David had with Mary as well.

The Moyers were biblical-based Christians; therefore, Joseph and Ida would have learned the biblical precept that required the head of the household to provide for his family in accord with St. Paul's instruction to Timothy: "But if any provide not for his own, and specially for those of his own house, he hath denied the faith, and is worse than an infidel" (I Timothy 5:8). David's father, Joseph, was a successful businessman, and he would have surmised that regardless of how wealthy Mary told them her own family was (we know this to be untrue), having David 24/7 would cause an extra expense for her, and that she should not be totally responsible for these extra expenses. We do not know if the Moyers were ever made aware of David's potential earning power. Once that potential became a reality, as it did, were they ever informed? More than likely, they were not. The Mennonite/Schwenkfelder cultural traditions that influenced their views regarding child labor would have included the role that children were expected to share in the domestic survival of the family and community by participating in farming and other chores appropriate for their ages. Employment of children where the remuneration was cash and outside of the religious/cultural framework may have been frowned upon. What's interesting here as well is that we have no record of Mary Walsh performing herself at these rather formal social gatherings. David was always the performer! As a matter of fact, there is no surviving documentation demonstrating that Mary ever performed in public in either Lima, Ohio or New York City, or anywhere, for that matter.

It is in November 1903 that we have evidence of David's first known public performance. At the corner of Bedford Avenue and Fulton Street lies Cooper Hall. The Bedford Political Equality League of Kings County, New York, advertised that a "fair" would be held on November 5, 6, and 7, 1903. A copy of the printed program has survived and was found in David's personal scrapbook.[132]

The Bedford Political Equality League was a suffragette organization that was flourishing in Brooklyn in 1903. The officers of this organization read like a who's who of women's rights activists of New York City: Mrs. Reba Talbot-Perkins, Mrs. Priscilla D. Hackstaff, Martha Wentworth Suffren, and Mrs. M.B. Talbot-Swain to name a few. From the program, it appears that the musical part of the "fair" was a small segment. From other literature of the period, these gatherings included several different activities advancing the group's endeavors. They had the usual panoply of speakers arguing the issues of the day, and one of these issues would have been cries for the enfranchisement of women. On November 5, 1903, David played four piano selections: Etude de Velocity No. 6 by Czerny, Scherzo No. 3 by Theodor Kullak, and at his second performance, he played Invention No. 8 by J. S. Bach and Waltz No. 3 by Chopin. Friday Night, November 6, David did not appear on the program, but on Saturday night, he did perform a solo piece, but no title is given. He also accompanied a Ms. Dolores Gamble with her vocal presentation. Performing a piano selection is a very different matter from accompanying a soloist. David must have been very clever to be able to do this at eight years of age. Personally, I know people older than him at the time, and with years and years of piano study, that could not and would not have accompanied anyone either playing another instrument or a vocalist.

The two evening performances that David participated in took place after eight in the evening. According to the program for Friday evening, in attendance where two well-known phrenologists—Jessie Fowler, daughter of L. N. Fowler, a noted phrenologist, and Dr. Cora Ballard. We can only imagine the scenes at this exhibition. The aristocratic women of Bedford, New York City, doling out literature to the participants regarding various goals they aspired to achieve for the good of society at large while David and a few other musicians performing with all their hearts and abilities and a few people in the back of the Cooper

Hall literally having their heads examined! Oh my goodness, what would David's parents have thought of this arrangement? They would have been in awe of their son's talents, but such a circuslike atmosphere in which he was performing would certainly have raised reservations about their original decision to allow him to go with Mary for further study. These Mennonite/Schwenkfelder descendants would have viewed such things as phrenology as superstition and probably would have had no background on the subject. Anything contrary to their learned faith such as phrenology would seem to be sheer idolatry and probably quite repugnant to their understanding of how good God-fearing people should behave.

Where were David's new adopted brothers while he is performing at this concert? We have no information regarding this. More than likely, Mary had employed either a mother's helper or part-time nurse to help with the boys or simply took them along. Any lack of arrangement for their care at times like this would have been so unfortunate.

David did continue to study with Mary, the Madame, for years to come and continued a rather rigorous performing schedule. It was August 28, 1903, when Mary returned from a trip to Germany.[133] Her two newly adopted sons were not with her on the trip nor was David. Perhaps, Ida Moyer, David's mother, took them in while Mary was away. Familial anecdotal evidence repeatedly suggests that David's mother was a very kind woman and would have kept the two younger boys if necessary.[134] We have no definite reason why Mary made this trip to Germany, but as further details evolve in David's story, it leads us to believe that she realized very early that she had found a real prodigy for herself and, probably, wanted to make contact with some people she had heard about for opportunities and advice as to how to proceed with the very talented David. Just as Mary had no reticence in approaching the wealthy of New York City and offering David as after dinner entertainment, she seemed not to have reservations approaching anyone else either. She was a very driven, determined, and single-minded woman. On page eight of David's "Reminiscences" he stated, "She was consumed with ambition and always was a little pushy." Needless to say, she had the financial means to travel to and from Germany, maintain the living quarters in New York City, and suspend her private music tuition business temporarily.

There are copies of advertising notices from newspapers and programs for David's performances in 1904. It was about this same time frame when David informs us that:

> She knew a lot of famous people who would come to New York and play. And, of course, naturally I had to go meet them—like Joseffy and Josef Hofmann—of course. I played for him. To me he was just a man. And Madame Carreño. Those names back in that era, I met many of them. She knew them all. She would have me play for them.[135]

In spite of the revelation regarding Mary's fantasies about knowing this one, that one, and the other as previously discussed, it is possible and believable that David did meet one musical notable in New York City mentioned in the preceding quote. Rafael Joseffy (1852-1915) was a Hungarian born pianist and composer. At age fourteen, Rafael studied at Leipzig and two years later became a student of Carl Tausig then moved on to Weimar and studied for two summers with Franz Liszt. Joseffy's performance debut was in 1872, and he was immediately recognized as a master pianist. In 1879, he entered the United States and made New York his home.[136] David must have played for Joseffy because in 1904, the following quotation from Joseffy appears on some of David's performance bills: "The most marvelous technique I ever saw in one so young."[137] It is doubtful that Mary made up this statement herself and credited it to Joseffy. She would have been seriously embarrassed if he ever questioned the validity of the quote.

Josef Casimir Hofmann (1876-1957) was born in Podgorze, near Krakow, Poland. Josef's father was an orchestra conductor, composer, and piano teacher, and his mother was an accomplished operatic singer.[138] In this familial milieu, Josef flourished musically and was always encouraged to participate. He started giving concerts at age six.[139] He is quoted as saying that he didn't mind giving performances as a child, a common outgrowth of "prodigism" even though the result is burnout, stunted emotional development, or both.[140] According to L. V. Kosinski, by age nine, Josef impressed the great pianists of the age: Franz Liszt, Camille Saint-Saëns, and Anton Rubinstein. At age eleven, Josef, under the parental supervision of his father, sailed into New York City to make his American debut in 1887. The audiences and critics went wild over this "musical phenomenon."[141] After some challenges to Josef's father by the Society for the Prevention of Cruelty to Children in New York City, Alfred Corning Clark, a local philanthropist, offered to provide needed financial support for the entire Hofmann family until Josef reached the age of eighteen. The following year, the family moved to Dresden, Germany, where Josef studied at the conservatory in Dresden for two years under the tutelage of Anton Rubinstein. By 1926, Josef became an American citizen and directed the Curtis Institute of Music in Philadelphia. Amazing as it may seem, Josef Hofmann was also an inventor. Upon his death, he held sixty patents in the United States with a few others in Germany. He is the man who invented our modern-day windshield wiper as well as the Hofmann shock absorber for the automobile. He died in California in 1957. It was impossible for David to have met Hofmann while in New York.

Maria Teresa Carreño was born November 25, 1862, in Caracas, Venezula. At age eight, the petite dark-haired girl gave her first public concert at the Irving Hall in New York City. Teresita (as she was called in her youth) was the grandniece of Simon Bolivar, and her grandfather, Caetano Carreño, was an important Venezuelan composer. Many biographers of Teresita claim that while she was a young girl, she was able to compose music, in addition to being an outstanding performer. Just as David would do, Teresa played at the White House although for a different president than David played for. She played for Abraham Lincoln. Briefly, she experimented with a career as an opera singer, but in the end, she decided to pursue her career as a professional pianist and settled in Berlin in 1889.[142] She led a gloriously busy life to the point that while staying in Boston for a long series of concerts, she introduced the extra concerts for children to be held in the afternoons as matinees. These children's concerts became so popular that other cities in the United States copied her experiment, and an entirely new phenomenon of children's concerts became very widespread. When Teresa wasn't performing, she was either teaching as many students as she could or getting married! She was married four times: to Emile Sauret, 1873; Giovanni Tagliapietra, 1876; Eugene d'Albert, 1892-95; and Arturo Tagliapietra in 1902. In case anyone is puzzled, Arturo Tagliapietra was the brother of her second husband Giovanni Tagliapietra. Of course, along with so many marriages, she had several children, educating all of them to the highest standards. One of her German critics is quoted as saying, "Frau Carreño yesterday played for the first time the second concerto of her third husband in the fourth Philharmonic Concert."[143] For Carreño, an average year of concertizing consisted of between seventy and eighty concerts. After her fifty-four years as a concert pianist, her final appearance in New York City was on December 8, 1916, with her final concert in Havana, Cuba, on March 21, 1917.[144] Carreño was probably the most popular female concert pianist of all time.

How did Mary Halter Walsh (or Madame Marie Berlino) really know these musical greats of the age? Joseffy did not arrive in America until 1880 as a concert pianist, and Mary was more than likely able to attend some of these concerts with her prodigy, David, in tow. It was standard practice for performers to meet the fans after the concert and sign a few autographs. Mary probably used the opportunity to convince Joseffy to give David's playing a listen, and he was impressed with the facility of this small young-looking child. In the case of Josef Hofmann, with the exception of his three-month performances in 1887, he did not return to the United States until 1926 long after David's time with Madame. David did meet Josef Hofmann while in Berlin after 1906, but prior to that date, meeting Joseph Hofmann in the United States was impossible.

Marta Milinowski, a former pupil of Carreño's, Vassar College graduate of the class of 1907 and later a faculty member in the music department, wrote the definitive biography of Teresa Carreño published in 1940 and has included a chronology of the life of Carreño.[145] This chronology demonstrates that during the years David was with Mary in New York City, Carreño was far away concertizing in Europe. When Carreño was performing in the United States (1862-1866), she only presented her artistic work in New York City, New Rochelle, New York, and Boston. Mary herself would have been between the ages of four and eight and living in Ohio during this period. Carreño's later tour in the United States was 1907 and 1908 when David and Mary were nestled in Berlin, Germany.[146] Yet again, we have another fantasy statement by Mary regarding whom she knew and didn't know. David cannot be held responsible for these falsehoods any more then he can be responsible for thinking he was younger at certain periods in his life then he actually was. He remembered, verbatim, whatever she told him as a child and just accepted what she said. Whether truth or untruth, her statements became a part of his memory bank forever. As his daughter-in-law, Betsy Moyer, said after knowing David for almost fifty years, "He swallowed her hook, line and sinker!"[147]

In 1904, Mary was promoting David as being only seven years old. But at the end of April 1904, David turned nine years of age. David was physically a small child. According to his United States military records and his U.S. passport at aged nineteen, his maximum height was five feet four inches. His demure stature as a child made him appear even more amazing to those who witnessed his performances. As a child, he never sat at the piano to play—he always stood.[148]

During 1904, David played in many venues. We have copies only of some of his performances. One way of promoting prodigies in the period was to present free public concerts at the piano manufacturer's showrooms or warerooms. Piano manufacturers were plentiful and always in competition with each other for sales. Pianos were extremely popular during this period. Almost every home in America had a piano, and if this item was missing, people would go to any length to own one whether brand-new or second—or even third hand. They were the equivalent of our modern electronic digital entertainment centers. Larger music stores would feature a particular piano manufacturer to increase sales, and special events and free concerts were given to the public. David was a natural draw for prospective piano enthusiasts. He was young looking for his age, small in stature, very handsome, and exceptionally capable as a performer. Surely, the many parents that attended these concerts or demonstrations imagined that if this small child they witnessed playing the piano so spectacularly, then so could their little John or Mabel. Of course, salespersons were always at the ready to sell their respective instruments at these free public gatherings. There is evidence that when people bought a piano, included in the price were a few free lessons taught at the local music shop. Free lessons for new customers would grow into paid lessons followed by the sales of sheet music and other learning supplies, i.e., more profits for the store. Mary was not slow on the uptake of involving David in these sales enterprises.[149]

Prior to these manufacturers'/sellers' exhibitions in 1904, David performed for the Rubinstein Club at Mendelssohn Hall in New York City on February 24. In addition to David's playing his own selections, he also had to fill in and play three extra selections because, as the hand written note in the margin states, "this one was ill so he played in his place."[150] On the actual program, the young man who should have performed was twelve-year-old, Master Allen Fenno, a boy chorister hailing from New Haven, Connecticut.[151] Under his name in parentheses, Mary had hand written "Earl" and the above-mentioned note. This program was shared with the Moyer family in Philadelphia. Mary seems to have only sent performance programs to David's family when his name as Earl appeared and never when his name appeared as David Berlino or David Moyer-Berlino.

David continued to play at any and all venues that were deemed acceptable by his mentor. Some of her decisions will appear questionable at minimum considering his status as a stage performer with an amazing facility for memorization of the musical selections; he was also so compliant that he would have played on a roof top if Mary had asked him. One of these performances was with the KIA Mandolin Club of Brooklyn. This performance was advertised for April 22, 1904, as a benefit for the St. Giles Home for Crippled Children, also in Brooklyn. A good cause, no doubt about that, and the attendees paid the price of $1.00 each for admission. It was quite common in those days for the "outside" entertainment to be paid by the club or organization that organized the benefit. David explained that "sometimes it might be a church affair where we would get half the money, and the rest would go to the church."[152] On the program with the Mandolin Club was David Moyer and Miss Isabel R. Franklin, soprano soloist. David performed the following selections: Invention No. 8 in F Major by Bach; Tarantella No. 2 in E Minor by Heller; Etude de Velocity No. 40 by Czerny; Scherzo No.2 by Kullak; and the Sonata No. 2, Allegro Moderato movement, by Mozart.[153]

The mandolin's popularity increased tremendously at this time. The eight-stringed instruments were held in the hands cradled by the body much like the guitar. It can be played with a shoulder strap from a standing position or from a sitting position with or without the strap. The instrument was introduced to America by Italian immigrants during the periods of the 1830s and 1880s.[154] The rise in popularity of the mandolin around 1900 was due to the amazing marketing techniques of Orville Gibson. The instrument was redesigned by him from the original lute-shaped, bow-backed instrument to a flat-back instrument. Gibson Company employees created mandolin clubs in the large cities as part of their jobs. Anyone could join and learn the instrument. It was cheap to purchase relative to other musical instruments of the day and could be learned quite easily. These mandolin clubs flourished for a time in the early twentieth century. Many colleges had mandolin clubs that students joined, and their public performances became very popular. Gibson also redesigned the instrument with a longer neck and added frets so it was easier to play for most people. The portability of this instrument also allowed for schools to include this as a learning instrument for young students prior to their taking up the more difficult instruments such as violin, etc. To some extent, the mandolin during this period rivaled the piano as home entertainment.[155]

David was hired to play at the F. A. North and Co. Music Stores in both New York City and Philadelphia. He played May 9, 1904, in Philadelphia and then immediately back to the North Store in New York City for the thirteenth, fourteenth, and fifteenth. During this particular week in May, David performed for six straight days in two cities. The newspaper advertisement for the New York performances listed his age as six. He had just celebrated his ninth birthday. The environment at the North Store on East State was unusual to say the least. David played the piano at night in the window of the North Store! [156] The advertisement states that a Lester piano could be bought for $209.00. We have no idea what David thought of this unusual venue, but one can't help but wonder if he felt like a marionette or a moving mannequin! David simply and obediently did what was asked of him. He was performing, and from his reminiscences, he tells us how he loved to perform. It is likely that David's mother witnessed his performance at the North's store in Philadelphia. On this occasion, the performance venue was less than twenty city blocks from where his family lived; therefore, it is unlikely that David's mother would have missed this important event. Hopefully, the venue was in a nice area of the store where she could sit comfortably and be proud of her son's performance. Although we have no written proof that either of David's parents ever heard him perform in public, we do have spoken memories of the stories of how proud his family was of his accomplishments. A family member (David's nephew's wife) does recall how Ida Moyer would "talk very often of how wonderfully Earl would play in public."[157]

On Sunday, June 22, 1904, the *New York Herald* newspaper, in the Brooklyn supplement, ran a large article entitled "Brooklyn Has Host of Very Bright Children Entertainers." The article tells a bit about each child performer, the instruments they played, or whether they danced, sang, performed impersonations or presented dramatic selections. What they had in common was their talent at young ages. All the children, except David, lived at home with their families. The largest part of this article is about David and his amazing facility:

> Of these performers Master David Earle Moyer, the pianist, of Brooklyn, occupies a position of prominence. He has been heard at intervals through the winter and spring, and those who have listened to his playing are loud in his praise. Master Meyer [sic] is only seven years old. It is believed by those who have observed the remarkable playing of this boy, and who are in a position to judge, that if he lives and continues his studies he will some day rank with the really great performers of the world.

Master Earle has a repertoire of some thirty selections and thoroughly memorizes everything before attempting to play in public. He plays with facility such selections as Bach's "Inventions"; "Perpetual Movement," by Weber; Mozart's "Sonatas" and "Concerto," with orchestral accompaniment; Chopin waltzes and Mendelssohn's "Spinning Song." He is now studying Mendelssohn's "Rondo Capriccioso." The boy's only teacher has been Mme Marie Berlino. She has instructed him for fourteen months. The little fellow lives with his teacher and is receiving a practical education at her hands. He displays remarkable aptitude for mathematics and some mechanical skill. Mme. Berlino has high hopes of making a great player of him.[158]

Egyptian Hall in Philadelphia was the venue for two concerts, both performed on August 26, 1904. John Wanamaker's was a large emporium with stores in Philadelphia, New York, and Paris. Wanamaker's Department Store was a unique place with many galleries including the famous Crystal Tea Room and certainly the Egyptian Hall decorated beautifully in an Egyptian motif and its Greek Hall where the famous Grand Court Organ is housed. David is not billed as the only performer on this program as he had so many times before. With him are Mary's two children, Robert and Clarence Berlino. They are billed for the first time that we know of as the Berlino Children. Clarence, aged three, played two selections on the piano as a soloist and two violin solos. Robert, aged five, played Gavotte in D Major on his cello, and David performed three solo pieces on a Chickering piano. The Berlino Children, as a trio, played Rondo by Haydn. The program for the morning concert, scheduled to begin at 11:30 a.m., began with J. Lewis Browne, a local Philadelphia composer and organist who four years later would become the director of Music at Wanamaker's.[159] This concert was followed by another the same afternoon at 3:00 p.m. in the Greek Hall also in Wanamaker's. If they attended, it must have been very exciting for David's family to witness such a concert in such a fine venue, especially in their own city. The venue itself surely was an improvement over the window performance at the F. A. North Music Store in New York the previous May.

The following month, David played in Bridgeport, Connecticut, at the Wissner Piano Warerooms on September 7, and then on the eleventh, he played at the Manhattan Beach Theatre in Brooklyn in September 1904. Manhattan Beach is on the Atlantic Ocean bordered by Coney Island, Brooklyn, and New York City. In addition to being a resort area, it was also a thriving Italian-American neighborhood with some Irish immigrants and Eastern European Jews as well making up the year-round population. The two performances, in which David appeared, one at 3:00 p.m. and one at 8:15 p.m, were the final concert performances for the summer season. The music was a mix of classical works by Tchaikovsky, Wagner, Rossini, Verdi, and David's performance of Bach's Invention No. 13 in A Minor and Mozart's Sonata No. 2, the Allegretto movement. He also played Rhapsodie Hongroise No. 2 by Liszt and Perpetual Movement by Carl Maria von Weber. Marching music and patriotic selections and "Irish Melodies," arranged by F. Godfrey, were played by Shannon's 23rd Regiment Band with Thomas F. Shannon, director. The mélange appears to have satisfied the diverse musical tastes of the audience. This concert must have provided a somewhat different musical experience for David.

The next day, it was back to Connecticut, this time to New Haven, for the Mathushek Piano Manufacturers at the Treat and Shepard Co. on Chapel Street at 3:00 p.m. and again at 8:00 p.m. At these two concerts, he was assisted by the eminent baritone Mr. J. J. Fisher. The actual program for these two concerts is reproduced here:

Program, New Haven, Connecticut, 1904
Photo: Courtesy of Moyer Family Archives

This program can be viewed quite humorously today, but at the time, I am sure some head rolled for the typesetter errors that it contains. David Clare Moyer? Below are two reproductions of the two programs, afternoon and evening as the above reproduction makes them unreadable:

Afternoon Program,	Evening Program,
New Haven, Connecticut,	New Haven, Connecticut,
September 12, 1904	September 12, 1904
Photo: Courtesy of Moyer Family	Photo: Courtesy of Moyer Family
Archives	Archives

The eminent baritone Mr. J. J. Fisher becomes Mr. S. S. Fisher. The correct initials for Mr. Fisher are J. J.[160] This recital certainly involved a fast train trip for David and Mary after the recital the previous night in New York.

For the rest of 1904, it appears that David worked very hard. He traveled to Elizabeth, New Jersey, where he performed a recital from 2:00 p.m. to 4:00 p.m. every day for a week at the Chandler and Held Piano Warerooms at the beginning of December. The programs of classical selections played for this week were divided into two parts, each supposedly taking approximately an hour to perform. Each part contained approximately eleven selections, a demanding repertoire for anyone, especially for a nine-year-old that was supposedly only seven years of age. The printed advertisement for this recital, at the very bottom, in italics states

Master Moyer, whose technique predicts for him a brilliant career, is considered a child marvel. He has recently been termed Paderewski Junior."[161]

This new title was bestowed upon David, and it is reasonable to assume that his mentor, Mary, may have had a word with the reporter for the *New York Herald*. David, all his life, even at the age of ninety-two years, loved to show everyone what fun music was. He paraded the music rather than himself.[162] On the same program, a quote from the *New York World* stated that "Master David Earl Moyer, seven years old, dashes off selections from Bach, Mozart, Chopin, Schubert, and Schumann with a skill surprising to his audiences, and shows great talent and careful training."[163]

There is no way to know if David ever read these programs or advertisements other than the musical selections he was to play. It is safe to say that these are pretty heavy duty plaudits to realize for a child so young. We can only wonder how statements like this would influence David at age nine.

Mary seems to have held very tight reins on David and his activities and his interactions. He may never have seen these statements until he reached maturity and sat down with the material. What is obvious is that most of David's recitals were sponsored by piano manufacturers or sellers in Brooklyn, New York, Philadelphia, New Haven, Bridgeport, Boston, and New Jersey. It is evident that it was Mary who made the contacts with these manufacturers and sellers and arranged these performance dates for David. Sometimes, it appears she was unscrupulous in the scheduling of these events, which certainly could be seen as somewhat draining for one so young. But David never voiced any negative feelings about this in his reminiscences. He was having fun, and to a healthy nine-year-old isolated from other children his own age, he probably didn't know anything different. David, it seems, simply took his life in stride and never made a fuss. It should be remembered that David was the working child in all of this, and it is doubtful that he had any knowledge of any earnings from his own labor. We now know this arrangement was simply accepted by society during this era. The well-published circumstances of child actors and performers who never saw ten cents of their earnings are widely known. David was no different. This was the way life was for David, and obviously, he accepted it. But was it right? Was it really acceptable for a forty-six-year-old music teacher to make most of her living from the tireless recitals and performances of one so young? Whether David was nine or seven years of age, as Mary claimed in his press releases and advertisements, he was still a child, and he merely followed the instructions of this woman on a daily basis. It appears she had full control, not only of his music instruction and development but also his total life. David continued this rather unbelievable pace of performances through October and November 1904. Gimbel

Brothers Department Store in Philadelphia ran a headline-style advertisement in the *North American* newspaper in Philadelphia. It read as follows:

Gimbel Brothers—Market: Chestnut: Eighth and Ninth
The largest Retail Store in the World
Master David Earl Moyer—the marvelous midget—plays fifteen minute
Piano recitals frequently between the hours of 10:30 and 12 and 1:30 and 4.
He is a seven-year old Philadelphia boy and he plays Mozart, Chopin,
Schubert, and similar music like a master.[164]

It would be nice to think that the Moyer family was in attendance at yet another of David's recitals and could find some humor in this advertisement, but this may be wishful thinking. They were probably in attendance but must have been quite annoyed at the advertisement by Gimbel Brothers Department Store. David was certainly not a midget! The suggestion in this statement by the local Philadelphia newspaper seems to imply that David was some kind of freak right out of a circus troupe. We know this is not an unusual viewpoint of young performers if they are over billed and unscrupulously portrayed by their manager. Two days later, David is doing more recital work back in New York. For November 13 and 14, he performed at the Siegel Cooper Co. in New York City, and the on fifteenth, sixteenth, seventeenth, eighteenth, and nineteenth, he performed for the Anderson & Co. Piano Warerooms also in New York City. Did he ever sleep? One thing for sure is that whenever David sat down at the piano for a recital, Mary was paid for his work. From this schedule, that seems to go on forever, David's earnings must have been supporting Mary's household completely. She couldn't give too many private piano lessons while she was on the road with David day after day after day.

On December 22 and 24 (Christmas Eve) David performed, for three hours each afternoon, recitals at the Bradbury Piano Warerooms at 500 Fulton Street in Brooklyn. Most other children, unless of course they were under the care of the state, would be at home with their families getting ready for the big Christmas celebration the following day with "visions of sugar plums dancing in their heads." It is doubtful that David was able to return home to wake up in his own bed for Christmas Day with his own family in Philadelphia that year. His family now consisted of Mary, her two sons, and his dogs and the cat. He must have felt the loss of not being with his own family. How could he not? Unbeknownst to David, his life as he knew it was about to go through some more major changes that would require him to rely totally on his own belief in himself, his talent, his deep desire to continue his musical studies, and his own wit.

Chapter V

Westward Bound

In January 1905, David and his mentor traveled to Washington DC. It is presumed that Robert and Clarence made the journey as well because David performed there for three continuous weeks. Chase's Polite Vaudeville Theatre, in Washington DC was a venue belonging to the B. F. Keith Vaudeville Circuit. David received wide press coverage of his performances during his twenty days in the nation's capital. The *Washington Post* dated January 9, 1905—under the heading "Symphony Concert" and subheading, "The Chase Audience Hears Master Moyer, a Child Prodigy"—mentions David's performance as "phenomenal."[165] David played at the de Koven Symphony Orchestra's weekly performance; however, the noted conductor Mr. de Koven was not present:

> And as a special feature a phenomenal piano performance by Master David Earl Moyer, a seven year-old prodigy hailing from New York.[166]

> The sensation of the evening was created by Master Moyer. The little fellow when standing erect just reaches the height to stretch his hands across the keyboard. He played Bach's Invention No. 8, F major, and a scherzo by Kullak and for an encore gave a brilliant etude of Czerny. He played with remarkable confidence and remarkable skill, even for one twice or three times his age, and fairly attested his claim to consideration as a child wonder. He was enthusiastically applauded and left the stage with every evidence of having achieved an artistic victory.[167]

David was not seven years of age, as advertised, but three months shy of his tenth birthday. Another article from the same newspaper, dated January 21, 1905, reads as follows:

> The Christian Endeavor Society of the First Congregational Church afforded its members and the public the opportunity of hearing Master David Earl Moyer, the seven-year old pianist of New York, in a concert Friday evening, January 20th. He was assisted by Col John Tweedale, as reader; Miss Edna Scott Smith and Miss Ethel Holzclaw, as vocal soloists; Mr. Elphonzo Youngs, Jr., coronetist, and Miss Lydia R. Hughes, accompanist. The mere mention of the numbers played by Master Moyer will uphold his claim to the title of "Paderewski, Jr." His first number included two inventions from Bach and a scherzo from Kullak, the second was the Fortieth Etude de Velociti from Czerny and the third was the beautiful allegretto sonata No. 2 from Mozart. The receipts are to be used in providing the society with the new Endeavor hymnal and for the purpose of increasing the missionary contributions.[168]

This is the first time in print that it is suggested that David had received the title of Paderewski Jr. The title was never claimed by David but was bestowed upon him by the reviewer. Always the quiet, humble, reserved, modest boy and, once he matured into adulthood, he remained a quiet, humble, reserved, modest adult—never one to blow his own horn. When viewed in its fuller context, it appears to be a powerful testimony given by the staff writer of the *Washington Post* who wrote a review of David's performances in Washington. It was written either after reading a prior review or after witnessing and writing the review of the concert performed by Eugene D'Albert where David was not simply in attendance but was invited to play one of D'Albert's encores.

Eugene Francis Charles D'Albert was born in Scotland in 1864 and was the son of the ballet master at Covent Gardens in London. He studied music at the National Training School in London that later became the Royal College of Music where he was awarded the status of Mendelssohn Scholar in 1881. D'Albert also studied in Vienna and Weimar. As a pupil of Franz Liszt, he became a piano virtuoso. Later in his adult life, he lived mainly in Germany and toured the world giving concerts. Subsequently, he became the court conductor at Weimar in 1885 and, in 1907, became director of the Hochschule für Musik in Berlin[169] where later David himself would study. According to the *Washington Post* for January 8, 1905, an article entitled, "D'Albert Next Friday," informs the readers about the concert to be held the following week by Eugene D'Albert with the Washington Symphony Orchestra conducted by Reginald de Koven at the

Lafayette Theatre. The unknown writer of this article states, "It goes without saying that the concert is of the utmost moment, musically speaking, as D'Albert is, admittedly and unquestionably, the greatest living pianist, even surpassing in technique and touch the genius of Paderewski."[170] David stated in his interview of January 1975 the following:

> Once when I was very young, Mrs. Walsh took me to the green room after a D'Albert concert in Washington, D.C. She frequently would take me backstage after a concert to meet such people. The audience was applauding; D'Albert already had given one encore. But the audience wanted more. He grabbed my hand and said, "Come on," and walked me out on the stage. He said, "Now play something." So I walked over to the piano and played, as I often did, standing up, probably, Mendelssohn's Spinning Song.[171]

With the attribution of the genius of Paderewski to D'Albert by the staff writer coupled with David's encore, it is more plausible that the journalistic Paderewski comparison was expanded to include the burgeoning talent of young David.

David Earl Moyer, Washington, D.C., 1905
Castle Photographers, 1221 Pennsylvania Ave.,
Washington DC
Photo: Courtesy of Moyer Family Archives

We have no hard evidence to suggest that David's family had current access to these newspaper accounts of his early or any of his future performances that involved the Keith Vaudeville theater chain or any other vaudeville group. His family would have been proud of him and his abilities while at the same time being assured of the integrity of his mentor at having him perform at such worthy causes as raising money to purchase hymnals for congregations at his performance on January 20, 1905, at the First Congregational Church, Tenth and G Streets in NW Washington and the evening before at Eldbrooke M. E. Church on River Road at 7:45 p.m.[172] However, the same family probably would have suffered some distress at any thought of their young son being involved with anything called vaudeville whether it is "polite" or otherwise.

While in Washington DC, David also performed at the White House for President Theodore Roosevelt:

> Then she [Mary Walsh] had me take a trip to Washington and play on the grand piano in the White House for Teddy Roosevelt. I think I remember I played a Mozart Sonata. I didn't have to sit down at the piano because I was just the right height to stand up. I simply walked up to the piano and played. You've seen pictures of that gold piano that was in the White House. I remember looking at it and thinking, hey, they didn't put any gold on the bottom of this thing. I was just a kid.[173].

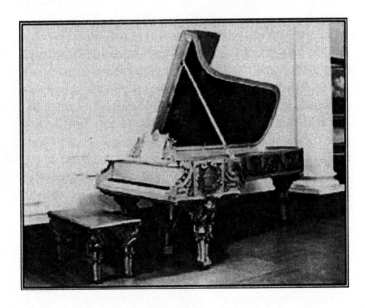

The Gilded White House Piano David played in 1905.
Photo: Courtesy of White House Historical Association, Washington DC

Although this event is not documented by White House archivists because the White House staff did not maintain the strict daily diary accounts of the President's day as they do now, it is typical of the mind-set of a child of David's age to remember something so significant as playing at the White House while the multiple week performances at Chase's and the various churches where he played seemed to pale in his memory.

Shortly after David's success in Washington, Mary Walsh decided that she wanted to take David and her two sons on a performing tour of the United States. While on a visit to David's parent's home in Philadelphia, Mary exclaimed, "Well, now we're going to travel." David recalls that Mary "was a restless individual . . . . We are going to make a trip through the United States." "It's perfectly all right to take him out," said Ida and Joseph Moyer. "She had told them she knew a lot of people way out West and that she was anxious to go."[271] But before leaving the New York area to begin the trip out West, Mary arranged another concert for David. This was a testimonial concert for "Master David Earl Moyer" (the Wonderful Boy Pianist), Thursday evening, January 26, 1905, at 8:15 p.m. The concert was held at the Anderson & Co.'s Recital Hall, 370 Fulton Street, Brooklyn. The program also states that Master John H. Jacobson, violinist, and Mr. Harry Wallace Steves, baritone, will assist. On the bottom of the program reads the following statement: "There will be a Silver Collection taken for Master Moyer's benefit."[174] This is typical of Mary Walsh's excessive enthusiasm. But was this excessive enthusiasm really directed toward David the ten-year-old child, his talent, and potential development as a virtuoso, or was it something else much more personal in the psyche of Mary herself? It is obvious that the proceeds of this testimonial concert were to provide the much-needed cash to finance the initial expenses of the tour. More than likely, it was this infectious excessive enthusiasm that swayed the Moyers decision to allow him to go with Mary from the beginning.

It appears that the vaudeville circuit provided a good deal of the work when there was not any other work scheduled with piano manufacturers or sellers Mary had contact with during their exciting trip around the United States. Few programs have survived from this time frame providing us little information regarding the totality of the performances. However, there are some newspaper archives that provide some tangible information.

Because David was so successful in Washington DC playing at Chase's Polite Vaudeville Theatre, Mary was able to develop contacts with the bookings managers at the individual theaters of the Keith Circuit. The procedure in booking acts was done individually at each theater through its local booking agent.[175] It was an effective network as managers knew other managers in other cities and towns and would give and receive recommendations regarding future employment of acts. The average vaudeville act could earn anywhere from $200.00 and upward for a week's performance of fifteen minutes per day, twice a day. The average cost of boardinghouse accommodation at the time was $15.00 per week for an apartment. Vaudeville performers were very frugal people and saved their money for the future. Many ended up wealthy![176] For Mary and the three boys, contact with the Keith Circuit or any other vaudeville circuit meant regular work and regular wages. The earnings were definitely needed for the survival of the four of them as well as money to save for the future. These performance experiences would have been enriching for David as he was now playing for audiences that probably did not have a particular interest or attraction to classical music per se. For David, as a youngster, this difference in audience was for him probably of little concern. He was a good professional child musician, and he obviously enjoyed playing. The change in audience composition was never really ever apparent to him.

> It was a regular circus act. We even were on the Keith Circuit, believe it or not, when we were out West, as it seemed like the easiest thing. There was nothing to it. Fifteen minutes on the stage. We would walk out, play a couple of numbers, and plunk that was the end of that.[177]

Before the troupe headed westward, David played what would be his last concert in Philadelphia until 1910. The venue was Grace Lutheran Church at Thirty-fifth and Spring Garden Streets, blocks from where he was born. The program that was handed out to the audience was several pages in length with advertisements from shoe stores, druggist establishments, candy shops, etc., all paying to support the concert.[178] The receipts from this concert must have been substantial, thereby ensuring sufficient funds to support the entourage for several months. It was by train that the happy troubadours would travel from one coast to the other with stops in between as they headed as far west as Hollywood. It must have been the journey of a lifetime for David, Robert and Clarence and for Mary herself as well. There are no previous records to suggest that Mary had ever traveled as far west as the troupe was now heading.

Train travel was enjoying its golden age between 1900 and 1945. The influence of the railroads was "all pervasive and utilization was universal."[179] Railroad travel prior to 1857 was considered a basic evil to be withstood. George Pullman invented the sleeping car in 1857 and the dining car in 1868 that improved the physical conditions for passengers, and thus more and more people traveled in luxury. Passenger cars by 1890 were considered "palaces on wheels" with the beveled glass, brocade upholstery and drapes, brass lighting fixtures and handrails, and the use of inlaid wood all adding to the luxury.[180]

The journey by train must have been an exciting event for David and the two younger boys. Robert and Clarence were born and reared exclusively in the city, and the opportunity to travel on a train and see so much of the countryside including cows, sheep, horses, and large farmlands, etc., things that they had probably never seen before, would provide an experience they would never forget. We know David had some experiences of country life as he used to visit his grandparents' farms in Pennsylvania when he lived at home with his family in Philadelphia. The younger boys probably would have been full of questions regarding the different farm animals that they saw, and David was right beside them to answer the questions and help to make the experience of travel even more exciting.

The first stop on the tour that we can document was April 24, 1905, Lima, Ohio. Although David tells us he performed in Buffalo, New York, this was probably before their arrival in Lima, Ohio. The *Lima Times Democrat* published the first of many articles extolling the virtues of the troubadours in a rather long article entitled "Tender Years: At Which Wonderful Talent Developed." The entire article from this publication is quoted below since it reveals the shift in status and changed mind-set of Mary Halter Walsh, now known as Madame Berlino, as being no longer just a music teacher, professional entertainment manager, or mentor, but now she becomes a mother in the fullest sense:

> Three precocious children, or, to use a stronger term, tots, in whom genius budded at an age so tender as to mark them as prodigies, are the guests of their grandmother, Mrs. Mary Halter, at 125 Northwest street. Accompanied by their mother, known in the world where talents are applauded as Madam Berlino, this wonderful family will receive from music lovers in Lima the attentions which Lima has bestowed upon them wherever they have appeared. Their stay is indefinite and the chance for some one of Lima's societies to engage them for an entertainment is too valuable to be lost sight of. That they will be much talked about, and as loudly praised as they have been in the East, is said without fear of contradiction, as the astonishing gifts these children possess lifts them in a sphere beyond their little world.

> The eldest of the three, and they are all boys, is Master David, just past his eighth year. He is conceded by the great musicians living to be the most wonderful performer in the world at his age, and they have gone so far as to say that he is even more wonderful than was Josef Hofmann, who created a furor with his surprising talents at even a more advanced period in life.

> When a *Times Democrat* representative called at the Halter home this morning it was in the midst of the masterful rendition of one of the youthful performers favorite selections. It was an interesting sight to

see the child standing before the instrument over which he has such strange command, executing arpeggios with a skill not to be approached by the ordinary musician of several times his age. When playing he does not occupy a stool, for when seated he could not reach the keys that bring out the harmony generated by Mozart, Bach, Beethoven, Chopin, Shubert and other masters, with all of whose music this wonderful prodigy is as familiar as other children are their A.B.C's.

He is a handsome youth, precise in his etiquette, courteous and gentle in his manner, and, like his equally wonderful younger brothers, schooled in a discipline that gives to the mother her share of the praise. But passing from Master David to Robert, aged 4 and Clarence aged 2, another remarkable development is brought to the surface. Possessed with astonishingly retentive memories, the two little tots name all of the presidents of the United States, the capitols of every state of the union, biblical facts and figures which would tax the mind of a theologian, and spell words that drive a newspaper man to the unabridged dictionary every day of his life. Master Robert plays accompaniments with his older brother, and never touched a piano until four months ago.

It goes without saying that Madam Berlino, who was formerly Miss Lina Halter, is a talented woman. She is a splendid musician and what she has discovered in her children is the result of painstaking care, and training since their babyhood. She has had her treasures before the masters and men and women of merit, and Joseffy says of Master David: "he has the most marvelous technique I have ever heard in one so young." He created a furor at the DeKoven symphony concert in Washington and received attention that would have turned the hearts of an ordinary youngster. President Roosevelt was one of his greatest admirers and had him at the White House in the presence of guests who were astonished at the gift of which he is an undisputed master.

Madam Berlino has engagements at Buffalo, Detroit, and Cleveland and will spend the winter with them in the South, being now on her way to the Pacific coast. One great event she is looking forward to with more than ordinary interest and enthusiasm is Master David's appearance next year in New York where he has an engagement to render Mendelssohn's concerto in G Minor, with orchestral accompaniment, the first time such an honor has ever been conferred on a child of such tender years.[181]

Lima, Ohio, was the hometown of Mary Walsh, and this appears to be the first time she visited her home city since she left for New York City in February 1900. What a wonderful way to return to your hometown! With three prodigy children that she claimed to be her own, she must have felt that local people would be impressed with her success as a musician and mother. How people reacted to these facts is questionable. Mary left Lima, Ohio, in 1900, a single woman with an obvious musical talent and returns in five years with a new surname (Walsh) and her nom de plume of Berlino and three children she claimed as her own, the eldest being, according to her, about eight years of age. It has been suggested that some of the townspeople must have been snickering and gossiping about this phenomenon behind her and her family's backs.[182] What else could they do? The locals could have perhaps more fully accepted the press reports regarding the origins of the three boys if she had informed the press of the truth regarding David as her prodigy and Robert and Clarence as her adopted sons. After all, it had been only five years since she left Lima unmarried and childless. Regarding the two younger boys, the truth was a bit more problematic. First, neither Robert nor Clarence resembled Mary in any way. They were of light complexion and she was dark, not unlike David's coloring. Adoption in this era was not something that people celebrated publicly. Mary could have simply included in the factual statement regarding David's identity that Robert and Clarence were also prodigy children placed in her care for tutelage purposes. Of course, this statement would not have been totally truthful but would have been understandable. Even in the present day, there are still suspicions that have been handed down as part of the oral folklore regarding Mary Belinda Halter Walsh Berlino. But Mary didn't give any explanation; therefore, the tongues did wag. Her own family went along with the fable quite easily. It was more likely easier for them to accept publicly and benignly her mythic hyperbole than to show any embarrassment at her audacity. Her mother, Mary Halter Sr., went along with the stories and claimed these children as her own grandchildren.[183]

Four days later, the same *Times Democrat* on April 28, 1905, ran another article regarding the intent of the female citizens of Lima and others to develop an Institution for Lima's Girls to match the level of service and participation that the young men of Lima had access to through the local chapter of the YMCA. It was stated that the fundraiser was scheduled for an afternoon matinee performance "in which Madam Berlino and her three wonderful children will be the drawing card and the opera house will be secured for the event."[184] The program was almost completely musical with Robert playing with David on the piano the selection by Czerny entitled Concert Etude in F Major (Allegrissimo) and Clarence performing a recitation together with Robert as well as one with David.[185] The *Lima Daily News* in their review of the performance stated

The music loving public that attended the performance of the Berlino children at the Congregational Church on Saturday afternoon were more than delighted with the artistic work of the little wonders. The program of classical music given by Master David was wonderfully executed, while the playing of Master Robert Berlino was of a like nature. Clarence, in his wonderful memory tests delighted his hearers, and three more charming little artists have never appeared before a Lima audience.[186]

David, Clarence, and Robert were hugely successful in their performances in Lima. The troupe of three performers continued their visit with periodic public performances around the area while staying at the home of their "grandmother," Mrs. Mary Halter in Lima.

The next stop that we have documentation for is the First M. E. Church in Kankakee, Illinois. The troupe performed there in early July 1905. The program we have relating to this concert informs us that David's piano performances were still the main event. We do know that Mary had purchased a small-sized cello for Robert and a small-sized violin for Clarence, but it does not appear that they performed these instruments at this time. Robert and Clarence were still the little masters of recitation. In David's "Reminiscences" he recalls how he knew all the railroad stations en route because he sat in so many of them:

The boys and I sat and played around in the stations while Mrs. Walsh went into town, found a place to live, and through references, arranged a concert! Sometimes it would be a church affair where we would get half the money. And the rest would go to the church. Other times, she came back and said, "Let's take the train to the next town." Sometimes we would stay at one place for several weeks.[187]

These various train stations where the boys waited for Mary to return with the news of what was going to happen next must have provided a false sense of freedom and, perhaps, some anxiety. They could sit together and play little games to amuse themselves while walking around the train station and could be fascinated with the architectural features and talk about the different things they were seeing. We can be sure that they found lots of funny things to see that entertained them. A simple exploration of the men's room must have caused some laughter and excitement for the three of them. Like all children, they must have found amusement and delight in the simple things. To be sure, David probably did his best to watch the two little ones while at the same time there was the train station manager on hand in case things got a bit out of control. Those were the days when people, perhaps foolishly, could leave three young boys for an hour or so at such a public place as a train station and not be concerned that someone would behave in an untoward fashion or interfere with the children in any way. Sadly, those days of trust have long ceased in most societies. However, it is a certainty that Ida Moyer, David's mother, or any other mother considered respectable would have never left any child in any train station on their own. How could Mary not know the inappropriateness of that act? Perhaps that is the difference in a mentor and a mother.

Photo of Kankakee Train Station, Kankakee, Illinois
Kankakee Visitors Guide

The next stop on the tour for the Berlino children and Mary was Colorado. Records available indicate that the wandering minstrels were in the state of Colorado for a minimum of five weeks, and because of the amount of performance work available, they may even have stayed longer. This western area is probably most famous for Pike's Peak or Bust gold rush boom beginning in 1858.[188] Like all mining areas, Colorado experienced booms and busts. In response to the busts, a large sugar beet industry was developed in the area of Fort Collins, not far from Colorado Springs. Because of the upswing in the economy of the area in 1904, tremendous building investment began to shape the area. New residences and businesses were constructed as well as buildings to house institutions for promoting culture. Company-owned coal camps were everywhere in Colorado.

These coal camps were specifically built to house the miners and their families, and the people had a constant desire for entertainment of any kind and, in addition, built many churches. These churches were always raising money from entertainment proceeds throughout the week, and many entertainment groups were hired to perform, following the usual arrangement of half the proceeds to the particular church community for the building fund and the other half going to the entertainers. For general entertainment purposes, most towns built their own opera houses. These opera houses were everywhere and did not restrict their presentations to pure opera. Minstrel shows, variety shows, vaudeville, and burlesque shows were extremely popular, and entertainers were widely valued by the audiences.[189] The Berlino troupe could have spent many, many weeks in the state and played many venues, therefore, increasing their funds.

The *Sunday Gazette and Telegraph for Sunday*, August 6, 1905, reported that Mrs. William Wells Price of 215 South Nevada Avenue, Colorado Springs, entertained on July 31 at 4:00 p.m. a group of invited guests to hear David Berlino "the wonderfully gifted 8 year old pianist."[190] This concert is billed as being in honor of David. Many other musicians were invited to the afternoon of musical culture, and one name in particular stands out to anyone who is versed in great violinists. Mr. Louis Persinger played at this gathering. At the time, he was only eighteen years old. Persinger trained at Leipzig Conservatory in Germany before he finished his training with Eugene Ysaye in Brussels.[191] Persinger became leader of the Berlin Philharmonic orchestra and the Royal Opera Orchestra in Brussels. In 1915, he was appointed leader and assistant conductor to the San Francisco Symphony Orchestra. He succeeded Edward Auer in 1930 at the Juilliard School in New York City. He taught Yehudi Menuhin, Isaac Stern, and Ruggerio Ricci.[192]

The three Berlino boys are mentioned in this article when they performed at this venue:

> Interest, though naturally entered in the playing of the Berlino children. David played a "Scherzo" (Kullak), "Spring Song" (Mendelssohn), and "Perpetual Movement" (Weber), with superb technique and temperament. No less remarkable was the playing of Robert, whose selections were "The Cuckoo Song" (Hummel), and "Spinning Song" (Spindler). Even baby Clarence played a selection, and all of the children gave an exhibition of memory training. They named the presidents together with dates of office, and the capitals of the United States, besides giving words suggested in five languages.[193]

Although David did not appear to remember this particular private venue, he remembered another venue where meeting the well-known musician, Alberto

Jonas, who would serve as a watershed in David's prodigious career. David explains in his own words:

> I can remember Colorado Springs. I went to somebody's home where I played for a man by the name of Alberto Jonas. He was quite well known. You will find his name in almost any book of musicians. He was a composer as well as a very famous teacher. He said, "Bring that boy to Europe. I'll teach him—for nothing, of course." And so, she (Mary) said, "All right, next year I will."[194]

We have no information from David in his childhood years to suggest that at that time he was ever aware of who Alberto Jonas was. Jonas, a Spanish-born pianist (1868) performed and taught extensively in Europe and the United States during his life of seventy-five years. He was a pupil of Arthur de Greef of the Brussels Conservatory and also studied under Anton Rubinstein at the St. Petersburg Conservatory. Jonas was himself a prodigy, and he made his debut in Europe in 1880 at age twelve.[195] While in the United States, he founded the Detroit Conservatory in Michigan,[196] held affiliations with the Juilliard School in New York City, the Curtis Institute in Philadelphia, and in Berlin, Germany, he also maintained professional association with many of the conservatories there as well as hundreds of private students, many of whom were taught for free. Although he did compose many small compositions for the piano, he is much better known for his instructive work written with Rudolph Ganz. *The Master School of Modern Piano Playing and Virtuosity* was published in six volumes during1922-1926. This series provided the student with a universal method of piano practicing methods that embraced all the technical, aesthetic, and artistic features to be mastered in order to achieve the highest level of virtuosity as a pianist. Included in this work are excerpts from the pedagogy of Clementi, Brahms, Czerny, Falcke, Germer, Herz, Hummel, Joseffy, Kullak, Liszt, Moszkowski, Phillip, Pischna, Plaidy, Rosenthal, Schytte, Tausig, Safonoff, and Wiehmayer.[197] Maestro Jonas concertized widely and was invited to someone's home in Colorado Springs to perform in late August 1905 where he was introduced to young David Berlino. This event was pivotal for David although he gives no clues just how pivotal this informal meeting in 1905 would be for him in his "Reminiscences" in 1975. For a musician of Alberto Jonas's stature to make such a commitment to David's mentor demonstrates how impressed he was with David's playing and his musical potential. Shortly after this meeting, Alberto Jonas did return to Germany where he directed the Hochschule für Musik in Berlin. David would become one of his private students. The Colorado visit by David and his two young companions and Mary Walsh Berlino ended on September 2, 1905, after the billed and advertised "Last Appearance, Master David Berlino, Boy Wonder

Pianist" was held at the Unitarian Church, corner of Tejon and Dale Streets, in Colorado Springs.[198]

The evidence provided by Mary's scheduling of the tour to be in one place or another at a particular time was to ensure that the proper contact with the selected individual she believed capable of advancing David's career, as well as her own, was on Mary's part a stroke of sheer organizational genius. It was no accident or coincidence that David, Mary, and the two boys were presented at this particular home on the appropriate day in Colorado Springs where Alberto Jonas, the virtuoso, was also in attendance. Obviously, their time in Colorado was very well planned by Mary, and it is believed she understood precisely who was who in the music world within the United States and, more importantly, precisely where they would be on a given date and was able to obtain an invitation for herself and the three boys to ensure that David performed. More than likely, it was her contacts with the piano manufacturing industry that provided her with this information.

If all Mary wanted was opportunities for invites to be in the right place at the right time to further David's career and to support her own desire to live and work in Germany, then there was no reason why the tour didn't stop in Colorado Springs that summer and return to the East and begin making the necessary travel and living arrangements to, in fact, take the next step, which was, of course, to go to Europe. The one thing Mary still needed was a substantial amount of money that would pay for the travel and living expenses in Germany. At the same time, she needed to be able to further convince the Moyer family in Philadelphia to allow David to go with her. Mary had, according to David, convinced his family regarding her status as a widow and that she came from a very wealthy family in Lima, Ohio. She could hardly at this point in time show up at the Moyer home looking for funds for the European experience and simultaneously produce her plan to remove Ida and Joseph's youngest son to a place so far away. Earning money to reach her target goal was still a priority for her, and she needed David's earning power to make it happen. The three children were totally unaware of this reality. They appeared happy on their tour, and to them, that's all that really mattered.

The small troupe continued their tour into Utah. Society in Utah seems to have rallied around the secular concerts and entertainments provided by traveling entertainers. Salt Lake City in particular was a very different experience from the other Western cities the troupe would have visited. "The city itself changed from an early pioneer outpost to a thriving urban metropolis. Much of this progress was due to the completion of the transcontinental railroad in 1869 and the subsequent spread of a network of railway lines throughout the state which forever changed it from its original, isolated area geographically to an area that rapidly developed a diversified economic and industrial area."[199] Salt Lake City was a very modern city when David and his traveling companions arrived in September 1905. The Mormons were no longer the majority of residents in Salt Lake. The very early twentieth century witnessed the arrival of many new immigrants to the community, and they represented many different religions and cultures.

> The Main Street was littered with poles and all kinds of wires; an electric streetcar system served over 10,000 per day. The city had full-time police and fire departments, four daily newspapers and ten cigar factories. Salt Lake City even had its own well established red-light district.[200]

The residents of Salt Lake carried on a love affair with entertainment. They loved theatrical presentations, concerts, dances—just about anything that they could enjoy. The Salt Lake Theatre was built in 1861 and "served as a center of community expression, much like a medieval cathedral"[201] that hosted religious meetings, political meetings, and many dramatic presentations, just about anything the community desired within the bounds of decency. The Salt Lake Theatre was the center of social life for all. The building could accommodate approximately one thousand five hundred in the audience. It was Brigham Young who insisted that the building of this theater was paramount in order to bring what he termed "civilization"[202] to this frontier outpost of twelve thousand people.[203] In an article by Walker, he explains that the main goal of this theater was to "provide proper drama in an uplifting atmosphere. Plays ranged from Shakespeare to the more common didactic melodrama. At the beginning, 'home' or stock companies, often supported by a professional actor or actress in a main role, formed productions. But the emphasis later shifted to touring stage companies, with little local participation."[204] Most of the eminent performers and lecturers on whatever circuit performed at some point in the Salt Lake Theatre. These notables included Oscar Wilde, the phrenologist Dr. Orson Fowler, and many notables from the American stage, including P. T. Barnum, the Barrymores, Sarah Bernhardt, Buffalo Bill Cody, Eddie Foy, Al Jolson, and Lillian Russell.[205] It is hard to imagine that David, Robert, and Clarence did not perform at this venue although we have no playbill or advertisement to confirm this fact. They did, however give two concerts at Phillips Congregational Church located at Seventh East and Fifth South Streets. On Monday, September 25, in the afternoon, and on Tuesday, September 26, evening performances were given. On the program are listed business sponsors of the event including the Clayton Music Company that advertised a "brand new piano for the small price of $135.00." David performed three selections on the piano, and Robert and Clarence performed their well-rehearsed recitations.

Congregationalism flourished in Salt Lake City as an opposing religion to Mormonism. Churches were being built throughout the area at an unimaginable rate. Fundraisers were an ongoing effort to raise money for the new buildings.

These buildings included not only the church nut also social halls and school buildings. Mary was able to offer the boys as entertainment for these endeavors, and they received 50 percent of the proceeds for their efforts. Their stay in Salt Lake City appears to have been a very rewarding one.

It is important to mention at this point in David's story that one requirement of all serious musicians is daily practice. This is paramount if they are to continue to maintain and advance their technique.[206] David never mentions, during this tour of seventeen continuous months, how this was facilitated. However, much later in his life, as an adult when he was professor of pianoforte at Oberlin Conservatory, he ran a piano summer school opportunity for some of his students at his summer retreat the Music Box on Vinalhaven Island off the coast of Maine. He encountered the same problem with his own students. The Music Box had a few pianos, but not enough for all the students to have adequate practice time every day. He sought permission and in some cases rented piano usage at various churches in the village of Vinalhaven. This is more than likely the same way Mary handled this problem for him while on tour. Robert and Clarence, in addition to performing recitations, were also students of the cello and violin as well as the piano. Although, the cello and violin were portable, it probably wasn't always advisable for them to practice within the confines of their temporary accommodation as it may have been disturbing to the other guests. More than likely, Mary sought the use of pianos and practice space at local churches wherever they were while on the tour.

The next stop after Salt Lake on the tour was Butte, Montana. Now, that must have provided a real shock for all the children and Mary herself. Butte is located in the southwestern corner of Montana. It was a mining town since its foundation in the late nineteenth century. Initially, it was gold and silver mining that dominated the area. After a few years, it was discovered that copper was in abundance, and the demand for copper to be used as wiring for electricity provision took over. Because of the intensity of the copper mining industry, people from all over the world came to work in Butte. Some came from as far away as "Ireland, Wales, England, Canada, Finland, Austria, Serbia, Italy, China, Syria, Croatia, Montenegro, Mexico and most of the USA."[207] Butte was a "wide-open town" where any and, it seems, all vices were available.[208] This hardly seemed like the kind of place in which Mary would have been comfortable with the three children. David was hired for a week of performances, twice a day at Orton Brothers Piano Store in downtown Butte, located at 213-215 North Main Street. Inside the program are listed twenty selections that David played. In addition, at the bottom of the program, it lists David as "Walter David, 8 year old pianist."[209] The timeline suggests that they didn't spend any more time there than was absolutely necessary for fulfillment of the agreement with the piano shop. Everything was unionized in Butte by the time David and the group arrived. The unions were a strong presence, and every walk of life seemed to be under the very watchful eye of the union bosses. "By 1900 there were thirty-four different unions organized in Butte and these unions represented the construction trades, brewers, teamsters, blacksmiths, and hack men. Even the musicians had a protective Union as did theatrical stage employees and theatrical ushers."[210] It was rumored that even the prostitutes had representation in a union. Now, how does a small performing group of three children with their mentor find other work to increase their income and live fearlessly in a place like Butte in 1905? The answer is simple: they don't. They do what they agreed to do and leave town on the first train, which is basically what David, Mary, and her two little boys did. All of them would have seen things they probably hadn't seen before, such as American Indians and Chinese people. They may have seen a few Indians at a distance in other parts they had visited, but in Butte, the Indians still lived on reservations close to the town, and the Chinese people had immigrated there in great numbers to work in the mines and on the building of the railroads. The sources used for this examination of Butte tell us that the Chinese still wore their traditional clothing complete with braided hair. The boys' eyes must have glistened at the wonder of all this!

The troupe departed from Butte and continued their journey in a northwest direction to Spokane, Washington. From what evidence is available, they performed recitations, and more than likely, David played his usual selection of piano arrangements at the Crescent Department Store for a full week. A copy of a letter of reference was found among the items in David's scrapbook stating that

> the Berlino Troupe has been with us during this week. They are wonderfully talented children and have proven an interesting attraction. We do not hesitate to recommend them to any store desiring such an attraction.[211]

Once again the boys were successful. There is no information available as to what other performances they gave while in the area. They continued on to Portland, Oregon, for more work after Spokane. The only evidence we have of their being in Portland is a photograph of the three boys and one of the dogs. The photograph that follows is interesting.

There is no way to make any definitive comment regarding this well-composed photo of the boys. However, David's eyes are downcast and his facial expression appears to be one of exhaustion. Clarence, balanced on the back of David's chair, appears forlorn, and Robert, standing to David's right, has the same serious, unenthusiastic look of his younger brother. Even the beloved Rexie appears sleeping. It is possible that there were multiple photos taken at this studio, but this is the only photo that has survived. This photo is a photocopy of the original that is part of a photo collage that hangs in the hallway of the William Moyer

The Berlino Boys in Portland, Oregon, 1905
Photo: Courtesy of Moyer Family Archives

home in Massachusetts. There is a period of approximately fourteen weeks when the boys were in the State of Washington that cannot be accounted for. The next time there is evidence of any performance is in mid-February 1906 in Hollywood, California. Perhaps Mary sent David to Philadelphia for the Christmas holidays. David does admit quite openly that he missed his brothers while on this tour. He stated during the taped interview conducted by his son and daughter-in-law in 1975:

> But then, every three months or so during our tour of the West, I would go to Philadelphia for a week or two, and then back I'd go. It was a pleasant life. Always I went home for Christmas.[212]

This statement of David's seems quite accurate. In 1903, the timeline suggests that he was free of performances for a few months between his appearances in Boston and New York. On Christmas 1904, David worked on Christmas Eve at the Bradbury Piano Wareroom in Brooklyn, New York, but he could have traveled on the following day, Christmas Day, to Philadelphia as the records indicate he did not appear in Washington DC until January 9, 1905. There is another gap of almost two and one half months between May 19, 1905, when in Lima till August 6, 1905 where he played in Colorado Springs for Alberto Jonas. The fourteen-week break between Portland, Oregon, and Hollywood, California, could have been spent traveling to Philadelphia and back to Portland as it took eighty-four hours to make the trip by train.[213] One fly in the ointment in trying to establish David's location during these various breaks is to account for the continuing pressure of raising funds to finance Mary's plan to move to Germany, which finally occurred in 1906. It is difficult to imagine that the money for David's travel expenses back home to Philadelphia was completely subsidized by Mary. Perhaps his parents paid his way home, or equally likely, he did not really return home at every break in scheduling.

The actual invitation to attend the "Musicale" at the home of A. G. Bartlett in Hollywood, California, is unique in the memorabilia collection of David Earl Moyer. Sadly the condition of the one-hundred-and-two year old invitation makes it unavailable for use. In addition to being the only formal invitation we have for "interested people" to attend such a performance, the boys were only at this home for four days. Mr. Alfred Griffith Bartlett (1850-1923) was a well respected member of the Hollywood Civic Community. In addition to owning several businesses, one of which was a music store, he was heavily involved as a contributor to the establishment of the Hollywood Public Library and was a charter member of Community Park and Art Association that helped to establish the famed Hollywood Bowl performance venue. At this time, Hollywood was not annexed to the city of Los Angeles as it is today; therefore, it had a separate identity. For sure, he was big money and big ideas! Mr. Bartlett's estate boasted of seven acres of rare shrubs and flowers from all parts of the world.[214] His widow and two daughters sold five acres of the property in 1927 for the sum of $1,340,000.

In an article appearing in the *Los Angeles Herald* for February 28, 1906, entitled, "Tots with Adult Brains Do Mental Acrobatics," written by Ethel Dolson, a staff writer, informs the readers that "three wonder children" have arrived in Los Angeles.[215] In addition to extolling great compliments to their mother-manager-"sole instructor" she also is very impressed with the memory feats of these children, "ages 8, 4, and 3." One of the many things Mary was good at was keeping their real ages a secret. David was two months away from his eleventh birthday, Robert was already six, and Clarence was five years old.

> The three, as well as being able to answer a multitude of questions in history, can name all the books of the Bible, recite psalms, and give numerous facts about it with a promptness that is astonishing.[216]

This fact stated by the author, Ethel Dolson, is remarkable because as an adult, David was a complete and total agnostic, according to his youngest son, Bill.[217] His parents would have been very proud of his biblical memory, but it appears that for David, in the long term anyway, these exercises had no real meaning other than superficial memory feats and nothing to do with religious belief. There is no way to ascertain if these exercises ever meant anything different to Robert and Clarence. In addition to the writer being impressed with these skills, she was also extremely impressed with David's performance repertoire:

> But most remarkable of all is the playing of David, the eldest: Only 8 and having a repertoire of over fifty compositions of the masters, embracing such works as Mendelssohn's "Spinning Song," Beethoven's Sonata Pathetique, Czerny's Concert Etude. Last night he played Kulak's "Scherzo" for one delighted listener with a finish that showed a technique and understanding one would hardly expect in a child.[218]

David performed in a concert at Blanchard Hall, located at 231-235 South Broadway in Los Angeles, on March 3, 1906. The concert venue was located in the same building that the Bartlett Music Company was located. Both were owned and operated by A. G. Bartlett. It appears that he must have performed several times at this venue vis-à-vis the *Los Angeles Herald* article quoted above. David performed three inventions by Bach, the Concert Etude in F Major (Allegrissimo) by Czerny, and two etudes by Stephen Heller and Perpetual Movement by Carl Maria von Weber in the first part of the program. The second part of the concert he performed Spinning Song by Felix Mendelssohn, scherzo by Theodore Kullak, andante from the Sonata in C Major by Mozart, Gallopade de Concert (presto) by Carl Czerny, and finished with the rondo from the *Sonata Pathetique* by Beethoven. It is worth mentioning that for this concert, the admission price was a simple "offering at the door." In the same article, the author, Dolson, expresses the following:

> To the normal adult there is something pathetic about the usual child prodigy. The head of a solon on the shoulders of a 3 year old seems out of place.[219]

A "solon" is defined as someone wise, especially an experienced and wise legislator or politician.[220] The point of Ethel Dolson's is well taken. Of course it's unusual, and Mary knew that these same normal people would either pay an admission price or make a monetary offering to witness such a spectacle.

By March 17, 1906, the traveling minstrels are found performing in El Paso, Texas.[221] The trip from Los Angles must have been long and colorful for the three children. More than likely, they would have traveled on the famed Sunset

Limited that ran from Los Angeles to Miami. The route was completed in 1883 by the Southern Pacific Railroad.[222] This trip begins at the main Los Angles Union Passenger Terminal where it connects the early Spanish missions. At the border with Arizona, the train crosses the Colorado River and follows the Gila River through the Sonora Desert. It is reported that the Sonora Desert is really five thousand square miles of pure silence. Today it is a vast eco-center and is well preserved. Before the train arrives in Phoenix, the Hassayampa River is crossed.[223] Legend from the area claims that anyone drinking its waters will never tell the truth again. The boys would have enjoyed hearing this myth. From Phoenix, the train travels onward to Tempe, Arizona, crossing the Salt River. From this vantage point, the Superstition Mountains can be seen. This is the site of the story of the Lost Dutchman mine where a German prospector Jacob Waltz found himself working an important silver vein during his youth. After the man's death, several prospectors tried to find the vein but apparently it had mysteriously disappeared. The train continues its journey through Tucson.

Tucson is an old city and sits in a large valley between the Santa Catalinas, the Rincons, the Santa Ritas, and the Tucson Mountains.[224] After crossing into the state of New Mexico, the children would once again see more mountains. The first group would be the Peloncillo Mountains famous for their booty of copper, gold, and silver. Following soon after is the Cochise Mountain where some say you could see the silhouette of the great Indian chief of the same name looking upward. There is the great Continental Divide to be crossed on this journey. This happens midway between the two towns of Lordsburg and Deming, New Mexico. The divide is crossed by the train at an elevation of 4,587 feet. The waters on the eastern side flow into the Atlantic Ocean while the waters on the western side flow into the Pacific Ocean. As the last leg of the journey begins to unfold, the boys would enter the Rio Grande Valley, see the Rio Grande River, and arrive in El Paso, Texas, safe and sound.[225] This journey would have provided the three boys with an educational experience hard to top. It would be nice to think that Mary would have had her tour book out and explained the different sites to the boys as they observed them. There is no way to know whether this was her style of travel or not. It seems she spent a good bit of time drilling them on historical and biblical facts while they traveled to keep their recitations in top form. But David leaves no information for us about this trip from Los Angeles to El Paso.

El Paso was a bicultural, bilingual city. When the boys reached El Paso, there was as much Spanish spoken as English.[226] This was another unique opportunity for them to experience something they would probably never experience again. They performed at the local synagogue on May 17 at 3:00 p.m. and again on Monday, March 19 at 8:00 p.m. A synagogue seems an unusual place to perform, but usually, the entertainers performed in either a building adjacent to the temple or in the basement. There was such a need for entertainment in areas like El

Paso that everyone wanted to get in on the hosting. The main sponsor of the concert was Middleton and Hudson, a local piano music store in El Paso. The musical program appears to be very much the same as the program performed in Los Angeles. David, Robert, and Clarence performed their recitations and all the music played solely by David. There are no newspaper accounts available regarding the concert, only the printed program found in David's scrapbook. The visit does not seem to have been a long one in El Paso as the boys performed in San Francisco on Monday, the March 26. They would have needed time to rest before their return journey to San Francisco.

David performed from March 26 to March 31, 1906, in San Francisco. Because of the earthquake that was to occur eleven days later, no newspaper reviews survive to inform us whether this performance was as impressive as his previous performances; however, there is no reason to suspect anything else.

The Moyer Family Archives hold eight large-sized photographs taken in San Francisco by Bushnell Foto. On the first photograph, in the lower right hand corner is a salutation: "Sincerely yours, David Berlino."[227] The actual handwriting is Mary's, not David's, and is consistent with other handwritten notations on other documents by her. David's cursive handwriting was probably not acceptable to Mary's standard for the purpose of autographs as he had not reached his eleventh birthday, and further explanation could have been the lack of time to put into practicing his handwriting. Copies of this photograph were presented to those concert attendees that requested an autographed photograph as a souvenir.

Sincerely yours, David Berlino, 1905
Photo: Courtesy of Moyer Family Archives

Another posed photo of the three boys praying had definitely been sent to the Moyers in Philadelphia. On the back of this photo is written in Mary's hand, "The Evening Prayer." Mary's use of David's name as Earl appears on the back of this photo (what the Moyers called him) appears to be used only by her when the Moyers received something she sent to them.

"The Evening Prayer" 1906
Photo: Courtesy of Moyer Family Archives

Five of the other photographs all contain, on the back, a message to either "Grandma, Grandmama, or Grandma and Aunt Helen." (Mary Halter Walsh's sister, Ellen, was always referred to as Ellen with the exception of these photos.) Mary probably had more than one copy of these photos printed, and it is plausible that the Moyers received copies with appropriate greetings on the backs as well. However, there is only one copy of each in the Moyer Family Archives, so perhaps David was given these photos by Mary herself in her later years when he was an adult. If nothing else, these photographs demonstrate that the troupe made sufficient money to pay for such a collection.

These photographs reveal how young these children must have looked because of their sizes. As mentioned previously, David was one month away from turning eleven years old, Robert six years, and Clarence was five years of age. The two younger boys look incredibly petite for their age, and this may be an effect from improper nutrition as babies, or perhaps, they simply had parents and ancestors who were diminutive. We know that David's First World War draft registration form listed him at five feet four inches in height, and we also know that all three of his brothers were approximately the same height as adults. It is not hard to understand how Mary could exploit the lack of physical stature of the three boys to market them as even younger. This offers some explanation as to why journalists reported the boys' abilities as more amazing than perhaps they actually were.

Following the performances in San Francisco, the group continued their journey to New Orleans, Louisiana. The trip by train began in San Francisco and crossed through Nevada, Arizona, New Mexico, and Texas into Louisiana. Once in New Orleans, they performed at the House for Incurables (Children's Annex) on April 16, 1906. The C Major Sonata by Mozart was performed by David although according to John H. Baron of Tulane University in his widely publicized article "Mozart in 19th Century New Orleans: Satchmo meets Amadeus," it was "one of the Berlino brothers."[228] It had to be David because he was the only capable pianist of the three children. There are no copies of programs or other information to enlighten us whether they stopped en route to perform or simply just made the journey directly to New Orleans. Mary's style was never to simply have one concert venue for such a long trip, so they more than likely did play in other venues either in New Orleans as well as along the way.

The chilling press reports of April 18, 1906, in Philadelphia, as well as in Lima must have created a fright unknown before by both the Moyer and Halter households. *The Evening Bulletin* newspaper's headline for Wednesday, April 18, 1906, read

Earthquake Shatters San Francisco; City in Flames; Hundreds are Dead[229]

The following day, the *Philadelphia Inquirer* didn't bring any good news regarding the devastated city:

Earthquakes and fire, which yesterday visited San Francisco and nearby towns on the California coast, left in their wake a terrible tale of disaster, death and destruction. In San Francisco the dead are variously estimated at from 700 to 1500; probably 1100 being a conservative estimate. The property loss will aggregate at least $100,000,000, possibly half as much again, in the city, while the outlying towns have also suffered severely.[230]

We do not know whether the Moyers were informed of the actual dates and places David was to perform in advance or not. Real fear must have hit the Moyer household hard. The only real form of communication was by mail or telegraph. Long distance telephone service was still in its infancy. Although the Moyers did have a telephone (Preston 6474) at their new residence, a large apartment located at 126 South Thirty-Fourth Street in Philadelphia, they would not have been able to receive or place calls to such a distant location as San Francisco. Even if they could, the telephone service was inoperable in San Francisco during this disaster. Hopefully, once Mary learned of the great tragedy in San Francisco, she immediately sent the Moyer household notification that they were all safe and sound. Later that April, the three boys are reported to have played in Atlanta, Georgia, first, at a benefit concert for the survivors of the San Francisco Earthquake, followed by two other concerts at the Cable Piano Hall also in Atlanta. The *Atlanta Constitution* for April 22, 1906, informs the readers of the talents and ambitions of the three boys.

> He [David] gave way at the piano to Master Robert, who looks like a cherub or like the little vestal choir boys one sees in pictures or reads about in stories of souls which have been uplifted by their song. Roberts little fingers hardly seemed as long as the breadth of the ivory keys, but he secured a good tone and played with unerring accuracy of noted time. Then little Clarence then formed with mother and brothers a quartet, for which he counted the time while he played the treble in a march for four hands, his tiny fingers climbing laboriously over the big keys but touching them correctly and producing genuine tone.
>
> The two smaller boys are quite as remarkable in other mental exercises as in playing, and an important feature of the baby's attainments is that he begged to be taught and is the pupil of the oldest brother, David.[231]

The unknown author of the above article also informs the readers that David "is bright and alert of expression and indicates not at all any undue mental strain."[232] There must have been theories about such young prodigies suffering from emotional difficulties brought on by performing at such an early age for the author of this article to mention such a thing.

Fanny Bloomfield-Zeisler (1863-1927) in an article entitled "Appearing in Public" states that when children frequently appear in public, it is more than likely harming them as potential adult performers.[233] Mrs. Zeisler would have been five years older than David's mentor, Mary, so, basically, she would have learned her craft and formed her expert view during the same period. There is evidence that Fanny Bloomfield-Zeisler was herself a child prodigy, born in Austrian Silesia and at age two moved with her family to Chicago where she studied with Bernhard Ziehn and Carl Wolfsohn, both noted teachers.[234] The first concert Ms. Zeisler performed was in Chicago in 1873 at the age of ten. She then traveled with her family to Vienna to study with Theodore Leschetitzky for the next five years before returning to the United States to concertize in many of the major American cities. For Fanny's teachers, during this period, the age of fifteen appeared to be an appropriate age for serious public performances. David, it should be remembered, was performing quite seriously at the age of seven. These facts beg the question, why was David doing all the performing that basically was offered to him at such an early age? The many performances we can document seem almost too much for such a young person. However, there were different reasons why David was doing so much performing: as it has been noted previously, he was providing much of the income for his mentor and her two sons as well as himself during this period. Without David, Mary would more than likely still be in New York City, demonstrating pianos for piano dealers and teaching many more children the basics of pianoforte. It appears that she herself may have been bored and unfulfilled with this more-meager lifestyle. David possessed that marvelous "rage to master" factor so unique to the prodigy that he couldn't say no. According to David, he was having a wonderful time and never complained about teaching little Clarence or about the amount of performing he did or the hours spent in train stations responsible for the two younger children and the dogs or about anything, for that matter. But during this tour period, did David's artistic ability, technique, and repertoire advance much from what he was playing the year before? It doesn't seem that any significant advance is evident from the records. The performances were concluded in Atlanta on March 25. The troupe continued to travel and possibly perform at every whistle-stop along the way till they reached Lima on May 15, 1906. Of all the information that has survived in print and in the family archives from the United States touring time of seventeen months, there is never any mention of any kind of educational activity such as reading, writing, mathematics, or anything resembling school subjects. The boys had to learn the answers to all kinds of informational recall topics to be sharp on the performing stage, but there is no mention of formal educational advancements for any of them. They had to have practice time built into their schedules, as previously discussed, but children need more than rote answers to rote questions, more than a plethora of successful performances and appreciative applause, more than knowing all the train stations from coast-to-coast to develop in the same way their peers were developing. They needed playmates, education, and something called home! They needed a base, and sadly never had this. David knew where his home was, although, he rarely saw the place and the people he loved most in the world, his own family. Robert and Clarence certainly had many experiences during those seventeen months that they would never forget, but they never had the rooted experience of that something the rest of us take for granted. Shortly after their last stay in Lima, Ohio, they boarded a boat in early July 1906 in New York harbor bound for Germany where they would finally be in one place and perhaps have some playmates their own ages and experience a real home for themselves, hopefully.

CHAPTER VI

Life in Berlin

The merry troupe of David, Robert, Clarence, and Mary set sail for Europe after their final concert in Lima on May 19, 1906. According to the *Lima Times Democrat*, they were to leave in early July. They traveled on the *Phoenicia 2*, one of the America Line ships from the pier at Hoboken, New Jersey,[235] on to Hamburg then by train across Germany to the city of Berlin to 19 Steigerlitzer Strasse where they would all reside until 1914. The journey across the Atlantic in 1906 would have taken approximately seven to nine days depending on weather conditions. Overland travel by train at this time was efficient in Germany, and the German railroad system from 1900 provided thirty-one thousand miles of overland tracks.[236] In 1900, Berlin had a population of approximately 2.5 million inhabitants, including many immigrants from mostly Eastern European cities.[237] Of course, there were some temporary immigrants such as Mary and the three boys as well as thousands of foreigners in the city there for the purpose of obtaining a musical education. At the time of their Berlin arrival, Germany appeared to be a quiet country under the guidance of Wilhelm II. The internal struggles and manipulations of the monarchy against the Reichstag (the elected governing body) probably did not occupy much space in the local Philadelphia newspapers available to David's parents and brothers.

There seemed to be no apparent reasons for the Moyers to refuse Mary's request to take David to Germany to advance his musical training. David's family seemed to have every confidence that this next step would be to his benefit. His recent tour of the United States gave no indication that it affected him in any negative way. Probably, Mary never discussed with the Moyers the day-to-day details of the troupe. David, as usual, just took these events in stride, and to him, they included no minor improprieties, just ordinary life as he knew it. David's parents seemed to be in agreement with Mary that his not attending formal schooling was appropriate since he was receiving a tremendous musical education.[238]

By the time David arrived in Berlin, there had been a fifty-year tradition of Americans coming to that city to pursue further musical studies.[239] What made David's arrival somewhat distinctive was his youth and the fact that he had an unrelated adult as his temporary guardian. However, he wasn't the only eleven-year-old who had lived that way. Artur Rubinstein, at age ten, also studied in Berlin without any member of his immediate family accompanying him. According to E. Douglas Bomberger in his doctoral dissertation *The German Musical Training of American students: 1850-1900,* the German Conservatory system had attracted over five thousand American students by the turn of the century: "Nearly all of America's influential musicians in the late nineteenth and early twentieth centuries were products of the German conservatory system."[240]

As mentioned previously, David was to receive instruction from Alberto Jonas as promised during David's informal audition before the maestro in Colorado Springs in 1905. He began to study with Jonas shortly after his arrival in Berlin. David's first comment in his "Reminiscences" regarding his teacher, Alberto Jonas, was that Jonas's teaching gave him a terrific technical facility. Jonas said, "If you are going to become a musician when you get older, you can learn all the sensitivities of music, but now you must be an athlete on the keyboard."[241]

Alberto Jonas, 1880
Photo: Courtesy of Hamilton Ontario Collection

The lessons involved David's meeting with Alberto twice a week, an hour each meeting.

> In the beginning, the lessons were all about technique, technique, technique. I had to learn to play every scale upside down, inside out and in all directions and at any speed. Every day I put in at least an hour on pure technique. I don't think students do that today any more. I couldn't get students to do that. I had certain exercises for going through all 24 scales in about 10 minutes time, a bit like an athlete trying to break a record.[242]

In addition to David's tutelage under the guiding eye of Albert Jonas, David had other things to learn and master. The most important item was that David, as well as Robert and Clarence, had to learn the German language to a reasonable level of fluency. This is, perhaps, one of the explanations for the absence of documentation of David as a public performer in Germany prior to 1908. From what David reveals, there were "teething problems" once they set up their residence at 19 Steigerlitzerstrasse.

> The police would come in and want to know all about you, where you were from. They had many questions. You had to have a pretty logical story. So, she said, "My name is Madame Berlino. My husband's dead and these are my three children.[243]

David's statement that the police were keeping an eye on strangers provides a small window indicating that being strangers in a strange country was not a simple matter. This was part and parcel of life in Berlin during this period. In 1891, the prime minister of Germany, Caprivi, persuaded the Reichstag to pass certain social measures deemed necessary. Included in these new laws was the prohibition of work on Sundays and more general restrictions on both child and female labor.[244] David, quite freely, adopted the same surname Berlino as Madame and the boys at this time. "I took her name simply to be part of the trio."[245] Prior to David's time in Berlin, Mary did on some occasions bill him as David Berlino, but we do not have any evidence that David was in agreement with her practice. This is the first time David mentions that he was part of a trio. While living in New York, he performed as David Moyer in the very early days with Mary, but subsequently, David Moyer gave way to David Berlino. Mary did, at a later date, formally refer to the group of musicians under her tutelage as the Berlino Trio.

Humpty-Dumpty Circus, Berlin, 1906
Photo: Courtesy of Moyer Family Archives

Mary's unquenchable thirst for photographs of the Trio must have spurred her to have the above picture taken in the early days of their stay in Berlin. She probably thought she would use the above photo for the purpose of obtaining bookings for the boys as a trio, although, David never played the violin. The photographer she chose probably did not have a piano on hand for David to pose with, so she just used what was available. The historical literature of the period regarding musical performances by children indicates that this type of advertising was frowned upon by the Germans in particular as they were very serious about their music and very particular as to who performed it in their country.

No. 19 Steigerlitzer Strasse is no longer standing in modern Berlin nor are any of the houses from No. 21 on down in the same block. There are many houses that appear to have been built in the same era as number 19 and are of the same design. This fact has been confirmed by the Landesarchive in Berlin. The place where No. 19 had stood is now a children's play area with rocking horses, jungle gyms, swings, and a few sliding boards. The rest of the space where other houses below No. 19 once stood is a waste ground. According to David, Madame had rented an apartment on the second floor of No. 19.

I lived in the same building with Madame . . . She had an apartment, and a very nice apartment, on the second floor, while I had a room on the fifth floor. Mine was one of those sky view rooms with dormer windows, a charming room; that's where I lived.[246]

David stated that the great pianist, Josef Hofmann, also lived at No. 19 Steigerlitzer Strasse.

21 Pohlstrasse (formerly Steigerlitzer Strasse)
Berlin, Germany
Photo: R. D. Moyer, 2005

He commented that Hofmann was always making things. "He made a bicycle from old parts which he collected and put together. All of us went to his apartment and I played for him. He was a nice fellow and a very small person physically."[247] It is easy to see why David was so impressed with Hofmann. In addition to being a great pianist, Hofmann physically was small like David. David always had an interest in building models, and to see how someone, not unlike himself, who could build a bicycle from random parts would have reinforced David's own desire to build many things. Later in David's life, he would build beautiful pieces of furniture for his home from his own designs and by his own hands. When he was nineteen, he built a model airplane that later was constructed as a full-sized flying machine.

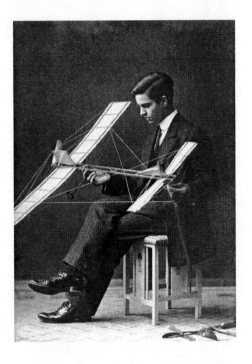

David and his model plane, Berlin, 1914.
Photo: Courtesy of Moyer Family Archives

David's model airplane becomes reality with the help of his friend
known only as Carral. Date unknown.
Photo: Courtesy of Moyer Family Archives

The Berlin census records for 1906 thru 1914 show that not everyone residing at No. 19 Steigerlitzer Strasse was a musician. Other tenants residing there were professional people that included medical doctors, nurses, and lawyers.[248]

No. 21 Steigerlitzer Strasse is still standing and occupied today although the street name has changed to Pohlstrasse. Pohlstrasse is a very long wide street; it is tree lined, and appears to be an ethnically mixed residential neighborhood within the area designated as the Tiergarten. The neighborhood appears that it was a comfortable place to live and must have been even more comfortable in the early part of the twentieth century when David, Mary, and her two sons lived there.

Bomberger's study, referred to above, included very important information for any American student thinking of traveling to Germany to study music in the second half of the nineteenth century.[249] Alexander Wheelock Thayer from Menden, Massachusetts, probably the best known nineteenth-century American music historian and the first reliable biographer of Beethoven contributed weekly columns to *Dwight's Journal of Music*.[250] Under the title, "Musical Correspondence," dated Berlin, September 17, 1858, and subsequently published on October 30, 1858, in Boston, he explained the curricula generally offered to all students of the German conservatories. Thayer also gives the readers thorough information regarding Sterns Conservatory in Berlin, its requirements, and even lists the "principal teachers" and their areas of specialization. The *hochschule* where David would eventually attend did not exist at the time of Thayer's writing, but his explanations regarding study in Germany provide valuable insights into what, in general, the prospective American student needed to know. Learning the German language was a priority for anyone going to any city in Germany for serious study. Thayer recommended that transatlantic passage should take place either at the end of May or early June to give the student adequate time to organize accommodation and, more importantly, hear and learn German before classes begin, usually around October 1. Furthermore, he lays out in full detail the monetary requirements for the prospective student and explains the amount of money needed for a year's study in Berlin. The normal conservatory course lasted three years.[251]

> Passage from New York to Bremerhaven, see the newspapers for steamships; but if you will do as I have done twice, take passage in a first class Bremen sailing ship, you will pay fifty dollars. At the end of the passage you will give as "drink money" to the steward a dollar or two. Reckon your passage up to Bremen on the steamboat

as another dollar; half a dollar will get you and all your baggage to the hotel and a couple more dollars will pay your hotel bill for a day and get you to the station, or ought to do so. Ten dollars is amply sufficient to carry you from Bremen to Berlin, where, for the two or three days which must elapse before you find rooms, you will be at $1.50 to $2.00 per day.[252]

Thayer cautions the future student that if the German landlords realize the possible tenants do not speak German and "do not know German habits"[253] they will be charged $12.00 per month for the same room for which a German would only have to pay $8.00. His advice is based on the fact that the German attitude toward those who speak English is that they are merely geese waiting to be plucked! The landlords are also afraid that the foreigners do not know the ways of the German people and will therefore cost their landladies too much trouble and expense.[254] No "hundred thousand welcomes" for English speakers in Germany during this period, that's for sure!

Most students intending to study a musical instrument in a foreign country normally had to transport their own instrument when they traveled. For someone intending to study pianoforte or the organ, bringing his/her own instrument would be impossible. Thayer's answer to this quandary was that the cost of renting a grand pianoforte would be $2.00 to $4.00 per month, and if organ study was the choice, organs for rent were not available at this time, but "a set of pedals adapted to the piano" may be rented for an extra $2.00-$4.00 per month." [255] Other expenses outlined by Thayer include, "daily portions of coffee and bread and butter need not cost over a thaler or a dollar a week. You dine at an eating house, as do probably 25,000 other persons daily, at an expense of 15 to 20 cents . . . Your tea or regular supper may cost you from 10 to 30 cents . . . Washing is about 50 to 75 cents per dozen depending if you have many small pieces or not. You must buy your own lamp and pay your landlady for the oil you burn. Your room has a great tile stove, which is heated with wood twice or three times a day, according to circumstances, costing 10 to 15 cents a day."[256]

These expenses, as outlined by Thayer in 1858, do provide a reference point for calculations to estimate the costs involved in 1906 when David, Mary, and the two boys traveled to Berlin, how much real money they needed to establish themselves and how much money it would cost them to live before Mary could realize any income. The chart below shows the purchasing power of the money in U.S. dollars in Thayer's time, 1858, David's time, 1906, and the approximate dollars and cents in 2005:

Expense Type For 1 Adult	1858	1906	2005
One Way Passage and initial settlement expenses	$71.00	$77.64	$1,800.84
Room Rent/Month.	$8.00	$8.75	$202.95
Room Rent/Year	$96.00	$105.00	$2,434.99
Piano Rental/Month	$3.00	$3.28	$76.08
Piano Rental/Year.	$36.00	$39.36	$912.76
Organ adaption/Month	$3.00	$3.38	$76.08
Organ adaption/Year	$36.00	$39.36	$912.76
Food, Laundry, Heat Light/Month	$25.78	$28.21	$654.33
Food, Laundry, Heat Light/Year	$309.40	$338.52	$7,852.00
Total Expenses/ 1 year	$548.40	$560.52	$13921.15

Chart: Travel and Living Expenses for one adult in Berlin
for the years, 1858, 1906, and 2005.[257]

The fact that Mary with the two younger boys lived together in an apartment while David had his own room on the fifth floor would require variations in these expenses. The monthly charge for an apartment for one adult and two children perhaps would have been less than the price of separately rented rooms for each individual. The daily living expenses would have varied as well because it's always cheaper to cook at home for three or four people than eating meals out. It is unknown whether the landlady would clean the large apartment unless, of course, Mary paid an additional fee for this service as well as laundry service through a supplementary arrangement. These costs, although not essential here, would make a difference in her weekly budget. Additionally, and unmentioned by Thayer in

1858, was the matter of taxes to be paid on all monies by Americans whether they brought the money with them, received it from home, or earned it working in Germany. The rate was two percent of all money over $300.00 per year for each person.[258] It is doubtful that David's allowance would have been $300.00 per year from the House of Ibach, his future sponsor. After all, he was only eleven years old and was being sponsored in part by Mary. If he received $15.00 per month as his allowance from the House of Ibach, then that amount would have amounted to approximately $180.00 per year. His family would send him money occasionally, but it is doubtful that he received more than $120.00 per year from them. It is more than likely that any money at David's disposal was kept under the minimum amount of $300.00 per year so he could avoid all taxes during at least his early days in Berlin. It is unknown how the German government would have known what amount of money he received from his family since more than likely they sent him cash inside a personal letter. If we assume a median cost of $20.00 for rent for Mary's apartment and add to it the additional estimated $25.78 per month for heat, light, and grocery expenses, the total yearly expense for her and her two sons would be approximately $549.36. However, the $300.00 government-imposed limit on each person would have reduced her individual money to a lower amount, approximately $185.00 per year. The same figure would apply to her two sons individually. Mary and her two sons together could have up to $900.00 per year in money, earned or otherwise, without paying taxes on any of it. This allowed her significant earning power as a music teacher without taxation. In Bomberger's study of American music students in Germany between the years 1850-1900, he quotes the outrage of a mother of one of these students, Maud Powell:

> I tell you the Germans who go to America and become what would here be called rich, and then grumble about taxes, had better come back here to refresh their memories as to how they were taxed before they went to America. Why it is something fearful the way they are taxed; all because of their immense army. The standing army numbers about 800,000, while the reserves swell the number to between two and three millions of men.[259]

Even though A. W. Thayer provides us with a basis for monetary estimation of what it would cost for three children and one adult to live in Berlin, the question of how Mary could organize all this across an ocean is still unanswered. So how does a single American woman, forty-eight years old, arrive in a foreign city with three young children, find a place to live, attract music students for herself and, hopefully, instrumental tutors for the boys so easily? Whom did she know? It has already been concluded that Mary did not know the musical greats that she led David and his family to believe she did know. The research suggests that she must have made contact with someone, some organization, or a sponsor. Alberto Jonas did give his word that he would teach David for free, that's a certainty! It is doubtful that Alberto Jonas had any time or any concern, for that matter, about how David would get to Germany, where he would live, or how he would live. It wasn't his problem. Jonas offered to teach David, not adopt him! How then did she manage?

Mary had made one trip to and from Germany in the summer of 1903. It is plausible that the trip was made solely for the purpose of marketing herself as a music teacher (after all, she was already entitled Madame Berlino) and marketing David as a promising prodigy to a piano manufacturer in Berlin (there were many) for the purpose of gaining monetary sponsorship. The sponsorship of David could and, in the end, did provide an income base for her to fulfill her dream of being able to live and teach in Berlin, the unofficial center of the world for music training and scholarship. Mary was not an unintelligent person. She fully understood the earning power of a prodigy as gifted and talented as David. For her to make the initial trip to Germany for the reasons explained was a stroke of sheer genius on her part. Just as the piano manufacturers that had outlets up and down the East Coast of America had provided David with what seemed to be endless public performances to demonstrate how wonderful their pianos were, they also provided Mary with several apartments to call home, all located over piano shops in New York City. They supplied an endless parade of students to teach, all for the end result: selling pianos.

As mentioned earlier, the Gibson Mandolin Company did the same thing with their sales employees, except that the employees had to travel around their area and start mandolin clubs in order to create a market for the selling of mandolins. Albert G. Bartlett of Hollywood, California, who sold pianos and owned his own concert hall, Bartlett Hall, provided performance work for David and more than likely had contacts with other piano sellers in the West that helped make the Western tour a financial success. Further, it is also possible that the reason Mary left New York City after only six or seven months was that the piano manufacturers wanted her to draw more customers into their sales premises to sell more pianos. In those days, many people could play the piano for demonstration purposes. That was nothing special. So many people could do it, and many could rival her piano playing and sound just as good with little training because they had a natural gift of playing by ear. There are people who can hear a tune once and imitate it. These people can make the same sound on the piano as the trained pianist, especially if the selections played are brief and already known by the potential customer. The piano manufacturers needed to market their goods on a wider scale, so they chose to use prodigies like David. Young small children that had a repertoire of good music to present could do that task on a larger scale such as in a large wareroom where several dozen people could attend or in concert halls or department stores where the manufacturers could, in essence, fill the place with potential purchasers. It was certainly a more productive method to increase sales than just using the available tune-playing salesperson in the sales shop for the individual potential buyer.

The House of Ibach in Berlin did the same. As a consequence of World War II, no historical correspondence records survived from Ibach to ascertain whether Mary actually sold to the company this rather unique idea of promoting a prodigy to enhance sales or whether this was common practice on the company's part. One thing that seems certain is that Mary had investigated the possibilities of some sponsor relationship with Ibach for David on that mysterious trip in 1903. The U.S. tour that followed had multiple purposes. A nice portfolio of David's press releases regarding his performances could have and probably were presented to the company by mail sometime during 1905 or early 1906 as proof of his ongoing artistic success. Mary may have been told by the piano company's representatives that real proof of David's success and abilities would be necessary for them to consider the kind of sponsorship she needed to realize her dream of becoming a part of the Berlin musical community. The favorable impression that David made on Alberto Jonas in Colorado Springs and Jonas's subsequent commitment to teach David was the equivalent of a gold seal of approval that, in the end, the House of Ibach needed to convince them that young David would be a worthy recipient of their generous support.

The Ibach Piano Company began humbly in 1794 when its founder, Johann Adolph Ibach, built his first piano for a local customer in Schwelm, Germany. The piano business proved very successful as more artisans were hired, and they began to manufacture organs. Over the years, the family had opened additional factories in Barmen and Berlin with retail shops and concert halls in Cologne, Düsseldorf, and Berlin, that magical center of great music.[260] The House of Ibach maintained a retail outlet in Berlin that was located at 27 Steigerlitzerstrasse, a few doors away from where David lived at No. 19. Ibach instituted a program of sponsorship in annual piano competitions and individual sponsorship of musicians. On their Website, they now publish from their limited archives a list in German of musicians they sponsored in past years including some names that might be familiar: William Backhaus, Berlino Trio, Johannes Brahms, Ferruccio Busoni, Teresa Carreño, Rudolf Ganz, Theodor Leschetizky, Franz Liszt, Ignaz Paderewski, Anton Rubinstein, Emil Sauer, and Felix Weingartner. The House of Ibach paid the tuition fees for David to attend the Hochschule für Musik in Berlin, beginning in 1911.[261]

The fact that the Trio was listed as one of the groups they sponsored accounts for the sponsorship that Ibach gave to David singularly and also covered whatever support Mary received as manager of the trio, which would include her two sons.

Years later when David was telling the story of his remarkable life to his youngest son's family in Wayland, Massachusetts, in 1975, he still could not understand how Mary (Halter Walsh) Berlino ran the tour with the three children in 1905 and 1906 across America, or how she had managed to arrange the transition of the troupe, including the dog, to Berlin in 1906, and once there, how she had supported them. Most probably the influential and financial role of the House of Ibach is the key to any plausible solution. David's free piano, Mary's use of a piano to teach her students, her recruitment of students, David's private room on the fifth floor, Cornelius Van Vliet's free cello lessons for Robert, and Albert Spalding's free violin lessons for Clarence, all bear the mark of Ibach. These expenses and opportunities would probably have exceeded Mary's economic possibilities as well as the range of her personal musical contacts at this early time.

Cornelius Van Vliet was born in Rotterdam to American parents in 1886 and spoke fluent English. There is not much information available to us regarding this musician, but years later, when David was teaching at Bucknell College in Pennsylvania, Cornelius Van Vliet was one of the performing artists to visit the area and appeared on a program with David. During this earlier part of his life, he was on tour in Berlin, and so he graciously agreed to teach young Robert.

Cornelius Van Vliet with the Trio and Madame, 1908
Photo: Courtesy of Moyer Family Archives

Albert Spalding, the nephew of the immortal baseball pitcher of the 1800s, was born in Chicago, Illinois, in August 1888.[262] Albert's uncle and his father formed the A. G. Spalding sporting goods company. Young Albert, according to his biographer, requested a violin for Christmas in 1895, and having received one, he began his studies with Ulpiano Chiti at his family's winter home in Florence, Italy. In 1902, Albert was fourteen years of age and entered the Bologna Conservatory with the intention of completing the coveted degree and title of Professor of Music. He passed his examinations with a total of 48/50 points. There was only one other student in the history of this conservatory who accomplished the same feat at the same age. That was Mozart![263]

Spalding's studies continued for two more years at the French National Conservatory in Paris, and he began a concert tour of French provinces, England, and Germany where he met the eminent violinist and teacher Joseph Joachim. Joachim, now seventy-five years old, refused to take Spalding on as a student as he, Spalding, was already on the path to great success and didn't require any further study.[264] It must have been around this same time that the eighteen-year-old Spalding somehow became involved with the household of Madame Berlino and taught Clarence for free. There are no records of how long this relationship lasted, but it did in fact happen and is not in conflict with Spalding's personality or drive. As stated in the biographical sketch provided by RCA Corporation: "He established not only personal fame in the world's finest musical centers, he was also a pioneer in bringing the finest classical music of Bach, Beethoven and Mozart to all States of the Union."[265] Spalding was so committed to spreading his joy and love of music to everyone that teaching a relative beginner violin student was not a problem for him.

David succinctly describes the routine of everyday life for the Trio once they became settled in their new home. Of course, in the first months, it is more than likely that becoming fluent in the German language was the priority for all of them. Mary already spoke German, so the task was probably hers alone to teach them. Mary's proficiency in German was more than likely acquired as a school student in Lima. According to Dr. Robert E. Ward, president of the German-American Historical Association of Cuyahoga County, Ohio, the state legislature provided for German instruction in public schools beginning in 1838. In later years, David told his family that he usually thought in German and translated into English what he wanted to say. It is also possible that on many of those tedious train rides across America in the previous years and during the voyage across the Atlantic, Mary may have already started teaching the children German. According to David, tutors were hired for academic subjects:

> My life during that Berlin Period was rather methodical. I would have a tutor from about 8-10 every morning in academic subjects. Then I would practice from 10 to 12, until lunch. In Berlin, I wasn't allowed to play the piano between 12:00 and 2:00 in the afternoon, because people took their naps then. I read or did other things after lunch. Then about 2:00 I'd again practice until about 4:00. After that I would do anything that happened to come along . . . Eight was the normal time for the evening meal in Germany.[266]

This statement by David reveals the tempo and structure of the household at this time. It must have been an adjustment for all of them after the somewhat erratic ad hoc lifestyle they had lived previously while on the tour. The other activity that would have been somewhat different for the boys was their attendance at public concerts and theater presentations as part of the audience, and not as the performers. Concerts and operas were plentiful in Berlin at this time because of the sheer numbers of students from all over the world studying music there.

On October 25, 1908, Ms. Marie Sloss, originally from Lincoln, Nebraska, had her "Letter from Berlin" published in the *Sunday State Journal*. Her letter informs the readers that she is studying at the Sterns Conservatory in Berlin under the direction of a Mr. Spencer. At the time of her writing, her letter home informs us that there are "116 teachers of pianoforte" employed at the Sterns Conservatory.[267] Ms. Sloss further states that regarding the current concert series, "The concert season is scarcely commenced but we have a feast of good things already and an astonishing array of choice material to choose from in the near future. Last Sunday's *Lokal Anzeiger*, announces nearly 150 concerts of importance to occur within the next few weeks."[268] Attendance at these public concerts in Berlin and the other major German cities that housed music conservatories cannot be underestimated for the aspiring music student. Alexander Thayer said it so pointedly in his 1858 article in *Dwight's Journal*: "One learns music, as he does the language, by continually hearing it 'spoken.'"[269] For David, Robert, and Clarence, attending concerts was a necessary part of their musical education. Prior to David's many, many performances beginning in 1903, when he traded his home life in Philadelphia for the life he was to lead with Mary, it is doubtful that there were many occasions for him to experience great music of the variety he was now able to hear on a regular basis. The availability of concerts must have been pure magic for David. He could now hear the music of the great masters played by the greats and, at times, the not-so greats and make his own judgments regarding the performer's technique, tone quality, and artistic expression. These experiences must have influenced him for the rest of his life.

David helped Madame with her teaching duties when her class was too large for her to handle. There were times when Madame couldn't teach for one reason or another, so he simply took over her students and did the job.[270] The teaching, practicing, and learning were all so much a part of David's life from his early days in Brooklyn, New York, that teaching in Berlin was just more of the same routine for him: "Even when I was a kid, I taught some, because I was already playing in public to some extent."[271] Just as he was her mainstay when they all traveled around the United States on the one and a half year "seat of the pants" tour the previous year, he was assigned duties to buy train tickets to places he had never heard of and took care of the two younger boys when Mary needed to leave them in train stations as she looked for work and accommodation in each new town.

Whenever David performed in public, an Ibach grand piano was delivered to the appropriate venue. His personal piano in his rented room was replaced with a new one every couple of years.[272] To a large extent, this arrangement with the House of Ibach permitted David a bit of space away from Mary and the two other boys. The single room on the fifth floor of the same building must have provided a much-needed refuge for David. The sheer noise in Mary's apartment could have been distracting not only to those in her apartment but also to those in the other apartments in the same building. There were children's piano lessons going on in the daytime. Robert needed to practice his cello, and Clarence needed to practice his violin, and David loved to practice and play the piano as well as build his models. Such a cacophony! The boys were getting bigger and probably required more space as well.

On Sunday, March 14, 1908, David, Robert, and Clarence performed in Berlin, probably a church hall or some similar venue. The printed program does not inform us where this "Grobes Konzert Nanu" actually took place.[273] Whoever made up this program had a sense of humor. Under the words *Grobes Konzert* the program informs the audience the concert is being "performed by the smallest orchestra of the world."[274] The translation of the German lists the musical presentations by the three boys. David performed Fantasia Impromptu by Chopin; Robert performed an aria from Martha by Friedrich von Flotow and a Concert Etude by Czerny. Clarence performed Invention in F Major by Bach; Scherzo in F Major by Theodore Kullak and "Big March Violin" by Hiller. "Nanu," prepared by Eulalia Jammeskloss, the poet, is a review of nine scenes as per Goethe for the "free stage Hansa." No evidence of reviews for this presentation is available, but it's refreshing to know that Mary's two young sons had made significant progress with their violin and cello playing that they were able to appear publicly with David. Life at this time appears to be settled and stable for the boys and Madame. David makes no references at this point to having any friends or the boys as having playmates. Perhaps there was enough socialization going on with students coming and going for lessons with Madame and the daily tutoring sessions that finally materialized were stimulating enough. David was used to having no friends his own age; it is difficult to know whether he had any opinion on the subject. He had his weekly lessons with Jonas and many matinee concerts to attend, so he probably considered himself busy enough. "That's where I lived. I'd get my own breakfast and my own lunch. Most of the time I had the main meal with her."[275]

In November 12, 1908, Mary and Clarence left the port of Cuxhaven, Germany, bound for New York City.[276] No records exist to suggest how long they stayed in New York City, what the purpose of their visit was, or even if they stayed in New York City or traveled elsewhere in the United States. There are no records telling when Mary and Clarence returned to Berlin. At the time of year they traveled across the Atlantic, the ten-day voyage would have been rough and cold, to say the least. Is it possible that Mary realized that in the near future, David would be progressing even further in his career, and this progress would, in fact, take him further away from her as he would develop into an independent performing musician? In her own mind, she must have been aware that by age thirteen, she had given him all the training she had to offer him. Earlier, David quoted Mary's philosophy regarding talent: "Oh, talent—it's 90% hard work and 10% talent." Maybe Mary was just bored with her life as music teacher and mother. That may have been the reason for the journey. David and Robert did not go on this trip, according to the arrival records.

David had not been home to Philadelphia since he arrived in Berlin in the summer of 1906. He must have yearned to go with Mary and Clarence, but per usual, David, Mary's mainstay, says nothing about this in his "Reminiscences." The implication that David stayed behind with Robert alone is mind boggling. David does state, in his own words, that he often helped Madame with her teaching classes, and there were times when she was absent from the Berlin home, and he would take her students and teach them just as she would. However, he never mentions whether any adult was called in to the apartment to mind him and the children during Mary's absences. Most likely in David's mind, keeping an eye on the boys was no different from teaching Mary's students. David was convinced of his personal status in Mary's eyes. He said in his "Reminiscences," "She [referring to Mary] never treated me as a child."[277]

David does however speak about the time Mary spontaneously announced a trip to Florence, Italy: "I remember once, the Madame said, I'm going to Florence. You three stay here in this apartment. David, you can take my students."[278] From Italy, the Madame wrote: "I've got some engagements here for you three. Get the next train from Berlin to Italy." So we went to Italy for about six weeks, playing in several places as a trio, and I played some solo engagements."[279] It was more than likely at this time that the Trio and Mary visited the family home of Albert Spalding's parents in Florence as David did make reference to visiting them. Hopefully, when Mary took these impromptu jaunts, she did have some adult supervise and help David and the boys in her own absence.

On the tour of the United States, when the boys were much younger, it appears she did leave them in train stations without adult supervision. Mary would have needed at least the better part of a day to get to Florence by train from Berlin. Any letter sent by her to the boys in Berlin would have taken another couple of days, at the minimum, to reach them. She would have needed, at the minimum, a day or two in Florence to organize engagements for the boys' performances. Added together, David may have been in charge for almost a week. Again, David never mentions any other adult looking after him or the two boys. Mary's style, thus far, seems to be one of thinking that David would totally cover or take over for her during her intermittent periods of absence.

In July 1909, David made himself absent for a while from the Berlino household. It was summertime; Jonas was no longer in Berlin as the *sommersemester* at the conservatories and universities had commenced and David's lessons with him had ended. One day, Mary asked David, "Would you like to go home to your parents?"[280] David did not hesitate in saying absolutely, "Yes!" David had not seen his family since the summer of 1906, so of course, he was anxious to go home. As David related the story of going to the Hamburg-American Packet Company located on the Unter den Linden to buy his ticket the day before he was to leave for home, he made it sound as if it were just another old ticket to purchase on any day as he had done so often for Mary in his previous eight years. This ticket had to be a bit more special to him. How did he keep his feet on the ground as he walked down the most famous street in Berlin? From David's telling of the story, he said, "It meant nothing to me to buy a ticket."[281] David was in for a bit of a surprise when he approached the ticket office. He felt so confident that there would be no problem that he simply went up to the ticket window and requested a ticket on the Hamburg-America Line for New York the next day. The ticket clerk surprised David with his response when he asked, "What is your age?" David responded, "I'm eleven." The ticket clerk responded with yet another question, "Who is your guardian?" David's instantly reacted by stating, "I don't have a guardian." The clerk then told David, "Well, we can't sell you a ticket that way; you can't get on that boat without a guardian." David must have been stunned both by the directness and absolute tone of the ticket agent. Who wouldn't have been shocked when, in fact, he was so confident that taking the trip across the Atlantic on a boat was nothing more than taking a ride on a streetcar? David then asked, "How can I get a guardian? I know the captain and the head steward." That didn't help either. The ticket clerk must have just looked at him and thought to himself, *Who does this kid think he is?* It is doubtful that the clerk ever heard the names of the captain and head steward that David mentioned. He was probably just following the rules of the company. The fare rules stated that a child was defined as between the ages of one and ten years and half fare would be charged.[282] So there stood David, puzzled. This had to be a new experience for David. Someone had actually said "no, you cannot" to him. It is doubtful that David ever heard many people say those three words to him. His parents allowed him basically to do his own thing with his mentor, travel anywhere and everywhere with her, and be her mainstay. The above interaction may have taught him a very valuable lesson; in the eyes of the public at large he was just a kid, nobody so special that rules would be relaxed.

However, it took more than an officious clerk to thwart David's desire to go home. The ever-resourceful David tells the rest of the story in his own words:

> I left but stood looking at the ticket office window when a couple of Americans came along. I heard them ask each other, 'Is that the boat we're going on tomorrow morning?' That was the boat I wanted to take. So I spoke to them, and I said, "I want to go on that boat tomorrow morning, but they won't sell me a ticket because I don't have a guardian. I've been on boats before. I'm an American. I want to go to Philadelphia.

I know my way. Will you be my guardian?[283] These people were total strangers, they were just tourists. I told them my story and said, "I have the money to pay for the ticket. I won't bother you a bit on the boat." The tourists said, "I guess it's all right."[284]

David handed his $30.00 to the tourists, and they bought him his ticket, and the next morning, he set sail on the Kaiserin Auguste Victoria homeward bound at last.

After about seven or eight days on board, the ship landed in New York City after its obligatory stop at Ellis Island, and David headed for the first train to Philadelphia. His parents did not know he was coming. The last person his mother expected to see on that hot July 31 day when she answered the door was David. "My mother opened the door and said, "Oh my God!" She just about fainted. That was marvelous."[285] That Moyer reunion in Philadelphia must have been a sight to behold. In addition, to his parent's joy, his brothers must have been so pleased to see him again. David left for Berlin a child of eleven years and returned a young man of fourteen years. David doesn't provide any details of his visit home, but he would have had a full two months to visit his grandparents and many cousins on their farms in Montgomery County and lots of time to catch up with his brothers and parents.

David prepared himself well for his return trip to Berlin. He was not going to be humiliated and challenged again by some anonymous ticket clerk at the offices of the Hamburg-America line:

> I went to the office (Hamburg-America Line) on Broad Street and said to the man at the desk, "Such and such a boat is sailing tomorrow. (I had already looked it up on the schedule.) "There is a party going on it tomorrow. I can't remember their names, but they live out beyond 69th Street. (That was the fine residential section.) Could you tell me who they are? He gave me their names—it worked! So I thanked him, called those people on the phone and took the elevated out to 69th Street to meet them and tell them about my problem. They were a little startled, perhaps, but were perfectly willing to be my sponsors. They were going the next morning, so I arranged to meet them at the pier in Hoboken, New Jersey. They said, "We're going down to confirm our tickets this afternoon." We went together. It was all kind of fun and didn't mean anything much at the time.[286]

David simply, efficiently, and independently accomplished his goal to get on the ship headed for Germany without fanfare. The family he contacted and asked for assistance must have been favorably impressed with his savvy, independent technique.

David returned to Berlin prior to October 23, 1909. On that date, he, Madame, and her two sons performed in the seaport town of Königsberg, located at the mouth of the Pregolya River that joins the Vistula Lagoon, an inlet of the Baltic Sea and the capital of the German province of East Prussia. After 1945, the area has been known by its Soviet name Kaliningrad named for Mikhail Kalinin, one of the original Bolsheviks, and became the administrative center of Kaliningrad Oblast, a Russian enclave that separates Poland and Lithuania. Since 2004, when Poland and Lithuania became full members of the EU (European Union), the residents have to make special arrangements to travel outside of the area, and foreigners who are permitted to visit as tourists must show passports at all the borders.[287]

The Trio performed a rather lengthy concert at the invitation of Handwerkerverein Königsberg. The program for this event provides a window to observe just how much the Trio as an entity, and the boys individually progressed musically since the days of the U.S. tour three years prior. There were no recitations! David's repertoire now includes the works of Robert Schumann, Adolph Henselt, Franz Liszt, and Mozart. The Trio performed two selections for eight hands, one by Bach and the other by Mozart. Mary played with the Trio for these numbers. Robert and Clarence played solo pieces as well as pieces set for three instruments, cello, violin and piano. The Trio ends their performance with a rendition of a Mozart symphony arranged for six hands. A ball followed the concert, but we do not know whether Madame and the three boys stayed for it. The boys may have had a chance to observe something different than they had ever experienced before and probably heard some great music that they were unfamiliar with as well.

(L to R) Clarence, David, and Robert
on board the S. S. Cleveland, 1910
Photo: Courtesy of Moyer Family Archives

It is obvious how much David has matured in this photo. He was now fifteen years old and his round face and boyish looks are starting to give way to the more mature man he is becoming. Robert and Clarence have finally shed their curls that were so distinguishing when they were younger, and what today would seem like girlish clothing has now been replaced by short trousers. They must have been happier than what the photo reveals. During the summer of 1910, the Trio and Mary traveled to the United States on board the SS *Cleveland*, one of the Hamburg-Amerika Line ships. While on board the ocean liner, Mary and another passenger, Marie Margaret Heinemann, arranged with the ship's captain to hold a benefit concert. The purpose of the concert was to raise money to help the widows and orphans of deceased sailors. A printed program of the event survives. Ms. Heinemann sang six solos while the Trio accompanied her and, in addition, performed selections as a Trio, and each member performed a few solo pieces. The concert was held in the second-class dining room of the ship. The passengers that attended must have enjoyed the event. If nothing else, it broke the monotony of the transatlantic crossing.

Mary may not have had the funds she was used to having while the Trio was performing across the United States in 1905-06. The usual financial arrangements were more than likely in place: half the proceeds for the deceased sailors fund and the rest for the performers. Leave it to Mary. It seems this woman could earn money on a desert island. There is no information to suggest that Ms. Heinemann received remuneration for her vocal services.

Despite the fact that David was a busy young man with his studies and concerts throughout Germany, Mary did manage to pry him away for a tour of England and Scotland to perform as part of the Trio prior to this trip to the United States. David mentioned in his "Reminiscences" that he had played at the Crystal Palace in London, England on several occasions.[288] He never mentioned performing in Scotland, but that may have just been a forgotten insignificant detail. Mary may have needed the revenue from these performances to finance the journey back to the States. In addition, the benefit concert on board the SS *Cleveland* provided funds to travel both to Philadelphia and to Lima after arrival in New York City.

The entourage traveled to David's family home in Philadelphia where Mary procured work for the Trio. The following invitation announced the availability of tickets to the Girard College performance and informs the reader of another performance in Philadelphia:

> You are very cordially invited to be present at a concert to be given by the Berlino Trio in the college Chapel on Tuesday, July 26, 1910, at 3 P.M.

> Madame Berlino brings her three sons to this country after four years of successful concert work in Berlin. After leaving Berlin they have

traveled over 20000 miles in Europe and America and next Monday commence their engagement at John Wanamaker's. They have played before all the Crowned Heads of Europe, and in the great palaces of Italy, and stand second to none as a trio in concert work in Europe. They are great favorites of the German Royalty. They appeared before a great many schools in London and throughout Scotland. Today they will favor us with the same concert that was given on the SS. "Cleveland", July 13, as a benefit for the Widows and Orphans of Sailors.

We gladly welcome them to our College home and thank them for this courtesy which they are showing us, the boys of Girard College.[289]

Girard College was founded in 1833 and opened in 1848 as an orphanage with the specific responsibility to educate "poor white orphan boys."[290] The institution was and still is totally funded by the generosity of its founder, Stephen Girard, a former sea captain. Today, the college is a private academic boarding school for both male and female students of all races.

One thing is certain: Mary still knew how to tailor the written word in order to attract an audience. After the week of Philadelphia performances, Mary, Robert, and Clarence traveled to Lima. There are newspaper articles from the local press covering the performances by Robert and Clarence. David was not part of this enterprise and spent his time in Philadelphia with his family.

When David arrived home in 1910, there was a small hornet's nest brewing within the Moyer family. David's next oldest brother, Townsend, had married a local Roman Catholic girl, Frances Danaher, the previous January. Schwenkfelders and Mennonites did not generally marry outside of their own communities, especially not Roman Catholics. At this time, it appears there was still a deep disdain for the Roman Catholic Church because of the sufferings the Schwenkfelders and others had experienced so many years before. Many Mennonite/Schwenkfelder members had married and moved away from the isolated communities of their youth. They tended to marry Lutheran, Church of Christ, or Reformed Church members as there was little opportunity for them to continue worshiping with the older traditional group. It wasn't easy for Joseph and Ida raising four boys and attempting to replicate their own value system without the support of the communities they themselves were raised in.

Townsend married a Catholic girl, and that was the last sin—or the first sin. Anyway it was a big enough sin that he almost was kicked out of the family. My mother never quite got over it because she was so extremely oriented regarding religion.[291]

The situation was possibly more complex than David's explanation. When Townsend married, he was only eighteen years and nine months in age and Frances, his wife, was five months shy of her seventeenth birthday. They were just kids. Frances's Roman Catholicism was difficult for Townsend's parents to accept. Their young age was another factor.

Their first child, Marie Ida, was born on July 6 and sadly died March 9, 1912. David informs us in his "Reminiscences" that Townsend was a very talented young man. "He did a lot of writing which he used to sell." Regardless of how distressing Townsend's situation was to his mother, she performed her duty by including the information regarding his marriage to Frances Danaher and the births of their children to the Genealogical Records of the Schwenkfelder Families just as she had added in 1918 the details of her other two married children.[292]

After the Trio and Mary returned to Germany in the autumn of 1910, Mary's brother John passed away quite suddenly that October. The *Lima Daily News* for October 7, 1910, states that Mr. Halter rose early and was found on the kitchen floor of his home sometime later in the morning.[293] He died of heart failure at age fifty-seven. He was Mary's only brother.

John was the owner of the Lima Marble works in Lima, and court records inform us that he died destitute. This event must have shocked both the family living in Lima as well as Mary in Germany. There was little Mary could do since making the trip home was out of the question. There is no information regarding his wife, Elizabeth, after his untimely death. They had no children. Researchers in Lima have tried to find out where John's widow went after his death, but she seems to have disappeared.[294]

After the New Year, David traveled to Leipzig to perform at the Alberthalle with the Winderstein Orchestra under the direction of Hans Winderstein. David performed Saint-Saëns's G Minor Concerto and the Liszt A Major Concerto. Even David commented that the Liszt piece was not an easy number![295] A review from the *Leipsiger Zeitung* stated: "D.M.B. [David Moyer Berlino] is master of a well developed technique, together with a great musical ability. His playing of the Saint-Saens' G-Minor concerto revealed healthy musicianship. His playing with the orchestra was marked with ease and a thorough knowledge of the concerto."[296]

In March, David performed with the Municipal Orchestra in Görlitz. The opening selection for this program was the Overture Opera, *The Marriage of Figaro* by Mozart to begin the Third Symphony for orchestra and cimbalo, a generic word for keyboard instrument, in F Major composed by W. Ph. (Wilhelm Phriedemann) Bach, son of the great J. S. Bach. David often mentions that his nerves were never a problem for him prior to such performances. The second selection David played with the orchestra was the Concerto G Minor by Camille Saint Saens.

Performing from memory with an orchestra requires thorough and accurate knowledge of the score, knowledge of the interplay and cohesion between orchestra and pianist, and a well-seasoned conductor and musicians to keep it all together. The next selection on the program for that evening featured the orchestra alone playing Tchaikovsky's suite from *The Nutcracker Ballet*. Next, David returned to center stage and performed three piano solos by Chopin: Ballade in A Major, Prelude in F Major, and Polonaise in A Major. The program concluded with the orchestra's rendition of the final scene from the opera, *Lohengrin*, by Richard Wagner.

Görlitz, a Prussian town, belonged to the province of Silesia, the very same province from which David's maternal ancestors, the Kriebels, hailed. It is doubtful that David knew this information at the time of his performance in Görlitz, but it completes one of those fascinating life circles. David returned 261 years after the progenitor of the Kriebel family had been born in Deutmansdorf, Lower Silesia, and 177 years after the first Kriebels immigrated to the small village of Towamencin, outside of Philadelphia. He performed again in Silesia as guest "Klavier-Virtuosen" with the local orchestra of Bad Flinsberg. Perhaps, the longest and loudest appreciable applause came not just from those physically in attendance, but from the spirits of David's long-departed, once-hunted, suffering ancestors who had to literally run from that same area to save their own lives and the future of the small band of Schwenkfelders. What a triumph! The press review that appeared in the *Der Neue Gorlitzer Anzeiger* announced David's success: "At the V. Symphony Concert the audience for the first time heard a young artist with magnificent talent. In certain delicate passages one could distinguish a wonderful musical feeling that existed within the young artist's soul. Remember his name, David Moyer Berlino."[297]

The Trio visited with Kaiser Wilhelm II twice prior to 1911. From what David says in his "Reminiscences," it was Mary that took them to Schlossplatz. During the first visit, the Kaiser was not present but the initial meeting with the rest of the family caused David a bit of consternation. His telling of the story is quite funny:

> The first time Madame Berlino took us there, Kaiser Wilhelm II was away. The Kaiserin was there, however, and Louise, their one girl, a charming young lady, and the four princes. This was about 1910. They had a beautiful home, and a lovely big living room with a magnificent piano. The Germans had told us, "You must click your heels together and you must bow, and you the women you must all curtsey." The American Ambassador, a man by the name of Hill asked us, "You're going to the Kaiser's Palace?" Yes, we said, how should we act? "Well," he said, "how do you act when you go into a wealthy home in the United States?" Say,

how do you do? I'm glad to meet you and shake hands." That's what we did. We didn't bow, we didn't click our heels. We just visited very simply. When we first met, the Kaiserin e asked 'What language do you wish to speak?" We said, we prefer to speak English. Then she said to all her household standing there, 'English." From then on there was never one word of German spoken. That was lovely and just as gracious as it could be. After we sat and chatted a while, she said to me, 'Would you like to play something for us?' I said I would and sat down at the piano and started to play, but the floor was so waxed that as I played my chair kept sliding away from the piano. It was terrible. The Crown Prince, who was right beside me, got another chair and sat in it with his feet against my chair to block if form sliding. I played first one of the slow Chopin waltzes, then the e minor one, #15, Posthumous, and I think I played some Mozart.[298]

From what David records in this vignette regarding his first visit to the Kaiser's Palace, all turned out favorably in the end in spite of the slippery floor. It must have been unnerving for David at the moment. There may have been a few laughs during the telling of this story to his family in 1975 as it was still comical to David sixty-five years later. The question of how Mary's other two sons interpreted the visit to the Kaiser's home begs to be asked. They were studying their violin and cello and had been performing with David as a trio. Earlier, David stated that this is about the same time the Trio began to break up. Robert and Clarence may have found these situations where they were present but not involved in the performance, a little hard to swallow and, therefore, may have felt second best to David as Mary, their mother, was the one creating these performance events. It must have been very hard for both of them to contain their feelings of disappointment in just being part of the audience as David performed.

When David performed as soloist with orchestras or other ensembles, it is doubtful that Mary was the organizer. From what he tells us, he traveled on his own to these venues and got the job done. These opportunities more than likely came about through the House of Ibach, the Jules Sachs Agency for Concert Direction in Berlin, or Alberto Jonas. On another occasion, David, the two boys, and Mary returned to the Schlossplatz, and again David entertained, but this time, the Kaiser was present and the issue of the slippery floor must have been resolved as it was not mentioned during the second visit:

We felt more at home. We chatted about everything. The Kaiser's birthday had just passed and there was a great long table full of presents from kings and royalty all over the world. One was there from Teddy Roosevelt, one from King Edward VII. We all looked at them, and the Kaiser was showing them just like any man: he was proud of all his presents. As we were leaving after saying goodbye, Madame said to me, "Here, take these upstairs and give them to the people." So I ran back upstairs with some photographs Madame had taken of us and rapped on the door. I was shown in to where the Kaiser was sitting at the piano, playing Weber's "Invitation to the Dance" and quite well too. I stood there by the piano not wanting to interrupt. He played about three or four pages, saw me standing there, and stopped. I asked, "Would you like to have this picture as a remembrance of our visit here?" "Oh, very nice. Thank you so much," responded the Kaiser. When I complemented him on his playing, he said "You inspired me to sit down and play."

They always said he had one short arm, and that is true, but it was short only by about an inch or two, and was perfectly useable.

For our education and as a gesture to the Madame, the Kaiser said, "Now any time you want to go to an opera, simply ask for tickets and you will get them." We could go to any opera, and there were always tickets for us, the whole family of us. We went often.[299]

In addition to David's comment about the Kaiser's short arm, which, incidentally, was something the Kaiser and his family never mentioned publicly, and some historians still debate its effect on the man, this is the first instance in which David mentions Mary and her two sons as being a family. He denied several times that she ever tried to mother him or tried to take the place of his mother. He never mentions the boys, Robert and Clarence, as being his brothers, but we do know that he always held Mary in high esteem and greatly respected her personally for what she did for him. The opportunity for free tickets to operas and concerts enriched all their lives and precluded any objections to attendance because of financial shortfalls in the weekly budget. David was about to undertake the next step in his career, and this would cause some changes in Mary's life and the lives of her two sons.

The year 1911 appears to be a significant year for David and the Trio. In his own words, David explains, "This is when the Trio began to break up." The two younger boys were progressing but David "outdistanced" them in his progress and was playing concert dates on his own with orchestras in distant places.[300] David has told us that he was signed up with the Jules Sachs Concert Management Agency in Berlin. Obviously, for David and the majority of performing musicians, whether either developing their careers or maintaining their careers, the concert agency was a must. There are no remaining archives of this concert agency or any other, for that matter, because of two major world wars. Much of the history of Berlin has been lost that it is difficult to paint an effective picture using primary sources of these and many other business organizations functioning in the early years of the twentieth century. However, William Weber of the University of Indiana at Bloomington, Indiana, has collected and edited several essays and published them as *The Musician As Entrepreneur, 1700-1914.* Weber has thoroughly examined the personal and professional files of American pianist Richard Buhlig and his concert life directed by the Hermann Wolff Agency in Berlin in his chapter "From the Self-Managing Musician to the Independent Concert Agent."[301] Buhlig was fifteen years older than David, and he also studied with Busoni and concertized in London, Copenhagen, Dresden, and Berlin during the same years as David. The concert agents controlled most of the scheduling of both the concert halls and the performers practically exercising a monopoly on who played where and when. In addition to having the Wolff Agency as his primary representative, Buhlig also had to deal with smaller agencies in each and every small town where he appeared as well. These agents did not work for free! They all charged a percentage of the receipts, and in the case of Buhlig and most other performers, the agency made more money than the performer. The *abrechnungen* or statement of accounts including the cost of each item that the agency spent for the particular concert such as, newspaper advertisements, printing of tickets, posters, programs, rental of the venue, fees paid to cashiers, attendants, hall police, other performers needed such as the orchestra, rental of instruments (if any), the mailing and distribution of free tickets to patrons, etc., down to the clipping and filing of reviews were included and sent to the performer after his concert by the particular agent.[302] According to the Buhlig records, the agency fees always had to be paid in full by the performer whether there were sufficient or insufficient receipts to cover the costs, which it appears, in the case of Buhlig as the available example, were always inadequate. Buhlig was only able to pay these fees and expenses because he had some financial assistance from private patrons, and frequently, the piano manufacturers made a donation as well.[303] These manufacturers knew only too well the publicity they were getting for their instrument when a pianist had a successful recital or concert using their brand of piano. Buhlig's records seem to show that the piano manufacturer gave considerably less than some very generous patrons. Also, the piano companies would arrange concert dates for performers in many different cities and towns, as most of them were international in scope, as early as 1900. Private patronage was still very important for the performers' basic survival needs. The out-of-town agencies would also require a cash deposit from the performer for future engagements. In 1913, Buhlig received a letter from the Wilhelm Hansen agency in Copenhagen requesting a deposit of 250 German marks for a scheduled concert he was to perform six months later.[304]

If converted and calculated to the U.S. dollar of 2007, Buhlig had to provide $1246.43 in advance to the agent in Copenhagen at least a full month prior to his performance. The concert agent was absolutely essential to any performer in building his performance reputation and maintaining it.

Without an agent, a person could find himself in the same humorous predicament as Ignace Paderewski did at age sixteen. According to Murray McLachlan, a modern-day Scottish concert pianist, Paderewski and two friends formed a performing trio of piano, cello, and violin with Paderewski as pianist in 1876. The trio went on tour managing the whole enterprise themselves and, actually, made a little bit of money but not enough to hire a piano. They would beg the use of a good piano from a local resident, and when successful, they still had the burden of moving the piano to the concert venue. The trio members could not afford the expense, so they would often be seen pushing the borrowed piano through the streets to the performance hall.[305] We can see clearly the necessity of engaging a performance agent to insure regular performances in order to build the reputation of the performer. Without the assistance of an agent, the career never became reality.

David's records indicate that at the same time he began his studies at the *hochschule*, Mary imported her nephew, Earl Wynne Davis, only son of her older sister, Virtue Amelia Halter Davis, to Berlin for study with herself. We know that Mary's mother, Mary Baker Halter, had died in Lima on March 18, 1912. Her obituary mentions that her daughter, Mary, and grandson, Wynne Davis, were residents in Berlin. However, it does not mention Mary's two adopted sons or David as grandchildren. This is a change from the previous press reports published in Lima where Mary's mother was practically crowned queen of grandmothers.

Wynne, as he was known by his family, was nineteen when he traveled to Germany to live with his aunt, her two sons, and David. Wynne had been a student of the piano and organ while he lived in Lima. It must have been Mary's idea to use Wynne as a replacement for David in the Trio as she knew all too well that David would be very busy with his studies once he entered the *hochschule*. David did imply that the Trio was waning since he was no longer available to simply pick up and travel with Mary, as in the past, on her whim. It seems that much of Mary's joy rested in the planning of performances for the Trio and traveling to the venues.

Never in his interview with his family or at any other time did David mention Wynne or indicate that anyone else had become a part of his life or Mary's Berlin family. In 1914, when David had to flee Germany, it was Earl Wynne Davis that accompanied him. His name is listed under David's on the ship's manifest. No program copies reviews or newspaper accounts exist to inform us if Wynne ever played with the Trio once David started his studies at the *hochschule*.

October 1, 1911, began the change in David's career that he would never forget. That was his first day of classes at the Königliche Academische Hochschule für Musik on Fasanenstrasse, Berlin.

Hochschule für Musik, Berlin, Germany
Photo: R. D. Moyer, 2006

CHAPTER VII

David's Student Days at the Hochschule

The Hochschule für Musik in Berlin held its first classes on October 1, 1869, in the northern wing of the Palace Raczynski in Berlin, Germany. This part of the building was loaned to the new institution by Count Athanasius Raczynski, a Polish art collector. The first term of the new institution began with twenty students and three faculty members, including Maestro Joseph Joachim. During the second term, thirteen more students were added to the registers and four more faculty members to the staff. Due to gross under funding and disputes regarding pedagogy by the then ministry of education, the new high school lacked the necessary administrative components for early success when compared to the similar institutions at Leipzig and Munich.[306] After a few years of struggle and the relocation of the *hochschule* several times, the institution soon found a permanent home on the Fasanenstrasse in 1902. Fasanenstrasse is still the home of the *hochschule*, and it is where David attended.

The *hochschule*, a state-run school, was free for German citizens to attend if they passed the *aufnahmeprüfung* or entrance examination. For foreign students, the costs were high, and David didn't have the funds to pay for his enrollment, so the House of Ibach paid his fees. In addition, each student had to be a minimum of thirteen years old and have sufficient general education and know the German language adequately in order to understand the lectures. Some level of musical talent and previous instruction had to be demonstrated. A certified record of previous good moral behavior was needed as well as parental permission to attend the conservatory if the prospective student was under the age of majority; proper travel documents for foreign students were also needed.[307] Because David was sixteen, not the age of majority in Germany at this time, Mary simply signed her own name to whatever form was required as she was so used to claiming that David was her own child.

He was registered as David Berlino. The level of general education that David had achieved by the age of sixteen is unknown, but we know it was haphazard to say the least. Other students who had attended regular schooling most likely achieved a higher level of general education than David since his learning environment was constantly disrupted, and from what information is available, the private tutoring prior to living in Berlin was sporadic. David's musical education was more than likely superior to others his own age that had had a more consistent general educational background. The five previous years that David studied privately under the supervision of Alberto Jonas, director of the *hochschule*, was a major plus for him in being considered for acceptance to the *hochschule*. It is doubtful that those responsible for admission decisions would have been able to ignore the input of Alberto Jonas regarding David's potential for success.

In his dissertation, Bomberger speaks of Riemann's opinion that a particular weakness of the conservatory system was its failure to demand completion of a thorough general education for all its students. Hugo Riemann (1849-1919) had received training in law, philology, philosophy, and religion prior to his attendance at the Leipzig Conservatory. Riemann was critical of the conservatory system because as he so aptly stated, "It comes to pass, then, that adolescent conservatory students can write a passable fugue but not an orthographically correct letter."[308] The *hochschule* followed the precepts of the already successful one hundred and thirteen conservatories in Berlin.

By the time David attended the *hochschule*, "nearly all of America's influential musicians in the late nineteenth and early twentieth centuries were products of the German conservatory system."[309] David would certainly do his part in adding something significant to this tradition by achieving the most from his studies. The academic regime was, on paper, demanding. The reality of it was that students had the flexibility to decide for themselves just how much effort they chose to exert. Attendance in classes in actual classrooms must have been a different experience for David since he had attended only very little school in his life up to this point.

Classes generally met Monday through Saturday every week. An individual course could have two or three meetings per week if that was the desire of the professor. All the various subjects in the curriculum were taught to small groups of students averaging between three and six per class. The pedagogical theory behind this was that students would challenge each other on their performance and their knowledge, and through this peer interaction, learning would take place.[310] This seminar style of learning in our modern experience is seen as more useful to students in graduate schools or later years of university than in early undergraduate classes. Again, Riemann as quoted in Bomberger criticizes the technique, especially in the area of applied music:

Three or more students are scheduled for one and the same hour, but one or two absorb the whole time; the others must be reassigned to another time (where they do not belong according to the plan), and naturally the number of prospective participants at this other time is still higher. Thus the timid, unassuming student repeatedly goes home empty handed. It has not happened to me that students at a famous institution complain of attending classes all week long without getting to play a single time.[311]

Riemann's criticism, however, is well taken. When David attended the *hochschule*, this practice was still common. It is doubtful that David would have been retiring and reticent in putting himself forward in these classes. He possessed that wonderful quality that is unique to the prodigy, as Winner calls it, "rage to master."[312]

One other potential pitfall for students attending the German conservatories was the loose attendance policy of the institutions. According to Bomberger, class attendance was never mandatory since the emphasis for the student was placed on the *öffentliche Prüfungen* or final performance of the student at the end of the year. This policy of nonattendance could have and probably did have a devastating effect on some students, especially those younger and less experienced. At most of the conservatories, including the *hochschule*, the *öffentliche Prüfungen* were public performances where local music critics wrote reviews of the performances for the press. It is doubtful that the professors would have allowed these reviews to influence their own assessment of the performances. It would seem unlikely that a student who never attended classes would be able to impress the professors with an outstanding performance sufficient to permit them advancement to the next level of study. There was, however, another *Prüfung* (in-house examination) that all students had to take that would demonstrate technical, particular proficiencies. The areas tested were in theory and history.[313] Perhaps this is where nonattendance had its greatest causalities.

The *Jahresbericht* (annual report) for 1911-1912 lists four hundred and eleven students enrolled for the academic year. Thirteen American students were listed in the school register including David Berlino, and the faculty listed sixty-one members of which ten were either *fräuleins* or *frauen*. The *hochschule's* academic faculty was broken into major areas of concentration. Composition and theory, including both *partiturspiel und zusammenspiel*, were required. *Partiturspiel* is defined in Cassell's *German Dictionary* as score reading, i.e., "when a pianist takes a full orchestra score and plays it on the piano, thus reducing about twenty-five lines of music to no more than ten—the number of fingers.[314] *Zusammenspiel* or *kammermusik* refers to chamber music, musicians playing instruments together as an ensemble.[315] *Gesang* or vocal studies, *orchesterinstrumente* or orchestral instruments and *kavier* and *orgel* or piano and organ made up the other three areas of concentration. David studied theory, composition, and *partiturspiel* with Professor Leopold C. Wolf in his first year at the *hochschule*, and during his second year, he studied composition with the famous composer Herr Prof. Engelbert Humperdinck:

> He was a tiny man and very badly hunchbacked. I don't think he was even five feet tall, a very charming little gentleman. It was advanced theory; we would write, oh, something in the form of chorales and chordal progressions, because that was the thing he wanted us to know very thoroughly—how to handle chords and voice leading.[316]

In addition to David's rather vivid description of Humperdinck's physical appearance, it is important to know something more about the professor. Engelbert Humperdinck was born in 1854 in Siegburg, Germany, and died in Neustrelitz, Germany, in 1921. His most famous work is the opera *Hansel and Gretel*. His sister wrote the libretto. Humperdinck's life was interesting and was always involved with music in some way. He was a phenomenal teacher, spent many years as a conductor, and wrote musical criticism. At one time, he was tutor to the son of the famous composer, Richard Wagner. It is his *Hansel and Gretel* opera for which he is best remembered.[317]

Nonattendance did rear its head in David's experience at the *hochschule*.

> We used to get history as well, but that was a very dull subject to me and I rarely went to class.![318]

David also did not attend any *gesang* or choral classes, but that was not necessarily his choice but the choir department's choice:

> If you were old enough and your voice was settled enough, you were supposed to sing in the chorus. Well, I would get notice about it and I would walk in the choir (master, sic) would say, "How old are you?" "Fifteen," "Oh, what do you come here for. Your voice is changing. Go on home." They wouldn't let me sing. So, I never got any choral work.[319]

Poor David! When he began his attendance at the *hochschule* in 1911, he was sixteen years and six months old, not fifteen as he more than likely believed was his age. Mary as we already know always had David, Robert, and Clarence years younger than their actual ages because when they were performing on the road, they were more appealing to audiences because they were so small in stature.

David's lack of choral work did not seem to hamper him in his long-term career, but perhaps he would have enjoyed the chance to learn about choral structures and other fine points that might have broadened his professional scope. His lack of accuracy regarding his real age probably deprived him of that opportunity.

David began his *klavier* or piano studies with Herr Professor Heinrich (or Hans) Barth, the notable pianist and teacher who had served as head of the department for piano and organ since 1910. According to the *Jahresbericht* for 1911-1912, David was assigned to another teacher named Curt Börner.[320] It is interesting to note that Herr Börner is not listed as a professor. David makes no mention of him in his "Reminiscences," and there is no information available regarding him.

Heinrich Barth was born at Pilau, Prussia, in 1847 to musically endowed parents and began music lessons with his father at age four.[321] Before his twenty-first birthday, he had studied with Steinmann in Potsdam and with Hans von Bülow, Hans von Bronsart, and Carl Tausig and was appointed professor at the Stern's Conservatory in Berlin. From what we know about Barth (there is little written), he concertized successfully in both England and Germany as both a soloist and as part of the Barth Trio with Heinrich de Ahna, violinist, and Robert Hausmann, cellist. He held the position of court pianist to Emperor Frederick of Germany.[322]

After David had proven himself to Heinrich Barth, he then transferred to Ernst von Dohnanyi, the Hungarian composer and pianist, during his second year of study. Dohnanyi was given his position at the *hochschule* at age twenty-four at the invitation of Joseph Joachim in 1905,[323] which was witness enough to his abilities. David had a memorable experience with Dohnanyi that more than likely influenced him for the rest of his life:

> I had been studying with Jonas who would tell me what piece to prepare, and I would perhaps play it at the lesson by note, that is by reading the notes. For my first lesson with Dohnanyi, he had asked that I bring a Beethoven Sonata to play for him. And so I did. I set the music up on the stand. And he said, "Oh, don't you know it from memory?" "Oh no," I said. I just learned it. "Well," he said, "When you have it from memory, play it for me."

> He handed the music to me, and that was the end of that lesson. I was embarrassed, of course, and therefore got busy and learned the first movement to, I think, the C major sonata, Op. 2, no. 3. I played it for him and he corrected it. He went to the other piano, (he didn't know which Beethoven I was going to play for him), made many suggestions and played the piece for me—from memory of course.[324]

David further informs us that the structure of the classes consisted of about eight students attending each lesson, and the class time lasted approximately two and one half to three hours each. "You never played anything for him until you knew it and could play it the way you felt it should be played with your interpretation. Then, he would perhaps correct it or recommend what else you should do."[325] From what David explained regarding these classes, attendance was the tip of the iceberg. Intense preparation was essential, and there is no doubt that David took all this preparation extremely seriously. It was probably fortunate that he had his own living accommodation on the fifth floor of the building he occupied as it gave him the environment to perfect his selections for class performances. David was also impressed with the piano Dohnanyi played during these classes. The Bösendorfer piano with the Clutsem keyboard was of great interest to David. This unique keyboard was curved rather then being straight. "It goes straight in front of you for about 2 ½ feet, then the treble and the bass start to curve towards you. As you got into the treble and bass, you did not have to throw your elbows out. It was a marvelous sensation."[326] Regardless of David's enthusiasm for the Clutsem keyboard, it was never produced en masse by any piano manufacturer because it was too costly, and other pianists found the technique of playing it somewhat of a challenge.

Another facet of David's developing personality emerged while studying with Dohnanyi. It is here that David first encountered Aline von Barentzen, two years younger than himself. It appears David may have experienced some touch of the heart. Aline, originally from Somerville, Massachusetts, "was the youngest pianist, at eleven years old, to have won the First Prize at the Paris Conservatory" in 1908. Although David thought she was Swedish, probably because of her name, she appears on the class roster of the *hochschule* as being born in Somerville, Massachusetts. From a ship's manifest for 1912, it appears that her mother was of Spanish origin, and from another source, her father is listed as being a native of Maine. There is little biographical information regarding Aline's origins other than at age of four she moved with her mother to Paris to study at the Paris Conservatory. "In one lesson she would play two or three Chopin Etudes, and, of course, that meant always up to tempo, always from memory, and as well as one knew how to play them. The next week, she'd play a couple more, and still more the next week until she went through the whole book."[327] David was obviously impressed with her memory and her ability to play such selections with such ease. One of her biographers remarks that Aline was interviewed by Clavier magazine, February 1981, and told "how she was programmed to play Chopin's B Minor Sonata and both volumes of the Etudes for the first half of a war-time concert."[328] This would be considered an absolutely amazing feat for anyone. Her online biographer, Rose Eide-Altman, remarks in her article for *Women at the Piano* that Aline had learned all twenty-four of Debussy's Preludes during a vacation and the Brahms Paganini Variations in just five days. Further, at one time Aline had an active repertoire of over five-hundred works.[329]

This amazing pianist was first enrolled at the *hochschule* in 1911 at the age of fourteen and continued there, completing her studies in 1913, unlike David who left the *hochschule* without completion at Easter in 1913. David ends his little story about Aline by saying, "I know she played in New York a few times, because I've heard people say they heard her play there. Then I lost her." [330] It would be safe to suggest that David may have been a bit smitten by Aline. The tenderness of his last remark about losing her suggests he may have thought she could, perhaps, be his friend or something other than just another student.

At the end of the winter term at Easter of 1913, David left the *hochschule* to play for Ferruccio Busoni at his Thursday sessions held in his apartment in Berlin. In David's mind, Busoni "was the God of pianists at that time."[331]

Ferruccio Busoni (1866-1924) was born in Empoli, Italy, to musician parents. His parents traveled extensively, and the young Busoni was left in the care of his maternal grandfather in Trieste.[332] It is in Trieste that the young Ferruccio first demonstrated his musical abilities. By age seven, he was touring as a pianist with his parents. His formal studies in piano took him to Graz and Leipzig. Later, he taught in Moscow, Russia, and the United States and, eventually, settled in Berlin in 1894 with his wife and performed as virtuoso pianist and conductor until war broke out in 1916. He subsequently settled in Bologna and Zurich teaching at the local conservatories. He returned to Berlin in 1920 and continued his intense performance and teaching schedules and died there in 1924.[333]

Busoni was controversial among music scholars of his own day and of today. He possessed an array of methods, theories, and skills; therefore, his work is generally recognized as being immensely talented while simultaneously exhibiting confusing interpretive paradoxes. He explored the depth of music's intellectual content and contributed a number of influential ideas in advancing twentieth century music. Born during the reign of Romanticism and dying during the rise of Neo-Classicism, his compositions and performances wavered between the alternative values characteristic of each movement. His major thrust was to liberate piano interpretation and performance from the exaggerations of Romanticism and return it more objectively to the composer's intention as the basic criterion of musical interpretation. When Busoni applied his theory to the music of Chopin, it was judged as too "heady" and the resulting rendition to be lacking in passion and emotion. Instead of the Romantic approach, he supported a retrieval of the absolute formal structures of Bach and Mozart. Ironically, he admired Liszt—the quintessential Romantic and the most programmatic of composers—and never tired of performing his compositions. This paradox explains why Busoni's own music displays such a volume of crosscurrents ranging from nostalgic Romanticism to the objectivity of Neo-Classicism.

Saddled with these paradoxical leanings, Busoni is difficult to define as a composer and theorist. In 1907, in his published work, "Sketch of a New Esthetic of Music," he anticipated much of the course of twentieth century music. Busoni pleaded for a music that would be utterly free from the constraints of rhythmic and structural norms, major and minor scale systems, and from distinctions between consonance and dissonance while urging exploration of microtones and electronic techniques. Yet in spite of his theorizing, his performances did not seem to have escaped the peculiar paradoxical blending of Neo-Classical objectivity with Romantic melody. Talented and brilliant as he certainly was his music never achieved the status of a consistent musical movement but remains a hybrid of counter musical currents.[334]

David was enamored with the opportunity to play for such an outstanding musician as Busoni. David was right to be so impressed, and his instincts were correct about the importance of being able to list Busoni as one of his mentors. Later in David's life, when he was professor of pianoforte at Oberlin Conservatory of Music in Oberlin, Ohio, one of his students, George Walker, said, when interviewed for this book, how impressed he was that Professor Moyer had studied with Busoni.[335] It appears that this was a major consideration for George Walker in choosing to study at Oberlin and with Professor Moyer in particular. David tells us that at the time he studied with Busoni: "He was the leading pianist of that type at the time and his style was absolutely fabulous—I mean the figurations and the dexterity he had developed. His playing was quite Lisztish, but his compositions were more classical."[336] On Thursday afternoons, David spent his time at Busoni's apartment with other musicians who would all play for the maestro and receive helpful criticisms. In spite of David's already-busy performance schedule in concert halls in Germany and Poland, arranged by either the House of Ibach or his agent at the Arthur Sachs Agency in Berlin, and his own entertainment performances for private parties where he was hired directly by the host or hostess, he put all his spare time into preparing for the Busoni sessions.[337]

David was earning real money for himself and making reasonable career progress. As the hired pianist for parties, David would earn twenty-five German gold pieces for each private performance. In today's money, that is equivalent to $96. Not a bad wage for someone seventeen years old! Gustav Hollaender, the head of the famed Sterns Conservatory in Berlin, had also offered David a teaching position for the autumn semester of 1914. But the world events that would unfold during the summer of 1914 brought David's professional career to a sudden halt.

Regardless of his performing successes, and there were many, David still held that the most important event at this point in his life was "being invited to play for Busoni in his private apartment on Thursdays." Fifty to sixty people would attend these sessions. Sometimes, famous pianists who had traveled from abroad for recitals would also be invited, so it was a great opportunity to hear these people play in a less-formal setting than on the stage. Busoni had these sessions for the sheer pleasure of it since it provided him with an opportunity to do some teaching for free. Refreshments were always served, and afterwards, people would stay and chat with each other informally. It should be noted here that most of these sessions were conducted in German. However, because Busoni was fluent in English and Italian, many did speak in English as well.[338]

June 23, 1914, was the day that Archduke Franz Ferdinand, heir apparent to the Austro-Hungarian Empire, and his wife were leaving a reception held in the town hall at Sarajevo and were both murdered by Serbian national Gabrilo Princip, a Bosnian member of the Black Hand, a Serbian secret group. This fact was not in itself a cause for war but, coupled with the intertwined and complex alliances among the nations of Europe since 1871, set the scene for the runaway-train effect that dragged the world into the war that was to end all wars.[339]

David was to find himself caught up in this turmoil, or as he put it, "the whole country went flukey."[340] Of course, it took a few weeks for the reality to sink in that Germany was really at war and for things to change in society. David's promised job teaching at the Sterns Conservatory was cancelled as were most of his performance engagements for the autumn of 1914. All David says about his departure was that he had to get back to the United States. There was nothing more for him to do in Berlin since it appears that recreational activities came to a screeching halt as people turned their attention to the war effort.

David's emergency passport was issued to him on August 26, 1914. He traveled from Berlin to Amsterdam and then on to London with Wynne Davis at his side. David was advanced $5.00 by the Relief Commission in Amsterdam. Arriving in London, both men were directed to the Savoy Hotel where they made contact with the Committee of American Residents in London for Assistance to American Travelers headed by the young American Herbert Hoover. Hoover became involved with this charitable enterprise at the request of Walter Hines Page, the United States ambassador to Great Britain. David and his traveling companion were not the only Americans left without any ships to return to the United States. It was estimated that over one hundred twenty thousand Americans were all in the same boat or, literally, not in any boat at all to return to the States. It was Hoover and about five hundred volunteers that provided food, shelter, clothing, and money for passage home to the stranded travelers. The Savoy Hotel in London was the main base for this operation, and both David and Wynne were given some cash and steamship tickets bound for New York from Liverpool.

David and Wynne arrived in New York on September 11, 1914. Wynne Davis listed his home address as Lima, Ohio, and David listed his address as his parents' home on South Thirty-Fourth Street, Philadelphia, Pennsylvania. By the time David arrived at his parents' home, he was indebted to the American

Relief Commission for a total of $48.50. The money was loaned and the tickets obtained by the Relief Commission for the use of the stranded Americans with a promise of payback of the money. Compliant David surely paid his money back to the commission. It would be totally out of character for him not to pay it back. One and one half million dollars had been loaned to stranded American travelers, and according to the Hoover Web site, all but $300.00 was returned by the recipients.[341] There is no evidence to suggest that Wynne Davis traveled anywhere else other than simply continuing his travel returning to his parents' home in Lima. Why was David without money? Previously, David worked, and he made good money and had a free place to live. More than likely, he had left whatever money he had behind with Mary for her support and the support of her two sons. There is no way to know how much money Wynne had at his disposal. There is no record of his having earned money while in Germany.

Chapter VIII

Back Home: A Different World

David found himself in a wholly different world back in Philadelphia from the childhood one he had remembered. Things had changed! His oldest brother, Vincent, had graduated from the University of Pennsylvania, Philadelphia, with a degree in veterinary medicine and married Cora Aldred in 1912 in Philadelphia and already had one child, a son named Charles (Skinny), and Cora was expecting their second child within two months after David had arrived home.[342] Vincent, naturally, no longer lived in the family home as he and his wife rented a small dairy farm in Lansdale, Montgomery County, Pennsylvania, where he was not only the farmer but also ran the veterinary clinic for neighboring farmers' animals who needed his assistance. Wilmer was employed in a local hauling company and had married a local girl, Susan Eshleman, in 1911, and they had a baby girl, Margaret, born in 1913. Townsend had already married before David's last trip home in 1910 and was employed by the Pennsylvania Railroad Company.

It must have been wonderful for David's family to have him back home once again, but for David, it proved to be trying times. He was a musician and a very accomplished musician, but in Philadelphia, he had to start from the beginning as if he had no past. This must have been a shock for him! While in Germany, he seemed to have the world at his feet. Back at home, he had no contacts, so he did the only thing he knew how to do, and that was to open a teaching studio. The only person David's parents knew involved in musical performance was Mary who was still in Germany, so they had no established contacts to help him either. One solution David did try was to go to the Judson Bureau in New York to see if he could arrange some performance dates. There was no chance of that happening as David found out from the beginning of his interview with Mr. Judson. David did show Mr. Judson his German press clippings and reviews, but Mr. Judson told him that he would need $10,000.00 to begin to rebuild his concert career. The money required would in fact cover his personal expense and agency expenses for concerts in New York at Carnegie Hall, some in Chicago, and San Francisco. Mr. Judson advised David that is how he would have to start out. If he got favorable reviews, then they would begin talking business with him.[343] To be honest, David must have been in shock at Mr. Judson's response. David didn't have the money, and he would not ask his parents for it. Up until this point in David's life, performances came very easy for him. Mary organized the entire concert performances in his childhood years, and in Germany, David had a performance agent as well as Mary; the House of Ibach and his own reputation made it rather simple for him to earn his living performing privately. He tried, however, to network with some conservatory people, but they were not interested, and the fact that he was only nineteen years old—he wasn't much older than some of their students. No luck there! He managed to get to know some of the local pianists at the Musical Arts Club, but these contacts never came up with any bookings for him. The Musical Arts Club in Philadelphia was in fact, the Musicians' Union Number 77.

He proceeded to rent studio space at Estey, Bruce & Co., the reed organ manufacturers, located 25 North Thirty-Fourth Street, half a block away from where he was born. Additionally, he placed advertisements in the local Philadelphia newspapers and attracted a reasonable group of private students who attended his studio for regular lessons.[344] This continued for about two and a half years, and it must have been somewhat boring for David as he was used to being a performer. He made enough money to support his studio and himself living in his parents' home. He never taught beginning students, so all his students had to have been more advanced in their training. The records reveal that David did perform a few times, but his performances were sporadic at best. In November 1914, he performed a public concert at the Hahn Conservatory of Music in Philadelphia. For this particular concert, he used the name of David Moyer, and "pupil of Busoni," on the program header.

The performance included selections by Bach-Busoni, Schumann, Chopin, Scriabine, and Liszt. The selections were popular with those who would attend such a concert, and possibly, David considered that to use his status as a former pupil of Busoni by opening the program with a selection of Bach arranged by Busoni would bring some attention to him as a serious and accomplished artist. He thought this might even open a few doors for him as a concert performer or a teacher at one of the many Philadelphia conservatories. He would, however, have to wait a few years before his dream became reality.

In the spring of 1915, David participated in both the Good Friday and Easter Sunday services at the St. Andrew's Episcopal Church at Thirty-sixth and Baring Streets, Philadelphia. The printed program does not give much information about exactly what David presented, but on Good Friday, he played the piano accompanied by some other musicians. On Easter Sunday, David and several other musicians were involved with the lengthy Holy Communion Service. It was a long program and high church in form as the music was redolent of pre-Reformation liturgical roots. David's experience of playing at religious functions in his boyhood days and as a young adult while he was with Mary was a good preparation for such participation. It is doubtful that his parents, Ida and Joseph, would have attended such an elaborate service since they would have found music reflective of Roman Catholicism as inappropriate. Later in the autumn, David would perform for the Godshall (Godshalk) Family Reunion in Worcester, Pennsylvania. David's own ancestry on both his paternal and maternal sides, was related in some way to the Godshall (Godshalk) Family. A copy of the program for the reunion survives, and David is listed as presenting a recital for the enjoyment of all. The cover of the Godshalk Family reunion booklet features a photo of David (taken in Berlin) with, among other remarks, the statement: "The foremost pianist in the Family."

David Moyer, Berlin, 1914
Photo: Courtesy of Moyer Family Archive

The concluding remark in the short blurb also states that he "played before the German Kaiser."[345] The (Godshall) Godshalk family reunion organizers were certainly proud of their David! The United States had not yet engaged in the war against Germany at this time, but it appears that the family reunion promoters were still quite proud of their German heritage. They obviously had no premonition of what was to come in the next few years.

David's continuing attempts to earn some recognition for the purpose of relaunching his performance career prompted him in 1916 to use the name David Moyer-Berlino. The change in name appears on a performance program in April 1916 where David was part of a musical presentation at the Central Presbyterian Church, Philadelphia. In August 1916, David performed at the Twelfth Annual Reunion of the Moyer-Myers Family in Perkasie Park located in Bucks County, Pennsylvania. The program suggests that David played one solo and played the accompaniment for the hymn singing as well. Here he could meet more of his immediate family cousins and interact with people that were, perhaps, closer relations than the ones he had met at the Godshalk reunion the previous year. On this occasion, he was simply David Earl Moyer.

He continued to use the name Moyer-Berlino well into 1917 when, it appears, some unknown person out of the great blue sky offered him a teaching position at the Bucknell School of Music at Bucknell College in Lewisburg, Pennsylvania. (In the 1980s, the school was granted university status.) Possibly, no one was more shocked that day than David himself. There was one proviso, however. David had to travel to Lewisburg and present a public concert. This was not problematic for David as he had every confidence in his artistic ability to impress both his prospective employer and the public, and he successfully accomplished the task. The newspaper review (newspaper name unknown) was found in the Moyer Family Archives along with the actual program for this performance. David shared the concert stage with Madame De Sylva Schoen, a mezzo soprano-contralto performer who also taught voice at Bucknell. On the program for this event, dated February 19, 1917, there is no mention of any accompanist for Madame, so it is presumed that David provided the accompaniment as well as performing his own selections. Madame Schoen opened the program and sang selections between David's two blocks of music. His selections for the concert were as follows: Bach-Busoni, Organ Preluden; Schumann, Romanze; Chopin, Polonaise in A flat Major; Turner-Salter, City of Rachel; Galloway, "O Heart o' Mine;" George Whitfield Chadwick, "Allah;" H. Ware, "I Had an Old Black Manny" and "'Tis Spring"; Chopin, Etude (Opus 10, No. 5); Scriabine, Nocturne (for left hand alone); and Liszt, Hungarian Rhapsody No. 12. Recently, in a correspondence from one of David's former colleagues at Oberlin Conservatory, Professor J. Fenner Douglass commented on the Bach-Busoni Organ Prelude as being a very popular piano selection in those days.[346] Busoni's transcriptions of Bach usually had "plenty of octaves and pyrotechnics."[347] David performed this selection true to Busoni's transcription!

Following his concert success, David was offered a position on the music faculty and would begin his work the following September in 1917. He still had some performance obligations to fulfill before beginning at Bucknell, so he had enough work to keep him busy during the interim. One of these commitments followed the Bucknell concert by only a few weeks. On March 2, 1917, the Norristown Schwenkfelder Church was the venue for his next concert for which we have a record. There may have been others. Norristown is a midsized town in Montgomery County, Pennsylvania, and serves as the county seat. From the name of this venue, it is easy to understand that David was connected to this church by his mother's Schwenkfelder relations. David seems not to have had much spare cash during his last days as a private music tutor in Philadelphia because he continued to use the same photo of himself in the trio although the two boys were cropped out by a local photographer. It was the last photo taken of him and the two boys, Robert and Clarence, as the Trio in September 1914 in Berlin (see photo p. 131). That David did not have a recent photo of himself seems unusual and contrary to habit as David was used to being photographed at regular intervals at the behest of Mary to keep the advertisements and programs up to date. However, another reasonable explanation for his lack of more recent photographs was that he was just plain sick and tired of the ritual.

Prior to departing his home in Philadelphia to begin his new career at Bucknell College, David had to fulfill his legal duty and sign the military draft register. This he did on June 3, 1917. When David was hired at Bucknell, he was still using the surname of Moyer-Berlino. The Bucknell University Archives list David as Moyer-Berlino for the academic years 1917-1919. However, under the 1918-1919 listing, the additional designation of "In Military Service" appeared under the name of Moyer-Berlino.

CHAPTER IX

Bucknell Life: 1917-1918

Bucknell College was originally founded in 1846 as the Lewisburg College in the town of Lewisburg, which lies in the center of Pennsylvania. Prior to its foundation, there were no other institutions of higher learning in the immediate area. It was literally "carved out of the wilds of Pennsylvania." The journey from Philadelphia in the early years took approximately twenty-five hours and was accomplished by traveling in a stage coach, canal boat, and an unheated train. It was a much shorter journey by 1917. Although, originally founded by the Baptists as a "school preparatory to the College," the Bucknell University Website makes it clear that this was not an attempt to proselytize for any religious denomination.

Female students were admitted as early as 1852 and attended what was then called the Female Institute. Prior to the opening of the Female Institute, both men and women were permitted to attend the same classes with the proviso that "while studying together, women were required to face east while men faced west."[348] Of course, this presupposes that each gender was seated on the proper side of the room from the beginning. If they were seated wrongly, this could result in their staring at each other! This was considered advanced educational method for the times, and it probably was. Since women could attend the same instruction as the men, there was some attempt at equality of education for both sexes.

In 1881, the college was in a dire financial situation, and local man William Bucknell, a charter member of the board of trustees, made a very generous donation to save the institution from ruin. He was aptly honored five years later by the trustees in their changing the name from Lewisburg University to Bucknell University.[349]

The end of August 1917, David packed his bags, and realizing he would never reside in his parents' home in Philadelphia ever again, he set off, belongings packed and well on his way to a college teaching career. It is doubtful that this caused him any undue stress. This departure was probably less traumatic for him than when he had to leave his established career in Germany to move back to the United States. He had originally left his home at approximately age five and a half and only returned for periodic visits until 1914. No apron strings had ever tied David to his family. That's for sure! Teaching music had been so much a part of him that it seemed a natural extension of his life thus far. David had arranged accommodation at the home of Mr. and Mrs. Bert Wagner located at 523 Market Street, Lewisburg, Pennsylvania. Lodging with strangers was no challenge for him as he had spent so much time in other people's homes throughout his life. The location of the house was only a short walk from the college

David was now enjoying the benefits of college life as a professor. For the first time in his life, it seems, he was actually interacting with young people his own age who shared his interest and commitment to music. Teaching at a college was a different experience for him than teaching private pupils in his studio in Philadelphia or helping his former tutor, Mary, with private teaching. The only time in his life that David participated on a sustained basis in what could be considered a school context was at the *hochschule* in Berlin. German educators, at any level, were rigorous, formal, and more demanding than David could possibly have been with the college students he was responsible for teaching. His interactions with other faculty members at Bucknell would give him some understanding of how an American college functioned and what would be expected of him as a teacher. This was an entirely new world to him. He was a mere twenty-two-year-old, and quite possibly some of his students were older than he was. Another twist in this teaching environment was that he was now teaching female as well as male students. With the exception of what may have been a brief palpitation for Aline von Barentzen at the *hochschule,* the only women he had experienced in his life until this point were the influential ones who exercised some control over him, namely, Mary, his tutor, and, of course, his mother. The new world had opened up for David, and from the information available, he met the challenge and complied with the protocols of a reasonably sized institution and did his job well.

It was at this stage that a young lady student at Bucknell caused his head to turn. Jessie Louise Cooper was two years younger than David and had begun her studies at Bucknell in 1916 where she devoted herself to piano, organ, and theory classes. Jessie was born in Ardmore, Pennsylvania, a suburb of Philadelphia, and was the daughter of Anna Magee and William L. Cooper. When she was about three years of age, young Jessie and her mother moved into the home of her maternal grandmother also in Ardmore. There is no documentation as to what happened to her father, William, but presumably he died young. Jessie and her mother lived with her grandmother until Jessie became a teenager.

Then they lived in Scranton, Pennsylvania, with her mother and stepfather, W.H. Cowles.

During this time, she attended a local Roman Catholic boarding school. She had some musical education with a Professor Cruthers in Philadelphia and with Professor Briggs of the New England Conservatory of Music located in Boston before attending Bucknell.[350] During this time, family lore reports that Jessie's parents lived in Scranton, Pennsylvania, wanted her close to home while she pursued her college musical education, and Bucknell was their choice. There is no documentary information, such as letters, etc., that have survived this period of David's early college teaching career or any evidence to suggest any depth of relationship between Jessie and himself. Certainly, there was some attraction between the two of them because while David was serving in the armed forces in France, he repeatedly refers to his "gal" and on some occasions refers to her as Louise and, on other occasions, Jessie. The probable attraction of faculty member/female undergraduate student had to be very discreet for both of them since the college would have had clear antifraternization policies.

CHAPTER X

World War I

David's teaching career at Bucknell was swiftly interrupted because of a mandatory order of the U.S. Army in the spring of 1918. Fortunately, for his family and this biographer, David kept a daily diary of his tour of duty beginning July 7, 1918, when his ship set sail from Hoboken, New Jersey, and did not return to the Port of New York until June 20, 1919.

Basic training for David and the rest of his regiment of the AEF (American Expeditionary Force) took place at Fort Meade, Annapolis Junction, Maryland, eight weeks before they were all shipped out to Europe to assist the French in the defense of their country against the German forces occupying French land. These AEF soldiers were more commonly known as the Doughboys! The academic year at Bucknell was winding down by mid-May 1918 when David had to report for basic training at Fort Meade. The eight-week basic training must have been physically grueling for all the new recruits who, like David, did not work in jobs that required physical labor. David does not leave a record of his basic training experiences in his diary. However, a photograph of him in a football uniform has surprised Bill Moyer, David's only living son. Bill has stated that his father was never a sports enthusiast and cannot really understand why his Pa, David, is dressed in such a uniform.[351]

The photograph below of David is perhaps his idea of a joke or a prank. The photo was taken by someone named Cooke and was a staged photo while David was still in basic training in Maryland. If the photo is viewed with a sense of humor, it is easy to see that David looks like he's holding up the large pants and his shoulder pads are on the outside of the shirt, not inside the shirt as they were meant to be worn. Bill, David's son, has often mentioned that his father, usually once a year, "would pull off a prank of some kind just to get a laugh." This, very well, may be one of those times!

David E. Moyer at Ft. Meade, Maryland, 1918
Photo: Courtesy of Moyer Family Archives

War, of course, was no laughing matter! In addition to the daily diary David kept for posterity, he also carried with him something called a "watch camera."[352] This very small camera resembled a pocket watch and appears to have been a rather popular novelty in its day. There were approximately three companies that manufactured these small unique cameras. The Expo Camera Company of New York City was one such company, and it introduced it in 1905. It was still available as late as 1939.[353] The camera cost $2.50, and a cartridge of film was twenty-five cents. A printing box (enlarger/printer) was available for $1.50. In David's war diary, there are instances where he talks about developing his film. The total weight of the camera itself was only two and three-fourths ounces; therefore, it was easily carried. The negatives measured 5/8" x 7/8", and one roll of film would produce twenty-five exposures.[354] David did record many images of war scenes in France and from the voluminous collection of photographs that have survived in spite of the horrible conditions in which he found himself; they did not hamper him from accomplishing this very personal task he set for himself.

For the diary entry of July 7, 1918, David does mention that when the troops traveled to Hoboken, New Jersey, they passed through Philadelphia, the city of his birth, at around 7:00 p.m. To his surprise and delight when arriving at the designated pier in Hoboken, David realized that the ship that he was about to board was the USS *America,* one of the ships from the Hamburg-America Line that he had traveled on previously going back and forth to Germany when he was a young student at the *hochschule.* The convoy of ships totaled five, and he makes a comment about how crowded the ship was with soldiers. David was assigned duty on the ship as an orderly and found himself running all over the ship doing whatever he was asked to do. As part of his duties, he was the waiter at the officer's mess. Once on board, David recalled that he wanted to see the first-class salon to investigate if the Ibach grand piano was still there as it had been years before. As a waiter in the officer's mess, David had access to the proper person to ask for this permission. Permission was given by the officer, and David found the Ibach in the salon just as he expected and began playing it. It wasn't long before he had attracted a "nice audience," as he recorded it, and he continued to play almost every day during the long journey to the shores of Brest, France.

The convoy of ships arrived in Brest harbor at about 4:00 p.m. on July 18, 1918. David remarks that Brest harbor was a beautiful site. For the next three days, the regiment hiked to and from the town of Brest and made camp, sleeping in very muddy fields as part of the daily routine. After three of these marches, they were boarded on to a train that was terribly overcrowded. He remarked that there was room for "40 men or 8 horses" in the freight cars; the space was tight, the scenery was beautiful, but the trip to Vaux was horrible as the train stopped at every crossroad along the way. Once in Vaux, they hiked five miles across countryside to a "little dirty village," Essonne. Their sleeping accommodation consisted of strewn straw on the floor of a farmhouse, but to David, this was the best night's sleep he had since he left Camp Meade.

David was assigned to the signal platoon, so his duties were clearly defined. The unit continuously hiked from, as David describes, one dirty village to another, and they completed some signal practice and other drills along the way. They were usually billeted in filthy quarters without sufficient food, with rats running around the places. He summarizes his early days in France as pure *hell!* The month of August would again see more hiking, signal practices, laying of telephone wires, and days of hard work. On some days, there was no dinner, yet on other days, there were great dinners when they would return from the long day's activities.

August 8, 1918, was the first mail delivery to the regiment, and this "brought tears to many an eye"; they also received their "first issue of tobacco"[355] after being without it for several days. Ten days later, August 18, 1918, David and his brothers-in-arms all received their first wages on foreign soil. His pay consisted of one hundred and forty-six francs and fifty centimes. He "felt rich!" Nice as it was to have some money, there was hardly any place where the soldiers could actually spend this money. However, the unit packed up and moved on again, only this time "half of the platoon was drunk."[356] Looks like some found ways to spend their meager wages after all! A few days later, David was informed that he was going to be transferred to the Army band, but it appears that this never really happened. In this foreign place and more than likely in a tent, he had his first tooth extracted. It seems his previous pain of the toothache was somewhat relieved because on the same day, he received five letters from his girl friend, Jessie Cooper, who had graduated from Bucknell the previous May.

September began for this AEF unit the same way August had begun. There was hike after hike, it seems, to nowhere. On Labor Day, the regiment had to hike eighteen miles each way with full packs, and during the return trip, two men died from the strain. Hundreds had to be hospitalized, and after receiving wages, the barely surviving members of the group wiled away the next few nights and got drunk.[357]

A few days later, the regiment left Essonne to march back to Vaux where they were loaded on trains once again for another long arduous journey, destination unknown. David, still not physically recovered from the previous days of strenuous hiking and other activities and the continuous lack of sleep since his arrival in France, actually collapsed and had to be placed in a sidecar and driven to Vaux. By four-thirty in the afternoon, the regiment left Vaux on a train that David described as "so crowded he couldn't even sit down." They did not arrive at the destination of Revigny sur Ornain located in the westerly area of the region of Lorraine, approximately thirty miles southwest of Verdun, until seven-thirty the following morning. After disembarking, the troops had to stand in a heavy downpour of rain for three hours, and then, after another one of the army's famous hikes, this one lasting six hours, they were eventually billeted in a "fine barn" at Lisle-en-Rigault where he "slept like a brick."[358]

The following days in September 1918, would be days that David would never forget, no matter how hard he tried. These events would mark his introduction to what is commonly called the Front. His regiment was billeted in mud dugouts with rats and without prepared food. The soldiers were able to cook a bit of food from their rations, but the sound of the artillery fire from the Germans was absolutely "frightening." One day, the regiment moved out of the dugouts and headed for regimental headquarters at La Voie Sacrée near Verdun. La Voie Sacrée was nothing more than a roadway with a parallel metric gauge railway that was used extensively in 1916 by the French to keep the front at Verdun Salient supplied with whatever was necessary to fight the German army. It was after the battles of 1916 that the road received its name of La Voie Sacrée or the Sacred Way. David and his regiment could see Hill 309 and 304 or, as he refers to them, "dead man's hill" from their dugouts. All seemed well for almost two days since there was little shelling near the 103rd Cavalry Regiment:

Great life! Nothing to do from morning until night. At 11:00 p.m. Germans started a bombardment. Two shells struck 10 feet from our dugout. Splashed dirt all around. Few fellows hurt. One very likely won't recover. Thought whole earth was falling apart.[359]

The following day, David was again sent to pigeon school. As a member of the Signal Corps, it was part of his job to gather the trained pigeons and have them at the ready to set them airborne so they could do their job of carrying messages from the fighting front back to headquarters. "The U.S. Army Signal Corps alone used 600 pigeons in France.[360] The French and British armies also used pigeons. Over the years, he spoke fairly frequently about the pigeons and their usefulness in communications many times to his children.[361] The time required to get to where the pigeon school and the pigeons were was a three-and-a-half-hour hike from his present position. He found pigeon school interesting and returned via truck to the encampment with pigeons in a cage. Four letters from Jessie "Louise" awaited his return, and he had to read them while wearing a gas mask. Two days later, he had to take the pigeons over to the First and Third Battalions and almost got lost in no man's land on the way back. He returned to his dugout, and while the German shells were whistling by David and his pals that he names as "Koenig, House, and Heist kept themselves busy making fudge and reading letters from home and waiting for orders to advance."

The orders to advance came at last, and in the middle of the night, the battalion moved further toward the front. That night, the American and French forces experienced an enormous barrage of fire launched by the Allied Forces. A French officer told the Americans and the French soldiers that it was the greatest barrage the world had ever seen! Later that day, the battalions made the big advance over dead man's land.

Saw lots of dead Germans and many of our boys. Awful sight. Cannon fire all day. German shells falling all around. Rainy, cold, nothing to eat. Slept out in the open.[362]

For David, the sight of dead Germans was as difficult for him to comprehend as seeing so many of "our boys," Americans, in the same lifeless condition. David had spent eight years living and studying in Berlin, Germany, and he always remembered with fondness and affection the German people and how kind and welcoming they were to him while he lived there. War and the great evil that it was as witnessed by him was something he could never really understand. In latter life whenever the subject of war came up in conversation, he would simply shake his head and remove himself from that conversation. For David, it was unbearable.

The next six days were so busy just staying alive that David mentions he had no time to write in his diary. When the situation settled down a bit, he does write at length:

> No time to write diary. Six days of awful battle. Under shell fire all the time. Dead soldiers and horses cover the fields and roads. Frightful! Slept in shell holes. Ate what ever we could find. Nearly starved. Took food from dead men's packs. In all, made advance of about 12 kilometers. Our Division lost in wounded and killed about 50 percent. Took many prisoners. Known as the Montfaucon drive in the Argonne sector.[363]

At the beginning of October, the battalion was relieved of their dangerous duty and began to return to where the rest of the regiment was stationed. During the return march, the shelling from the Germans continued, and many more in David's regiment were wounded and killed. The destination was a "rest camp"; however, they still continued to sleep in dugouts and suffered from the effects of lack of food. After seven days of continuous marching, they finally arrived in a small village that resembled a ghost town. They were billeted in a barn, which to us sounds like a nice change from being billeted in dugouts and shell holes, but according to David's diary entry, it was cold and damp and felt more like an "ice house" than a barn. He was so disgusted, hungry, and cold he never even tried to find out the name of "the dump." After about eight more days of hiking and poor conditions, they finally arrived at Thillombois, another small village in the Meuse area of the Lorraine province. The troops were hoping that since there was a hospital at Thillombois, they would receive some medical help because most of them were very sick, more than likely from poor food, too much physical exposure to the cold, and the incessant damp and wet conditions in which they had lived for so long. David writes in his diary that they received no relief from the hospital's pills that were distributed. David, by this stage, is certain that the hospitals have "only one kind of pill" to distribute to the soldiers for all illnesses, and they are useless.

As mid-October approached there were rumors of a possible peace. However, David and his battalion appear to have continued to march from place to place with no known apparent destination. All they seem to know was that they were marching toward the front lines once again. Sometimes, these marches went on for more than twelve continuous hours without a break. When they were billeted, it was usually in horrible, wet, cold conditions, and rest was hard to come by, especially when they reached the front at Death Valley.

Death Valley, a sector north of Verdun called Bois Belleu, was very near the German zone referred to as the Hindenburg Line. It was here that the French and

Americans incessantly attacked the German strongholds but with little success for the most part. This is where David and his comrades found themselves.

On one of the last days of October, the battalion was marching along a road in the middle of the night, and David wrote in his diary that they had to march wearing gas masks while they were also tripping over dead horses along the way. On October 30, David was called to ration detail about 4:00 p.m. He and others that had received this order had to spend the rest of the day lying around on roads with shells "falling thick and fast. The rations didn't come until nearly 7:00 p.m." At the end of that day, there was little to eat and the soldiers were not permitted to light a fire to cook their bacon, so they ate it raw.[364] The following day, however, some of the uncomfortable-ness was relieved as the "signal crowd" was able to move into better dugouts where they had a stove to cook meager rations of bacon and make coffee while the German army (Fritz or Jerry, as David refers to them) continued to drop shells all around them.

November 1 began as another harrowing day for David. He was instructed to go to the 316th Regiment and collect a basket of pigeons. Part of his responsibility was to get the other pigeon men from the local battalions to come and get their birds. None of these men showed up, so David had to carry the birds himself. "The men were scared to come out. During the whole time, Fritz kept sending GD cans over. It was an awful job." Sunday, November 3, 1918, David had a new group of pigeons to work with:

> Had six messages to send out with pigeons. Tried to get the relief of pigeons out to battalions in the morning, but Jerry was peppering Death Valley so heavily it would be suicide to try to go though there. About 2:30 p.m. tried it again. Got half the way down the valley when a German plane came sailing over very low. It was so low, I thought it was an Allied plane. No one was bothering it. When it got nearly over me I looked up and saw the big black cross. I dived for a bush to hide myself and the large basket, but too late. The plane dived directly towards me and turned its machine gun on me. There were a few exciting moments with bullets whistling and splashing the ground all around me. Not one found its mark only a few bullets went through the basket.[365]

After this rather harrowing experience, David, the ever-compliant person that he was, did not retreat to the encampment but continued to try to complete the mission with the birds. As he continued down the valley, an enemy shell landed about twenty feet in front of him and the vibration knocked him off his feet. Realizing how close he was to death and escaping it for a second time in one afternoon, he finally returned to his camp.

Once back in the safety of his camp, he realized again that there was no place that was really safe. "Jerry tried his best to put a shell down our smoke stack, but missed, but then he (Jerry) managed to fill the dugout with mustard gas." If the dugout had been the successful target of the mustard gas, then it would seem improbable that any of the soldiers would have survived. They must have been exposed to some of the fumes from the remains of a mustard gas bomb that had exploded outside of the dugout because now, still wearing his gas mask, he proceeded to write in his diary. He wrote how beautiful the valley once was when completely covered with nice green grass. "Now the whole valley is nothing but mud and shell holes. The entire surface of the ground has been destroyed. The little village of Moley Farms is nothing but a mass of stones. Not even a street can be recognized."[366]

The constant shelling of the area around the temporary dugout quarters must have been deafening, especially for someone with such sensitive hearing as David. His last words for that day in November are that he was "never so close to death. Thought at times, I would never see girl or home again."[367]

David seems to have had no problems obtaining the pigeons, but he did have difficulty getting someone to assist him in attaching messages and taking the birds out to a defined place. The other signal corps members from other battalions seemed always to disappear on him. Many times he had to handle the pigeons by himself and make treacherous journeys on foot carrying a large basket of pigeons. Perhaps it was just the lack of individual discipline of some of the AEF members who allowed fear to overcome them and prevent them from fulfilling their duties. Before David was discharged from the army, he had been promoted to the rank of second lieutenant. Surely, he had earned that rise in rank by, at times, his own courageous efforts.

After several days of living in dugouts, the American troops, including David's unit, marched forward to Etraye, France, where they hoisted their regimental colors on the side of a formerly occupied German shack. The hills along the Etraye valley were littered with German shacks and dugouts. Compared to the conditions in which the American soldiers had been living, David found the formerly occupied German encampment, including the dugouts, to be "very comfortably fixed; no wonder they didn't want to get out."[368] He went to sleep in one of the shacks that night and again wrote that he "slept like a brick." The next day, David was back again on duty retrieving pigeons from the division and making boxes for the birds.

November 11, 1918: When David awakened together with his regiment, they were informed "by their lieutenant that the Armistice had been signed and all firing would cease at 11:00 a.m." From wake-up time until just before 11:00 a.m., the American, French and German regiments continued the barrage of fire against each other so severely that he describes these last barrages as "letting the gates of hell open." On the exact minute of 11:00 a.m., all the firing ceased! "The American troops almost went crazy with joy!" In a few minutes, "Old Glory was flying over the field and how good she looked!" Sadly, the great cheers of joy were silenced for David's battalion when they were informed "that our good Sergeant Jenkins was killed by a shell just twenty minutes before 11:00 a.m. He was the one man that everyone had a good word for, and the signal men would do anything for him. It brought tears to many of our eyes and when hardened soldiers cry over a fallen comrade, you know he was dearly loved. For a time, even the joy of peace was forgotten."[369]

As his final act as a Signal Corps man, David let the birds fly free before leaving Etraye as they were of no further use to the army.

The regiment moved from Etraye to Damvillers, another small French village a few miles away. Most of the time, David spent in Damvillers was taken up by military drills, "real Camp Meade stuff" entertaining the troops. Occasionally, military maneuvers were practiced over and over again. David was now participating in regular Sunday services conducted by the chaplain by playing an old organ found in an old theater. There was little to keep these tired soldiers busy during peacetime in a foreign country.

One annoyance all the soldiers underwent was official inspections. One general, in particular, demanded that all the soldiers lay out two full sets of underwear on their cots. David, in his diary, finds this demand rather humorous. "We had orders that if you haven't two suits of underwear, take the one off your back to lie out! Some Army!! Had to use a blue print to lay the stuff out. They inspect our borrowed equipment about three times a week, but they never inspect us for cooties, bugs, etc. and we surely are loussey!" It's refreshing to know that David never totally lost his sense of humor. The rigorous inspections, however, really did annoy him: "They think more of the equipment than they do of us. You haven't time to wash and shave, and then if your face is dirty you get a week extra duty! Yesterday, we had an overseas inspection. We didn't even have time to get our pants down before they shoved us in past the doctor. It was a joke!"[370] Knowing what these men had been through, it does seem David had a few valid points to make regarding the inspections and the futility of it all. His point about the equipment being of more value then the fighting men is well taken. The U.S. military had never before in history had so many men in one place after the peace was achieved. Perhaps by keeping the men critical of the institution of the military, they would not have time to get into arguments and scrapes with each other.

The U.S. Military commandeered a YMCA hall for the use of the soldiers, and David was very involved there presenting musical programs and activities for the troops. He seemed to enjoy these events and in using his pocket camera. The following photo was taken in Damvillers by one of David's friends using his pocket camera. It was eventually sent home.

David E. Moyer in Damvillers, France, 1918
Photo: Courtesy of Moyer Family Archives

By December 22, 1918, David's diary revealed how disgusted he was with his life in this "mud hole." When he returned from his maneuvers that day, Jessie's Thanksgiving letter had arrived.

> Oh, how I wish I were back. This is an awful place to spend Xmas and with no idea when we will leave for 'God's Country'. There are many rumors about leaving the 28th of this month and being home some time in January, but I put no stock in rumors anymore. Every one is very discontented with mess and conditions. Will start this week and write what our menu is for each day. It will be interesting after getting out of this man's army to look back and remember the many times we came from mess with a hungry gut and being utterly disgusted.[371]

On Christmas Eve of 1918, David's spirits began to lift a bit. He was assigned as an orderly to an officer named Spierling. He did simple little jobs all day. This had to be better than being outdoors in the mud and rain laying telephone wires and then having to rewind them for no apparent reason. His unit spent the day cutting down whatever trees they could find to decorate the rooms of the barracks. "The officers of the regiment held a big feed in the theatre and the band, Spierling, and I helped to furnish the music. Rain had gotten in on the piano (due to holes in the ceiling of the theatre) and it was impossible for me to play, but I came in on the eats and oh, how good the goose was! Before the evening was over the officers were pretty well stewed from the champagne."

On Christmas Day, he played for the chaplain's service in the morning, and the chaplain asked him to make up a program for entertainment to be held in the theater at 7:00 p.m. the same night. David had a hard time getting any entertainers to sign up at short notice since most of them were already in Etraye entertaining. From what he says, the entertainment never happened. The army did provide a fine Christmas dinner for the soldiers consisting of pork, beans, potatoes, tomatoes, bread, butter, "really good coffee," and a few nuts, some chocolate, and grapes. David contrasts the actual meal with what the Government Issue meal was to be, "corn Willie."[372] The corn willie David speaks about is actually tinned corned beef.

The local YMCA provided the soldiers with gifts of cakes, chocolates, one package of Piedmonts, a cigar, and a bottle of wine for each man. David makes mention of the fact that by the time the evening was over, they were all feeling quite happy. Beginning the following day and continuing for the next five days, the units were sent on marching exercises. The first stop was Thierville-Sur-Meuse, and all David can tell us about this march is that it was truly horrible—dead bodies, dead animals, obliterated towns, and villages along the way. He does remark how poor the morale was. The days of endless marching in cold, constant rain and the poor sleeping conditions didn't help morale at all. David remarks that for warmth, he slept between two other soldiers named Sheridan and Dougherty for several nights. The food was also very poor, mostly his least favorite, cold corn willie, bread, and cold coffee.

The next stop is the little town of Souilly. His feet were cold, and he swore there was a quart of water in his boots. At Souilly, they were billeted in a reasonably good barracks that had electric lights. "It was a large hospital, but they forgot to leave the bunks." Again, he had to sleep between his two pals for warmth. The regiment marched further again to Chaumont-sur-Aire where, at last, they had sleeping accommodations that were dry. The rumors had started again, and this time David heard that they had to stay at Chaumont-sur-Aire, "received new equipment and then start for the port." His only comment is, "I hope it's true."

Nineteen hundred and eighteen ended harshly for David and the regiment. They were all stuck in the middle of nowhere, no dry clothes to change into, poor cold meals, no heat, and pointless hiking maneuvers, which seemed to never end. So far, all the rumors about leaving France and going home had amounted to nothing, and more than likely, added to the feelings of desperation all were experiencing.

The regiment continued to remain at Chaumont-sur-Aire until February 6, 1919. During this period, David was assigned to the orderly room and seems to have been run off his feet most days. He put together many musical programs to entertain the troops and was playing the music for the chaplain's services on a regular basis. Letters from Jessie Louise and a few chocolate bars arrived during this period. David seemed to keep very busy, and when he had time on his hands, he wrote to Jessie and his mother and worked on developing some of the photographs taken with his camera. From the tone of his diary, his and the other soldiers' spirits had lifted considerably.

February 6, 1919, David and two hundred others were given a pass to travel to Nice on the Cote d'Azur. The journey was unpleasant as the train was made up of third class German cars without lights or heat. David and the troops used candles for light while traveling at night. Upon arrival in Nice, he received instructions to check in at the Hotel Windsor, and that's exactly what he did. When he and the others left Chaumont-sur-Aire, the weather had been extremely cold and snowing, and on arrival along the Cote d'Azur, he found the heat intense. He felt absolutely rotten and just lounged around the rest of his first day there in the hotel room. For ten full days, David was ill. He did attend the local military infirmary and received some kind of pills, but as usual, they didn't help his condition at all. It is not surprising that he became ill in light of the nature of his diet during those last few months together with the constant marching and maneuverings in the wet, cold hills of France.

Finally, on February 17, 1919, he felt well enough to take a trip to Monte Carlo and Monaco. He found the scenery beautiful and refreshing. His one opportunity for some real rest and relaxation was mostly spent in bed. After the side trip to Monte Carlo and Monaco, David was faced once again with the ordeals of traveling back to Chaumont-sur-Aire. On top of that, when the unit reached the train station and saw the military rations they were given, it seemed all their hearts sunk simultaneously. They returned to their base of operations sixteen days after they had first left.

Once back at base camp, David was again working in the orderly room. Upon seeing fifteen letters from Jessie had arrived, his heart must have almost leapt out of his chest. There was also a letter for him from Jessie's mother, Mrs. Cowles. He never wrote in his diary any comments about this letter from Mrs. Cowles, but he did say that he would start answering some of them in the evening when he was off duty.

March arrived with good news for David. He became aware of an order from the AEF University seeking a music instructor. Instantly, he submitted his name. The very next day, the good news of his assignment arrived, and he was to leave for Beaune at once. He had to pack his gear very quickly and get himself to division headquarters in Souilly. When he arrived there, he was then informed that his train for Bar-le-Duc (the first stage of the journey) would not be leaving until the following morning at 6:00 a.m. One of the obstacles that David faced trying to get to the university in Beaune was that he had little money in his pocket. He was, however, able to draw three days rations that consisted of nothing but a bit of bread and corn willie. David tried to secure money owed to him by the army from his pay book, but he was refused by the quartermaster. He had a total of three francs to his name. Once he had arrived in Bar-le-Duc, he tried to borrow money from the local YMCA, and of course, the answer was no again. While on the train from Bar-le-Duc to Toul, near Nancy, he met another soldier who offered him a place to sleep overnight at a local army camp, and this proved to be "one of the finest camps I have ever seen in France." Again David started the rounds to the quartermaster then to the pay master and so forth. Again, he had no luck getting any money. When he finally boarded the train toward Dijon, he was lucky enough to be on an American train with a kitchen car, and there he was able to eat a good meal for free.

The train from Dijon to Beaune was French and although the journey was brief, there was commotion. All the American soldiers piled into a second class car, and once they were "nicely fixed, a Frog conductor arrived and started an awful line of talk. We all knew what he meant, but we put him out and then he called an M.P. Out we had to go, but only into another second class car." David does not expound on the reason they had to move from one car to another, but it's easy to be sympathetic to the American soldiers feeling that they were in some way being insulted by the French conductor in spite of what the Americans had just completed, namely, returning the country to French control some months earlier.

David and the others heading for the university arrived and realized what a great camp they were assigned to (the AEF 766), and as he stated it, "the life of Riley begins." The billets were very comfortable, a hospital was on site, and the mess was much better than anything he had experienced thus far. The music course in which he was soon to participate was fully comprehensive, but he would quickly learn that there were many pitfalls that would discourage him once again. "Got acquainted with the music faculty and a general outline of the work and I think it will be great. It is a bigger movement than I had thought possible. A-Z in music will be taught and all instruments. Dr. Robinson of New York is in charge of the College of Music and he is a thorough musician."[373]

David did not write in his diary on a daily basis from March 12 to June 13. Instead he tended to summarize the happenings in his life at his new assignment as a faculty member of the AEF University.

> During these months very little of importance happened. Pianos never
> arrived although we were promised many times that they would come

and that they were on the way. For the first month most of my time was taken up with office work; registering students and dropping those who left. It is absolutely impossible to keep a strict roster; the registrar's office sends us all kinds of reports and none of them are complete.[374]

For David, with his previous experiences as a teacher of music, both privately and within a college context, it is easy to see why he became so distraught over the system at the AEF University. In addition to these frustrations regarding his work, he also became disenchanted with the accommodations. The brass of the AEF decided that his unit should be moved from the comfort of the 766 Camp to the Fourth Camp. When showed the proposed quarters, the unit squawked at the filth and the dark conditions and the lack of flooring (the floors were simply compacted dirt) of this proposed facility. David realized that the colonel was angered by the response of the men. However, he did have concrete floors installed, and other improvements were made in the billets, so the disgruntled troops eventually moved in as ordered. In addition to the new billet, a clubhouse consisting of two rooms and a kitchen was opened for the music instructors. "The club house was fixed up to be 'very homelike.' It was managed by two YMCA women, a Miss Turner and Miss (name forgotten) were stationed there permanently and every afternoon lemonade and sandwiches were to be had."[375]

For the next two months, David never attended the College of Music, and quite frankly, who could blame him. He was always a man of high integrity and dedication who loved to teach, but the lack of pianos and other factors frustrated his spirit. There was really little else he could do other than sleep, read, attend occasional dances, which were held on the base and also in the village. At the AEF University, the kitchen staff was made up of French civilian employees, and not military men. David invited Mademoiselle de Grisie, one of the kitchen staff, to both dances on the base and in the town. He remarked that she was a very good dancer; however, "She was empty headed."[376] Mademoiselle must have spoken some English for David to make this judgment. David did not speak French. Obviously, David's experiences had not been with empty-headed women in the past. However, she was very kind to him, and she had a piano in her home; she invited David to come and practice on her piano at any time he chose. At the college, he was able to locate classical music scores, which had previously been his old standbys, and with anytime access to a piano, he could begin to get his playing back up to standard.[377]

The troops at Beaune had received two visits from General Pershing and one visit from the secretary of War Newton Baker before they began their long journey south to the port of Marseille where they would board a ship and begin the long trip home. David recorded in his diary that these visits from the notables required about three days of preparations and always ended with a grand review and speech from the distinguished visitor "in which he always told us what good boys we were now and what we had done for our country." Generally, the boys shouted back to the speaker, "When do we go home!" "When do we eat?" Needless to say, the colonel in charge was embarrassed by the troop's responses. David expressed his thoughts on the reasons why the men of the Educational Corps responded to the speakers the way they did:

> A great deal of hard feeling exists between the officers and men and the Educational Corps. The men of the Army feel that this whole educational program is to promote the interests of the civilian men who come over to give us education and receive extravagant salaries.
>
> The director of our college received $625.00 a month and we do the work. He seldom comes to the office and during the whole term he gave out one hour lessons on one day. He then promptly turned the class over to one of us. We receive our $1.00 a day for our services!
>
> When we get back to the States it is the idea of these Educational "cooties" to continue the work in the form of Educational compulsory military service. An organization has been formed to counteract this movement by the officers and enlisted men and although at the present time we are forbidden to do any active work, a great deal will be heard from this organization when we are civilians.[378]

David, while being away from home, away from his girl, and making no progress with his career, was obviously disgusted and frustrated. He had high hopes when he submitted his paperwork for the music teaching job in Beaune, but the lack of organization and the feelings of being exploited were too much for him to bear. He was not the only one of the AEF soldiers stationed in Beaune that felt this way.

June 14, 1919, was the day he learned for certain that he and many of his corps men were finally to leave France for home. The twenty-four hour ride by train to Marseille must have filled them with joy but also some anxiety while they wondered were they really going to leave the southern city or just be recamped for a longer stay. When the train pulled into the local train station, he and the other men were marched to another camp, and according to David, the only things worth mentioning "about this place was the mess hall and the dust. All roads were made of some sort of coal dust and within a half hour we looked like black men. The mess hall was large enough to feed from two to three thousand men at once and within a very few minutes." There were days of paperwork yet to be completed, and the soldiers were informed that if all the paperwork was completed before the next morning, they would be able to sail for America. This required personnel to ask each soldier many, many questions and to change all of their French money into greenbacks. But early the following morning, the soldiers had their final field inspection and started the march to the pier where they would board the ship. David said, "The walk was not hard but it was slow" and took about four hours. Once they were at the pier, the men boarded the Italian liner *America*.

"At five o'clock p.m., the ship started to leave the port of Marseille and everyone wore a smile as the coast of France passed by." The journey continued, and the following day they had a good view of the coast of Spain. The first stop for the *America* was the harbor at Gibraltar where recoaling seemed to take forever. The following evening, the ship was once again ready to continue the journey through the Strait of Gibraltar, which connects the Atlantic Ocean to the Mediterranean Sea and separates Spain from Morocco. David's final entry in his diary states, "And now our next port will be the long hoped for and dreamed of Port of New York."[379]

David never discussed his time in the U.S. military with his family until he mentioned on a tape recording in 1975 that he, in fact, served in the army. Like the rest of his life prior to these events, he just never discussed these things with his children. He returned to Philadelphia to his parent's home after disembarking at the Port of New York. Their reunion was joyful, but David had other matters to attend to. He needed to notify Bucknell University that he would be returning to his teaching post in early September for the beginning of the autumn term. And, of course, there was Jessie Louise to see as well! David and Jessie were able to see each other almost as soon as he returned home. He was still using his pocket camera to record notable events!

David with his parents after his arrival home, 1919, Philadelphia
Photo: Courtesy of Moyer Family Archives

Jessie Cooper with David's parents, 1919, Philadelphia
Photo: Courtesy of Moyer Family Archives

This is the original sized photo of the images David developed from his pocket
camera during his military service in France, 1918-1919
Photo: David E. Moyer
Courtesy of Moyer Family Archives

Enlargement of preceeding photo
Photo: David E. Moyer
Courtesy of Moyer Family Archives

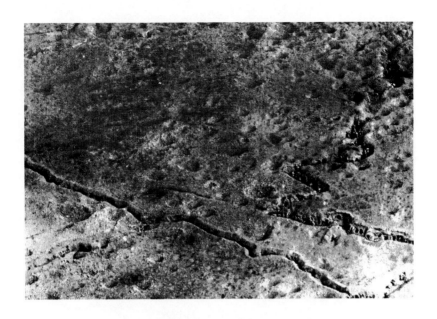

Arial view of Trenches, the Argonne, France, 1918-1919
Photo: Courtesy of Moyer Family Archives

A German Bunker, France
Photo: David E. Moyer
Courtesy of Moyer Family archives

Chapter XI

Mary and the Boys in Berlin

While David was struggling in Philadelphia to get his career back on track and prior his military duty with the AEF in France, Mary, his former tutor, and her two sons' lives in Germany changed drastically. There is no way to know the actual reasons for the changes that took place, and David didn't seem to know either. From the records available, however, it is possible to trace their movements.

The boys and Mary, their mother, appear to have stayed in Germany until July 1916. Although Mary had applied and received a passport for 1914 that was valid for one year, she never traveled to the United States or anywhere, for that matter, during the valid period that this passport was in force. Robert and Clarence also had a passports issued in 1915, but they never used them until 1916.

Just how Mary, Robert, and Clarence survived during these last years is unknown. They no longer had David on hand to help with the finances! Germany was at war, and inflation was rising rapidly, so all she could really do was teach students privately, if any were available. Mary may have had some savings, but when she had the opportunity in 1914, after David was safely in America, why did she not choose to leave and bring her two sons back to the USA beggars belief. What was keeping her there?

Her passport dated August 22, 1914, reveals a mysterious fact. Although her passport included both Robert and Clarence, there is also listed someone named Elvine born October 15, 1910.[380] There are no further records regarding Elvine, but it is possible that Mary had found herself yet another potential prodigy and wanted to bring this child with her to the States. Elvine would have been four years old at this time, according to the passport record. The reason for the application was stated on the passport: she wanted this passport for "protection."

It is very possible that whatever family Elvine had, if any, or if she was from either a local adoption agency or orphanage, someone had the good sense not to allow this German born child to leave the country. Mary was aged fifty-six in 1914; therefore, she could hardly have claimed this child as her own offspring. Perhaps, she just wouldn't leave Elvine behind and stayed on in Berlin to try to figure out another plan of some kind that would permit her to take Elvine with her regardless of where that would be. Mary's passport for 1915 is not on file at the National Archives in Washington, so we have no record of exactly who was supposed to travel with her even though she apparently never made the journey to the USA at this time.

On July 5, 1916, Robert and Clarence were given individual United States passports in their adopted names to travel back to New York City. The ship's manifest records for Robert and Clarence proves that Mary sent them to Rotterdam, Holland, where they boarded the ship *Noordam* July 29, 1916, on their own to make their last crossing of the Atlantic Ocean toward home. Home to these two adolescent boys is probably a word that most people would think could cause some confusion for them because of their backgrounds. But maybe not. Robert (Paul) was old enough to remember something about his life before life with Madame Mary, and surely he informed his little brother, Clarence (Arthur) about whom they really were and where they came from. They had to know that they were American and spoke American English and that German was something they had to deliberately learn. They also had to know that Madame and David were American as well. Both Robert and Clarence were still using their adopted names that Mary had given them. The boys were sixteen and fourteen years old respectively.

Interestingly, the ship's manifest arrival record for August 5, 1916, at New York there is a handwritten notation above the name of Robert Haggerty, "arrv. to child society."[381] When the boys had to tell the immigration officer where they were to go in the United States, they gave the name of G. A. Gauthier of Santa Ana, California. How they came up with that name we will never know. Perhaps the boys told another passenger on the ship of their dilemma that they didn't have an address to go to and that passenger kindly gave them an address to use.

The two boys had every reason to be fearful of what might become of them. We don't know what Mary may have told them to expect, if anything, upon their arrival in New York. They must have been frightened and anxious! Mary, in effect, abandoned the two boys between the date in July she chose for herself to travel to Copenhagen, Denmark, from Berlin to board her own boat on July 13, 1916, and the date the boys boarded the ship from Rotterdam, July 29, 1916. There is no evidence to suggest how the boys got from Berlin to Rotterdam and if anyone was put in charge of them at this time. From the unknown date that Mary left Berlin for Copenhagen until July 29 was a very long time for two boys to have no protection and to physically survive on their own. This must have been very emotionally painful for them, but in some sense, depending on their actual relationship with her, it may have been a bit of a relief as well. After all, it was the second time in their young lives that they had been abandoned by their parent. For both boys, Mary was the only mother they had ever known. It is common knowledge that children from any kind of abusive household always maintain an emotional attachment to their parents regardless of how devastating the environment is for them. Both boys were the real losers in all of this, for it seems certain that once David returned to the USA, the Trio became a mere figment of Mary's imagination. The boys must have realized that she favored David, the one with all the natural talent, but it appears Mary had other fish to fry and wanted to continue her life without them. On the reverse side of Robert's 1916 passport, next to his photograph, is stated:

> The applicant was issued above mentioned passport [#1897, dated, June 29, 1916 in the name of "Robert Berlino." He and his brother Arthur Haggerty, bearer of Emergency passport No.A.15473 of July 5, 1916, were brought up by Mrs. Marie Berlino, but she can produce no evidence of their legal adoption by her.[382]

Robert Haggerty and Arthur Haggerty
1916 Passport Photos
U.S. Records Administration, Washington, D.C.

The notation on the reverse side of Arthur's 1916 passport simply states, "The applicant was brought up by Mrs. Marie Berlino and has always gone under her name."[383] Whether Mary ever had any legal document to prove that she, in fact, did adopt the boys cannot be ascertained. Adoption records belonging to the State of New York are locked away forever and cannot be accessed. It should be remembered that at the time of the boys' adoptions, Mary was already using her nom de plume of Madame Marie Berlino, but legally, no such person existed.

Mary's behavior during the summer of 1916 and her traveling arrangements lead to suspicions. She sailed alone from the port of Copenhagen, Denmark, July 13, 1916, and arrived in New York City on July 25, 1916. On the ship's manifest, she listed her place of residence in the USA as 85 Berkley Street, New York City. We know Mary had not lived at that address for many years. She managed to enter the USA before the two boys arrived and would not have been questioned regarding their supposed adoptive status or anything else for that matter. She was just another passenger on the ship. Just as she avoided the issue of the subpoena served on her regarding her divorce petition from her former husband, John H. Kunneke in 1885, by simply not responding, she made sure she would arrive in New York prior to the boys' arrival and not have to answer any difficult questions for anybody. Mary obviously had no intention of continuing to raise these boys.

Once in New York, it appears she made the journey to Lima, her hometown, possibly to seek some financial help from her two sisters who still lived there. When her mother died in 1912, Mary was left one third of her mother's belongings, not including the house in Lima. Consequently, she may have gone to Lima to try to raise money from her sisters by selling what she could. A newspaper article from the *Lima News* May 10, 1919, states that Mary was in Columbus Grove, Ohio, in the summer of 1916. Columbus Grove is in Putnam County and is adjacent to Ottawa County where Lima is located. Exactly why she traveled to Columbus Grove at this time is a mystery. Perhaps she had a friend living there at the time, but if she had any hopes of gaining help from her former husband, John J. Kunneke, she was out of luck because he died in 1907. According to legal documents, we know that Mary traveled to Philadelphia, and more than likely, she went to the Moyer household at 126 South Thirty-Fourth Street where she sought to seek refuge. She needed refuge! No records survive to document what she might have told the Moyers about her situation and the whereabouts of the boys. On September 23, 1916, she appealed to the deputy clerk, District Federal Court, Eastern District of Pennsylvania, with a signed affidavit stating

> I, Marie [a large ink spot covers something] Berlino, being duly sworn according to law depose and say that in the summer of 1906 she went from Philadelphia to Germany for the purpose of imparting musical education to David Earl Moyer, minor son of Joseph A. and Ida Moyer, residing at that time at 126 So.34th Street, Philadelphia, Pa., that on her arrival in Berlin April 1915, she executed a lease for premises on

Lutzow Street, No. 10, in the City of Berlin, said lease expiring on March 30th, 1917; that all of her household goods, musical instruments, clothing, etc., remain on said premises and that it is necessary for her to return to Berlin to dispose of the same and to settle up other business affairs.[384]

In the sworn affidavit quoted above, there is no mention of her two sons being with her in Germany. From what David has said, Mary did not "impart musical education" to him from 1906 onward because he was then studying with Alberto Jonas. During this time, she acted only as his temporary guardian, and not as his musical instructor. It is clear that the content of her affidavit does not conform to the facts as we know them from the available documentation. It seems that being "duly sworn" meant nothing to her. In addition, she had to submit a certified description of herself to accompany this appeal, and this Description of Applicant was issued by a neighbor of the Moyers, James L. Monihan, who lived at 119 South Thirty-Fourth Street, Philadelphia. Mr. Monihan was an officer of the court in Philadelphia. Her contact address, which was required information, is listed as 25 No. Thirty-Fourth Street, Philadelphia. This address was the same address where David had his studio. No one actually lived in this building since it was a manufacturing place of business with a few rooms rented for music studios and other business people. Whatever Mary told David about her situation, we will never know. She must have told him some kind of story to justify her being in Philadelphia in the first place.

It must be stated that without Mary in David's life, he would never have had the opportunity to receive the superior musical education and training that Berlin afforded. The five years of private study with Alberto Jonas, study at the *hochschule*, and the opportunity to play for Busoni would never have happened if Mary wasn't so committed to him and his development as a concert pianist. She really was the prime mover in launching David's musical formation. The Moyers probably took pity on her and helped her, perhaps with a bit more than just hospitality at their home while she was in Philadelphia.

Beginning on December 9, 1914, and continuing throughout World War I, the U.S. Department of State issued passports only for specific purposes and to specific countries. "No passports were issued for travel in Germany and Austria from then until July 18, 1922, and none for the Soviet Union until approximately September 1923."[385] Mr. Monihan, the Moyers' neighbor, must have had some serious influence with people in very high places because Mary actually did receive a passport that was personally signed by Robert Lansing, secretary of State in the Wilson administration, to travel on September 21, 1916 back to Berlin. This passport was only valid until March 21, 1917, when it would expire. Additionally, the *Republican-Gazette*, a Lima newspaper reported

April 1, 1917, that "Madame Berlino, concert singer and former Lima woman who is now in Berlin, probably will not be allowed to return if war is declared between the United States and Germany. She has applied for and received German naturalization."[386] Wonder what Secretary of State Lansing would have to say about that information? In another article in 1919, *Lima News* stated that Mary's family had not heard from her since 1918 and feared she had disappeared. Mary did return to the United States in October 1922 (without a passport) and retired to Lima.

We will never know the exact circumstances of where Mary spent the remainder of her time in Europe. It has been suggested in later newspaper accounts regarding her European flings that she spend the unaccounted years in Copenhagen, Denmark, but she is not listed on any census records available for the period in Denmark under any of her names. Why was she so intent on not being in the United States during the World War? The above details concerning her behavior provides some clues. She probably could have stayed in Lima with her sisters in 1916 when she went to visit them, but she didn't choose to do this for whatever reasons. Perhaps the only reason was that her false identities and her fantasies about her own position and her significance in European society was what the poor soul clung to for survival. If she had remained in Lima in 1916, she would have had to change her persona and be just another piano teacher and live in a more realistic world with her sisters and her extended family. Obviously, she just could not do that. After 1922, Mary lived in Lima, gave piano lessons privately, and also was a private tutor in both French and German. The supposed reason for her return to Lima according to press reports at this time was that her next eldest sister, Ellen, who had become quite senile needed her assistance. Mary's eldest sister, Virtue Amelia Davis, had passed away a few years before so Ellen was basically on her own. According to Margaret Fry, also of Lima, stated in an interview that Mary was brought back to the United States by the American Red Cross. Mary had made an appeal to them while she was still living in Europe that her sister was severely ill, and she was the only person who could take care of her.[387] Ellen Halter, Mary's sister, did not die until May 1937 when the initial report of her death was published in the *Lima Times* and stated that she had been ill for the last three years.[388] The following day, May 18, 1937, the same newspaper printed a larger article about the death of Ellen with many details regarding the Halter family:

> Miss Halter, one of the last members of a long line of German aristocrats, was widely known throughout this section as a business woman. She at one time conducted ladies hat shops and ready-to-wear establishments in Lima, Chicago, Muncie and Indianapolis. She was also active in real estate.

> She resided with her sister, Mary, known professionally for many years in international music circles as Madame Berlino.[389]

It looks like Mary really did believe her own fantasies! It is obvious from what the reporter wrote regarding Ellen Halter's life that her sister Mary was the informant.

The boys, Paul and Arthur Haggerty, after their return to New York City in 1916, were returned to their mother, who had married Mr. Edward Dunn, and to their sister Gertrude, born in 1902. Arthur died from tuberculosis in 1920 while resident in the Fox Hill Hospital, Richmond Borough, and New York City.[390] On the census record from that hospital he was listed as "soldier." His medical condition was listed as tuberculosis. In 1937, Paul worked for the Federal Music Project located in New York City. It appears from the documentation that he had worked in music since his return from Europe. He married Lottie Feldman, a local New York journalist. It seems that Lottie was offered a much better job in journalism in Chicago, so she and Paul moved there and remained there until their deaths. Paul worked for Baldwin Piano Company as both a salesman and a liaison for local and visiting musicians. Additionally, he entertained in night clubs and died of acute bronchopneumonia in 1973 with no issue. His wife, Lottie, predeceased him by seven years.

CHAPTER XII

Bucknell: 1919-1925

In the autumn of 1919, David returned to his teaching responsibilities at Bucknell College in Lewisburg, Pennsylvania. Jessie Louise Cooper also returned to Bucknell as a graduate student studying voice and teaching piano. She taught in the junior department at Bucknell, which would have been the equivalent of high school or secondary level, and also did some college teaching at her alma mater in the college department of music.

David and Jessie were now able to conduct their courtship in public and spend the much-needed hours getting to know each other once again. David's academic responsibilities included the teaching of piano and advanced harmony. Jessie and David performed many duo piano recitals, both on the university campus and off campus. According to the press reviews, they were a smashing success. In David's studio at Bucknell, he had two pianos side by side, and that's where he and Jessie would practice their two-piano selections to be performed at public concerts. On May 26, 1920, both David and Jessie had piano students performing in piano ensembles in the same student concert. What joy this must have brought to both of them!

On June 16, 1920, the couple were married at a private ceremony held in the family home of the Lawshe's, friends of both the bride and groom. Dr. Emory W. Hunt President of Bucknell College and a Baptist Minister joined the couple in matrimony. Jessie's mother and her husband, Mr. Cowles, were in attendance, but for reasons unknown, it appears that none of David's immediate family attended the ceremony. There is no indication that this was a problem for David.

David and Jessie Moyer on their wedding day with Mr. and Mrs. Lawshe,
host and hostess, 1920
Photo: Courtesy of Moyer Family Archives

After the wedding, the happy couple took the traditional honeymoon and set up their home in Lewisberg, Pennsylvania. David bought himself a Steinway grand piano for their first home. He lamented in his "Reminiscences" how it took him three years to pay for it.[391] There are no records of Jessie's continuance as a performer with David on the same program once they were married, or any evidence to suggest she continued as part of the faculty at Bucknell. In the United States in 1920, only 15 percent of white women with employed husbands worked outside the home.[392] Perhaps Jessie and David felt it was best that she not continue to teach at the college now that they were married. Societal norms would probably have been more of an influence on their decision than anything else. Jessie and David were both compliant people and were never ones to rock the boat, so to speak. The newlyweds entertained themselves in their first home by making music together. David and Jessie would play duet numbers on the piano, and many times, Jessie would sing. Her favorites were German Lieder and Wolfe songs and Shumann and Brahms.[393] David makes the point that if they didn't make their own musical entertainment, there was not a sound in the apartment because there was no radio in their home, and of course, television had not been invented.

By 1921, David had been made head of the music department at Bucknell, and along with his new job title, came additional responsibilities. He became fully immersed in the concert performance season now more than ever. Besides performing, he now had the major responsibility for the scheduling and promotion of these concerts. Newspaper clippings from the Lewisburg and Williamsport areas reported that more people attended these public concerts in Williamsport more so than those held in Lewisburg. However, this audience factor never seemed to affect the avid concertgoers in Lewisburg when David was on the program. There were many instances of packed auditoriums when he performed.

David received great public support and acclaim as a performer. "Moyer Recital Crowns Season," was the headline of an article published in the *Lewisburg Journal* on April 15, 1921. The venue for this concert was the Baptist Church where, according to the article, the numbers in attendance "taxed the capacity" of the Baptist Church. "His concert was a triumph, closing at the highest pitch a season of artist recitals. Fully six hundred musical people entered into the event and cheered Mr. Moyer to his best efforts, recalling him repeatedly and remaining at the close, not a person moving until he responded once more."[394]

Another concert was held on September 28, 1921, at the Williamsport High School Auditorium. It appears that most of the Williamsport concerts were arranged by a Mr. Harry S. Krape, a local agent. Listed on the program for that concert was an old acquaintance of David's from his Berlin days. Cornelius Van Vliet, back in 1906, had been the cello teacher for young Clarence Berlino. They must have been so happy to be reacquainted again after so many years and to perform together for the very first time. Public concerts that had been organized by independent agents—and therefore were not for the benefit of the college—paid the individual performers handsomely. David was paid for his performances, and these engagements must have added a little extra for the family budget.

Saint Paul by Felix Mendelssohn was performed at Bucknell College in June 1922. David provided the piano accompaniment, and Jessie sang soprano in the chorus. The four lead soloists were professionals hired for the event. Marie Stapleton-Murray sang the soprano solos and had previously sung the title role of Verdi's *Aida* in the opera of the same name in 1920. She was later to become the mother of actress Jean Stapleton, a.k.a. Edith Bunker, in the very popular, *All in the Family* television series in the 1970s.

David performed in the Historical Memorial Concert with famous Luella Melius at the high school auditorium in Milton, Pennsylvania, on Thursday, May 3, 1923. The concert was to pay tribute to the world-famous opera star Adelina Patti, who had died just a few years prior.

Adelina Patti was born in Spain to Italian parents and had taken the world by storm (when she was very young) with her incredible voice and singing style. Adelina's parents were poor, but they were a performing family. They had moved to America to find better performance situations and more opportunities for serious training for their prodigy daughter. In fact, the family had three daughters that all excelled as opera singers. At the age of sixteen, Adelina made her operatic debut in the title role in Donizetti's *Lucia di Lammermoor*, and her career blossomed from then on. Much of her fame in the United States was because of the amazing support she received from the Italian community in New York when she was very young. Adelina, as an adult, based herself in Europe and performed in Leningrad and even Buenos Aires. In American circles, she is probably best known for her rendition of "Home Sweet Home," lyrics by John Howard Payne and music by the British composer Henry Rowley Bishop. She sang this song in the White House for the grieving Abraham Lincoln and his wife in 1862.[395]

At the concert given in humble Milton, Pennsylvania, Luella Meluis, former opera singer, wore gowns that duplicated those worn by Madame Patti in Chicago in 1870. It seems strange in today's world that working-class people would attend such a function in large enough numbers to finance the concert. But they did! Entertainment of any kind was appreciated by people in the small towns of America and always proved to be successful events for the promoters. Certainly, if these concerts were not financially successful, the promoters would have never arranged them in the first place.

In January 1923, "Momentous Announcement" press release was distributed in Williamsport announcing the appearance of Erwin Nyiregyhazi, the eighteen-year-old Hungarian pianist, at the local high school auditorium. It is apparent that David was involved as a ticket seller/promoter in support of this. His enthusiasm is evident as he, in his own hand, printed across the top of the announcement, "Leave your order with David Moyer. Join the party!" To David, a concert was a party, a social gathering, to be enjoyed by all who attended and performed. Although he was always a serious musician, he loved the gathering of the audience, and he entertained them superbly. To him, it was always a celebration.

Even before David's marriage to Jessie, he had been fully aware that Bucknell's music department was not what he considered to be "outstanding." He felt the students were not serious about their musicianship, and when he approached the president of the college, Dr. Emory W. Hunt who had previously presided at the marriage of David and Jessie actually agreed with him. The president of Bucknell expressed his view that the purpose of the Department of Music was to simply "offer a little music to the college girls if they were so inclined."[396] This was not good enough for David! His own experience of learning music was much more serious and rigorous, and as a teacher, he wanted to be part of something that reflected the depth of his own training and experiences. He clearly saw that staying at Bucknell would only be a continuation of the frustration he was experiencing. He requested a recommendation from Dr. Hunt for his career advancement, and the president graciously agreed.

Another factor, although David never mentions it in this context, is that Jessie was pregnant with their first child, and perhaps, he was aware that a more professionally minded, serious Department of Music would provide him with a higher salary. Sonia, their first child, was born January 17, 1924, in Lewisburg. The birth of Sonia was very difficult for Jessie because she encountered serious physical difficulties immediately after the birth. Jessie became ill with phlebitis after already spending three months in the Geisinger Memorial Hospital because of blood poisoning. Both David's mother and Jessie's mother rushed to their apartment to look after their new granddaughter while Jessie was recovering. Jessie's progress was long and drawn out. One of Jessie's aunts from Ardmore, Pennsylvania, also arrived to help with Jessie's care in the hospital. Jessie's health crisis eventually passed, and David continued his search for a more challenging teaching position, and he was successful.

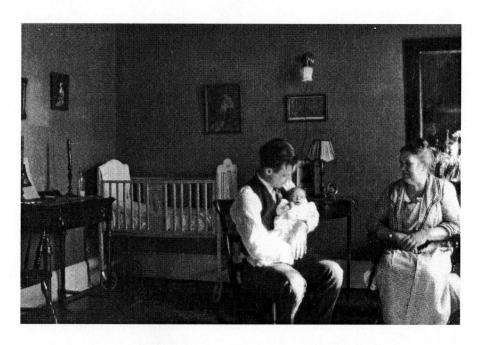

David holding newborn Sonia as his mother looks on,
Lewisburg, Pennsylvania, 1924
Photo: Courtesy of Moyer Family Archives

CHAPTER XIII

The Early Oberlin Years

Mr. David Moyer
Lewisburg, Pa

Dear Sir:

I have the honor to inform you that at the meeting of the Prudential Committee of the Board of Trustees of Oberlin College held July 8th, you were appointed Assistant Professor of Pianoforte for two years with a view to permanency. The salary for the two years to be $3,150 per year.

Yours truly,

July 13, 1925

Above is the unsigned letter received by David on approximately, July 15, 1925, at their residence in Lewisburg near Bucknell College. It must not have been easy to pack house and home, a piano, and a small child for the 320-mile trip to Oberlin, Ohio. Although David owned an automobile at this time, the trip to Oberlin must have been challenging. There was a lack of major highways at this time, and the infrequency of gasoline stations would have been a major concern as well. They rented a small apartment at Merwin Apartments within walking distance to the conservatory.[397] Traditionally, housing for both faculty and students at Oberlin was always difficult to find. One rented what was available. A year later when their second child, David Earl Moyer, Jr.,(always called Bud)

168

was born on July 4, 1926, the four of them moved to larger housing at Howard Apartments at 20 N. Pleasant Street, Oberlin.[398] Two years later, in 1927, David Sr. was promoted to the rank of full professor.

The establishment of Oberlin as an educational institution seemed essential to the founding of the community of Oberlin as a town. In the early 1830s, the Mississippi Valley was colonial territory in the United States where communities there were founded mostly by New England Congregationalists who settled the area adjoining what was to become the town of Oberlin, then a five-hundred-acre tract of level tree-covered land privately owned by a few Connecticut residents promoting the establishment of a utopian community for preaching the gospel to the non churched West.[399] Eleven families arrived from Vermont, New Hampshire, and Massachusetts to begin a new colony named Oberlin in honor of a renowned French-Alsace pastor whose Christian philanthropy had just become known in America.

To guarantee success, only pioneers of high character were chosen. Those chosen freely and voluntary entered a covenant whereby the "degeneracy of the church was lamented, the importance of building up of institutions of Christian learning was emphasized and the dependence upon the counsel of the Lord was acknowledged."[400] These pioneers pledged themselves to own only the amount of land they could profitably manage to practice economy and industry so that they would have sufficient surplus supplies to support the religious cause of preaching the gospel. They vowed to eat only plain wholesome food and to renounce all bad habits—in particular, to avoid tobacco and alcohol usage, even the drinking of tea and coffee. Dress was to be plain and durable. All should build their houses without ostentation providing for widows and orphans of the colony as they would for their own families.[401] These same Christian ideals of the founders of Oberlin were very much in continuity with the ethos of the Schwenkfelder/Mennonite communities who informed and guided the way of life pursued by David's parents.

The Oberlin Collegiate Institute opened December 3, 1833, accepting both male and female students. It was the first collegiate institution to admit women in the United States. The first circular promoting the school stated that it was the intention of the founders to "elevate female character, by bringing within the reach of the misjudged and neglected sex all the instructive privileges which have hitherto unreasonably distinguished the leading sex from theirs."[402] In 1835, a further decision was made to admit students "irrespective of color" as well.[403] The inclusion of persons of color to the school brought with it tremendous financial support from the abolitionist movement that ensured, for a time, the financial security of the fledgling institution.

The Oberlin Conservatory of Music, founded in 1867, later became well known for its excellence in producing highly qualified musicians. The history of music at Oberlin College began in 1835 when the college added a sacred music course to the curriculum, albeit for only one year by hiring the Reverend Elihu Parsons Ingersoll as professor of sacred music. Never before an American college offered such a position.[404]

After Reverend Ingersoll's sacred music instruction, George N. Allen took over the task. There was no shortage of students participating in these courses. In 1837, Oberlin Musical Association, later named Oberlin Musical Union, was founded. The musical Union was a choral group of about 150 singers from the entire school. The chorus performed all the major classical works, i.e., B Minor Mass of Bach, Brahms' Requiem, etc., and was accompanied by the Oberlin Orchestra. The Musical Union is still an important presence on the campus. The Oberlin College trustees became suspicious of George Allen's insistence that secular music was as worthy of study as sacred music. This included the teaching of piano as part of the curriculum. At the time, only string instruments were acceptable in accompanying the choir. During these early years, music courses were limited, and students did not receive college credit for participation in these courses.[405]

The music department at Oberlin continued to have difficulty in obtaining proper recognition from the trustees. However, George Allen continued his teaching of natural history, and his work in the music department was on a voluntary basis until 1864. It is believed that he not only worked diligently to expand the music department but also invested his own funds in the purchase of many instruments and expended great effort building the music hall. He compiled Oberlin's first hymnbook containing approximately three hundred harmonized hymns.

The 1865-1866 academic prospectus for Oberlin College announced the creation of the Oberlin Conservatory of Music. "This Institute, which has been established for supplying a want generally felt by those interested in the cause of art, to the furtherance of which it is devoted, began its first term the fifth of September of the present year [1865]."[406]

By the time David was hired for his position as assistant professor of pianoforte, the conservatory had been running successfully for sixty years. In 1900, it was considered one of the leading music schools in the United States and was viewed as comparable to the leading conservatories in Germany regarding its admission and educational standards, as well as for the equipment available for student use.

David's teaching assignment primarily was in applied piano studies for accepted piano majors plus others majoring in other instruments. In addition to teaching piano majors, he also taught piano proficiency in other areas such as organ, voice, clarinet, flute, harp, cello, composition, music education, school music, violin, theory, trumpet, and trombone, etc., for those needing help in understanding musical theory. During David's thirty-five-year teaching career at Oberlin, he taught a total of 574 individual students—a number calculated from the handwritten teaching register that he compiled after his retirement in 1960.[407] In addition to conservatory students, David also taught college students desiring to take a semester or more of piano instruction as elective courses or to pursue a dual degree program that led to both Bachelor of Arts and Bachelor of Music degrees. A few faculty and staff members who desired instruction were also accommodated.

Until 1930, the highly esteemed European system of teaching applied music instruction at Oberlin Conservatory was class teaching.[408] This system was not problematic for David to adapt to since it was the same system he had trained under during his days at the *hochschule* in Berlin. According to Skyrm, this method persisted in order to accommodate more students at a cheaper tuition rate.[409] Later, however, the class method gradually disappeared and was replaced with the private single half-hour or full-hour lesson.

The issue of nonattendance for classes, concert rehearsals, and recital concerts by students became an issue at Oberlin Conservatory just as it had been in the German Conservatories prior to, during, and after David's attendance 1909-1911. Oberlin was not inclined to follow the German practice of leaving it up to the students when to attend and when not to attend. The administration tried on several occasions to control student absences from necessary participation. Students were individually deciding when to leave and return from vacations. One remedy tried was to penalize students by making them wait to register for preferred classes until the second day of registration. It was at this registration period that students also chose their practice rooms as no one really wanted an undesirable room. Nevertheless, this seemed to have little effect on students' attendance. Later, the faculty adopted a method of financially penalizing students if they either left early for or returned late from vacation time. The penalty was a $3.00 fine. Eventually, the administration introduced a system whereby a student who had more than the number of allowed absences during the semester would forfeit all credit earned during the course. Because no one wanted to forfeit credit for their work, it appears that this system finally brought absences under control. The religious Protestants who ran the conservatory were not about to be lax in their administrative duties. They definitely were not willing to allow the situation that existed in German conservatories to exist at Oberlin.[410]

In 1925, when David was hired as assistant professor of applied piano, the new director of Oberlin Conservatory, Frank Shaw, had been in his position for one year. A problem existed in the Department of Applied Piano because the conservatory had maintained a regulation that all students, regardless of their major course of study, had not only to study piano, but had to develop sufficient ability to perform a student recital on this instrument in addition to their chosen instrument as well. In addition, the two twenty-minute lessons per student were abandoned in favor of two half-hour lessons. This regulation created an overload in teaching hours for department faculty.[411] One of Mr. Shaw's priorities was to tackle this problem by hiring more piano instructors.

One of Oberlin Conservatory's commitments was to develop performing musicians. David possessed an incredible resumé as a successful performer. His training under both Alberto Jonas and at the *hochschule* in Berlin provided David with the performing credentials that Oberlin was seeking. His recent teaching experience at Bucknell was equally impressive. David was well aware of the responsibilities involved in being a faculty member: individual advising (students and fellow teachers), committee consultation, faculty meeting attendance, etc. It seems David was one solution to Frank Shaw's problems.

Prior to David and a few other teachers hired in 1925, the average teaching load for professors of applied music was thirty hours per week. With the increase in faculty, the thirty hours decreased to twenty-four hours per week. Extra time was always needed for piano majors preparing for major recitals, so the teaching load at times seemed very high. According to some of David's former students, he was always at the ready to give whatever additional time was felt necessary by his students. All conservatory professors had to attend Wednesday night rehearsals for students preparing to perform their formal recital later in the year.

The art of performing requires practice in the same way that mastery of any instrument requires practice. Future performers have to get used to performing in front of live audiences. These Wednesday night events helped to prepare students for live performances by having them perform in front of what was probably considered a very friendly audience made up of other students and faculty members.

Faculty meetings and other committee meetings also took up valuable time. Needless to say, it was a busy life! In David's first two years, he only had three students in 1925 and four students in 1926 assigned to him. More than likely, this was because of the fact that he was busy fulfilling performance contracts made prior to his employment at Oberlin and playing local concerts in the Oberlin area. Over the following years, his class register indicates an overflowing influx of students, many of whom were transfers from other professors. The system of transfer from one professor to another was not uncommon. There were also students who transferred from David to other professors.

The conservatory continued to grow during David's thirty-five-year tenure, and it appears that as time passed, his teaching responsibilities grew in terms of hours per week. The highest number of students he ever taught in one twelve-month period was sixty-one in 1956 from a total conservatory student population of approximately four hundred fifty students. David's own teaching registers list 1,373 names of students who attended his instruction studio during his thirty-five-year tenure at Oberlin Conservatory.[412] Many of these students appear multiple times over many semesters and years depending on the type of major the student had chosen, i.e., whether they were dual degree students or piano majors under his tutelage. On top of all of his teaching responsibilities, he continued to concertize in and around the town of Oberlin and sometimes farther afield.

Faculty concerts performed at the conservatory appear to be part of the contractual duty for some. David performed many times with the conservatory orchestra and as a solo performer during his early years. In a newspaper review entitled "Delightful Piano Recital on Tuesday: Professor David Moyer New Faculty Member Appeared in Warner Concert Hall" by W. T. Upton, 1925. The published review was recovered from the Moyer Family Archives and stated the following regarding David's earliest concert at Oberlin:

> With an extremely interesting and unhackneyed program, Mr. David Moyer, one of the latest additions to the Conservatory's piano faculty, made an uncommonly felicitous introduction of himself as a concert pianist to his Oberlin friends at Warner Hall last Tuesday evening.
>
> Mr. Moyer's style is particularly attractive in that in addition to abundant technique he possesses poetic feeling of a high order, a true sense of balance and perspective, rare sensitiveness to line and color, and an unfailing sincerity in all that he plays.
>
> A refreshingly large portion of the program was devoted to novelties—the Bach-Busoni organ chorals, the Griffes Scherzo, the Sonata Heroic by Campbell-Tipton and, if my memory serves me rightly, the Jonas pieces, never having been heard here before. And the best of it is that each in its own particular way proved its right to be heard. Busoni has long been considered the leading Bach authority of his time and these chorals are effective transcriptions. No less effective was the skill with which at all times Mr. Moyer was able to disentangle the thread of the choral [word unreadable] enmeshing counterpoint.[413]

David concertized throughout the Oberlin area whenever he was invited. He traveled as far away as Missouri for performances in his early days in Ohio. He performed a concert on the local Cleveland radio station WTAM with other musicians in 1928. His reputation as a fine performer was spreading all the time.

On September 16, 1929, David and Jessie's third child, a second son, William Cassel Moyer was born in Oberlin. The family was now complete, and needless to say, Jessie's life was very busy and full with three children less than six years of age coupled with her involvement in various community activities. The Moyer household was organized like most other professional families of the era. David tended to his professional responsibilities and was the breadwinner of the family while Jessie reared the children, kept the house, and performed all the necessary chores to keep things running smoothly. Her mother, Mrs. Anna Cowles, after the death of her husband, WH in Maryland, moved to Oberlin, Ohio as a trial to see if living with her only daughter was what she really wanted. "Gee Gee Ma," as she was known to the family, must have been a welcome addition to the Moyer household. Her presence afforded Jessie some freedom to become more involved in her numerous charitable activities and social clubs outside of the home. Gee Gee Ma's presence in the Moyer household was not permanent and would not be for several more years as she had not made up her mind that she wanted to give up her new found independence, but she did make herself available to Jessie and the children when she was needed. Gee Gee Ma was a woman ahead of her own times in many ways. She was strong willed and wasn't the easiest person in the world to live with, but she was Jessie's mother and they did manage to co-exist as needed.

Although never written in stone or anywhere else for that matter, there were customary expectations and protocols to be observed by faculty, spouses, and children regarding social behavior. Colleges, universities, boarding schools, private academies, at least socially, all appear to have had these same social expectations of faculty spouses. In Oberlin, a relatively small town built around the college and conservatory, the expectations for spouses and children would have been quite commonplace and seen as the norm. Jessie more than likely was subtly encouraged to become involved to some extent, but she accepted this challenge without fanfare or question and joined various clubs and organizations and, in some cases, became a very active officer in some of them. She sang in the choir and organized a quartet at the First Congregational Church for both local Sunday services and concerts in nearby towns and cities. The First Congregational Church had a longstanding affiliation with the conservatory and the college; therefore, it was not unusual for faculty wives to be involved there.[414] She was associated with the Cub Scouts, Boy Scouts, the Girl Scouts, the Young Women's Club of the First Church, the Calendar Club, the Nineteenth Century Club, the Allen Hospital Auxiliary, the local Parent-Teachers Association, and the local bridge club.[415] In June 1931, the *Chronicle-Telegram* newspaper reported in the personals column that:

> Rev. and Mrs. William Muir Auld, Miss Elizabeth Rich and Mr. and Mrs. Otto Greene were guests at a dinner party last evening at the home of Mrs. David Moyer in Oberlin. Other guests were members of the bridal party of the wedding of Miss Harriet Carr and S. Norman Parks, which will take place today.[416]

The bridegroom, Mr. S. Norman Parks, was the son of an Oberlin professor with whom David and Jessie were close friends. We do not know from the above article exactly how many people were present, but we know it was a minimum of seven. Jessie was a very organized and generous person to take on such a dinner party with three young children in the house.

In spite of her busy volunteer schedule and numerous involvements, Jessie's dearest activity outside the home was singing at funerals. She was well known in the area as a soprano soloist and was prepared to sing at any funeral and in any church or other venue when requested. Her family remembers her as always crying during the funerals, which increased her demand. A woman of real heart!

Moyer children did not take piano lessons from their parents in the home. They lived in an intense musical environment, but lessons were never forced upon them. Bill learned the trombone, and Bud learned to play the flute, both through a local public school music education program. Bill never studied the piano until he was a conservatory student and had his father for his piano teacher for a year or two.

All three children, Sonia, Bud, and Bill, were educated at the local Oberlin public schools. One of Bill's fondest memories was riding his bike home for a fully cooked meal for lunch, always including a daily homemade dessert! Then he would return by bike to Prospect Hill School and later Oberlin High School for the remainder of the school day. David would walk home every day for his fully cooked dinner. His dear friend, Professor Maurice Kessler, an Alsatian violinist and teacher of conducting, would walk with him as he lived around the corner from David's house. These two professors had much in common and often conversed in German instead of English since they were both fluent speakers. Maurice was six years older than David and had attended the *hochschule* in Berlin as a violin student a few years before David's own attendance. Maurice too had been a child prodigy. There were times when Mrs. Kessler was not at home to serve her husband his dinner, so Maurice occasionally would join the Moyer family for the midday meal. Jessie was always gracious and well prepared for impromptu guests. Every day, after lunch, David would lie down and take a short nap before returning to the conservatory to complete the remainder of his daily teaching assignments. This was a routine he had followed since his days in Germany when quiet hours were officially enforced. He would continue this habit for the rest of his life.

According to Bill, his mother did everything for them as a family. She was the disciplinarian and kept things running smoothly just as did the mothers in all the other households he knew. His father put great effort into his teaching and other conservatory responsibilities and into concertizing while spending his leisure time in his woodworking shop in the basement of the family home usually alone. David would periodically help his sons with their attempts at model building, boats, and airplanes, but for the most part, he just loved being alone with his projects in his basement workshop when time would permit. David had spent so much time alone during his early years in Brooklyn and living in Germany that he had learned to enjoy his own company. It simply was second nature to him.

There is one incident that Bill vividly remembers when his father did step into the role of disciplinarian. In his own words:

> My friend, Fredrik Christiansen, and I were about eight years old when we decided what fun it would be to break into the Prospect Hill School through an unlocked door one Saturday morning with our roller skates on so as to zoom up and down its echoing corridors. We did this with much shouting and high spirits until we were caught by the school's humorless maintenance man. He phoned our two fathers and reported our aberrant behavior. I have a very clear memory of my father threatening to "nail my tongue to the floor" if ever I lied again about doing such horrible misdeeds. Ironically, my friend, Fred Christiansen, later became an architect and designed among other structures, many public school buildings![417]

This singular event is Bill's sole memory of his father ever disciplining him.

In 1933, the Moyer family moved into a three-story wood-framed house at 280 Elm Street, still within walking distance of the conservatory, so David could continue walking to work. That year, the Moyer household would include another family member.

Muriel Moyer of suburban Philadelphia, David's eldest brother Vincent's daughter, was accepted for study at Oberlin Conservatory. She roomed at her Uncle Earl's home in Oberlin. Muriel and Sonia, David's daughter, shared a bedroom there and became good friends in spite of their age difference of ten years, Muriel of course being the elder. Muriel majored in music education but, sadly, was only able to complete one year of study because of a nagging back injury she had suffered while in high school. She used to say what a fabulous teacher Uncle Earl was and she would have known since she was one of his students at the conservatory.

After returning to the Philadelphia area and having her much-needed back surgery in the summer of 1934, she fell in love with a local young man Albert F. Geiger whom she married and, consequently, was unable to return to Oberlin for further study. Muriel continued her involvement in music for the rest of her life. She assembled and directed a local community orchestra, directed church choirs as well as community choruses, and was a church organist for over thirty years at the same church. She was a well-loved and respected woman!

The house on Elm Street contained an apartment on the third floor. David and Jessie usually had someone living there; sometimes people paid a nominal rent, and other times, it was given in kind to a needy student. These impromptu tenants simply became part of the extended family. During the late '40s or early '50s, one of David's female students found out she was unexpectedly pregnant. This young woman was naturally quite frightened and confused. Being unmarried and pregnant was a serious situation in those days. Without a second thought, they offered space and comfort in their home until the student could muster the courage to inform her family and make the necessary plans for her and her child's future. All worked out well for the student and her child, and she was able to continue her conservatory studies and graduate.[418] Jessie and David would remain in this fine house until 1961 when they rented another house at 103 E. College Street also in Oberlin. The large house on Elm Street was no longer needed as their three children were all married and living away from home. Their tenure at this house would be short lived as it would be the last home in which they would both reside in Oberlin.

David took a six-month sabbatical in 1937. The sabbatical was not restricted to a simple family adventure. A "sabbatical" is defined as a period of leave from work for research, study, or travel, often with pay and can be granted to university professors every seven years. However, most faculty members at the conservatory were not able to get this leave at the seven-year interval as the word implies without having a professional reason for the leave of absence and had to take the break when the time was available. The official reason for this sabbatical was that he had been invited to perform multiple concerts in California. David and Jessie also decided to use this opportunity to take the entire family on a tour of the United States. One of Sonia's friends who had been suffering some teenage angst was permitted by her own parents to join the adventure. David had recently purchased a seven-passenger Plymouth automobile and attached a York Cruiser camper to the back of the car, and off they went down the East Coast to Florida, then in a westward direction to California, and then eastward again to the Moyer family summer retreat at Vinalhaven, Maine.

Bill remembers this tour very vividly. As he tells the story, his father had borrowed a clavier or a practice keyboard from the conservatory. A clavier is a silent instrument where the mechanical action of the keyboard could approximate the physical feeling of performing on a keyboard instrument. If nothing else, it would enable the user to maintain physical strength and flexibility in the fingers, wrists, and arms while away from a piano or organ for long periods. The conservatory owned several of these clavier/keyboards, and in the past, they were rented to students for silent practice.[419] Since he was five and a half years old, David had never lost proximity to a keyboard of some type.

There was always one available, wherever he was, even while he was on tour with his young family, albeit, one producing no sound. But by the time he and his family had reached the Grand Canyon, David had more than enough of this annoying partner which, in utter frustration; he literally (and silently) hurled it into the Grand Canyon, wondering what the keyboard might say to the one discovering it there, perhaps, fifty years hence! [420]

David seemed to know exactly where to go and what to show his children on this six-month trip. Jessie must have been a well-ordered person to have been able to keep meals going and sleeping arrangements clear for everyone to have a good time. Lengthy hotel stays and restaurant meals could not be a daily occurrence as most professors did not have such money to spend. Hardships—no doubt there were some—have been long forgotten. From what Bill has said, he realized years later that the route of the trip in 1937 bore a great resemblance to the route his father took in 1905-1906 with Mary Walsh and the two boys.

In the autumn of 1938, David and Jessie attended the yearly faculty/student social function at Oberlin College where all could meet a non-academic setting. A young female student from Lima, Ohio, Margaret Fry, who was just beginning her studies, also attended.[421] She was majoring in liberal arts at the time. Maggie, as she liked to be called, had heard about David Moyer when she was about fourteen years old from Mary Halter Walsh (Mme. Berlino). Maggie had wanted some extra tutoring in the French language she was currently studying in the local high school, and her family knew of Mary's fluency in the language in addition to being a local piano teacher. Maggie would travel across the city of Lima on her bicycle to Mary's house for her weekly tutoring sessions. The French tutoring went very well; Maggie was impressed with Madame's knowledge and her way of expressing particular phrases. In addition to the French tutorials, Maggie also took a few piano lessons. She had already been studying the piano with her aunt who was a professional musician in Lima. One day, her aunt asked her if she could see what selections she was preparing for her piano lessons with Mary. Maggie complied and showed her aunt the selections she was preparing for the next lesson with Mary and her aunt's response was stark: "She's nothing more than an old fashioned piano teacher"![422]

At the Oberlin reception, Maggie sought out David and Jessie Moyer. She approached them and introduced herself. She did inform them that she was from Lima and had spent some time as a private student with Madame Berlino studying mainly French, but she did have a few piano lessons. In the midst of the pleasant conversation, Maggie innocently informed David and Jessie that Mary was wondering when they were going to come to Lima and bring her to Oberlin to live with them. "Their faces suddenly dropped with expressions of embarrassment and fear. They really didn't know what to say. Mrs. Moyer looked unhappy and distressed. The impromptu interaction ended rather abruptly! I was so embarrassed and I think they were as well."[423]

Many decades later when Maggie consented to an interview for this book, she spoke freely and openly about her feelings and impressions of Mary Halter Walsh Berlino:

> She was a tall woman, very spare in size. She was toothless, had dyed greasy hair and seemed to have no concern for her overall appearance. She spent a lot of time muttering to herself in German while giving intermittent commands, also in German, to her dogs. She always said the dogs were a gift to her during her German days from Kaiser Wilhelm. These dogs appeared to be her playmates. She talked endlessly sometimes about her life in Europe with her son, David. She never actually mentioned any other children other than David. It was well known in Lima at the time that she would go out of her home late at night and visit the back doors of the kitchens of the hotels and, at times, private homes to beg for left over food for her dogs. She was really destitute, poor woman. People used to speculate as to whether the food was really for the dogs or, perhaps, for herself. I never had the impression that she studied in Europe, but she did have large trunks in her home and she used to say that they were full of court dresses from her days living in Europe and her associations with the Royal families there. Mary did have a few nice items in her home. There was one painting on the wall in her living room that I always thought was nice. It would be what was called a 'living picture' in those days. It was a painting of a man and his skin looked like it was pure marble.

> I was of two minds regarding Madame. I admired her ability to be so independent at a time when most women were not able to be independent. On the other hand, I also found her somewhat repulsive and sad to be around.[424]

After two years of attendance at Oberlin College, Maggie returned to Lima and attended a college closer to home and graduated with a degree in English literature. She subsequently taught English for fifteen years, married, and had a family of her own. Maggie never forgot Mary Halter Walsh Berlino. "Madame to me was very much like the main character in Willa Cather's short story *Paul's Case*."[425]

In this story, Paul, a Pittsburgh, Pennsylvania, teenager works as an usher in the local Carnegie Music Hall. He is a troubled young man and has great difficulty fitting in with his classmates and, in general, the society in which he lives. He feels he is better than his peers and most people in the town, and he creates a fantasy life in his own mind to avoid the despair in his soul. Once he earns some money and the trust of his employers at the music hall, he steals one night's proceeds and runs off to New York City, buying fine clothes for himself, attending concerts at the real Carnegie Hall, living in a fine hotel, and drinking the finest wines for all to see, and finally, is completely broke in eight days. His despair deepens with the arrival of his father to New York City to find his shamed son, and he tries to bring him back to Pittsburgh. The stark reality for Paul regarding just who he was and how he lived in Pittsburgh was too much for the young man to bear. Instead of riding the train back home with his father, he chooses to jump in front of a moving train, ending his sad life.[426]

Mary never deliberately jumped in front of a moving train ending her life. Ironically, her end, according to press reports came in 1941, while crossing a busy street in Lima without ever raising her head to see if it was safe to cross. Most of the documentary evidence available does suggest that Mary had also created a fantasy life for herself and lived it much longer than poor fictional Paul. She seemed to have manipulated everyone everywhere she went, including David Moyer's parents and people of influence who reached out to help her at various times in her life: David Moyer, the Children's Aid Society of New York City, the two innocent Haggerty brothers, the little boys she supposedly adopted, members of her own family, and peoples of her hometown on her various visits posing as a successful mother and teacher. For sure, one person she was not going to manipulate was Jessie Moyer and her husband and treasured children.

Bill Moyer recalls that on one occasion, his entire family drove to Lima, Ohio, where they were introduced to the woman known as Madame Berlino. "I was quite young at the time, about seven or eight years old. She lived in a one floor, run-down house. It was more like a shack than a house. When she opened the door to greet us, her two dogs ran out the door. She simply said, 'See what you've done, you've let the lurchers out!'"[427] Bill doesn't remember much else about the visit to Lima, but he never recalls going back there or hearing that his father ever returned to Lima.

Although David's family have repeatedly stated that whenever he talked about Mary, which wasn't until he was practically eighty years old and never that often, he gently spoke of her with great fondness in his voice for what she had done for him. On June 2, 1988, Maggie wrote a letter to Bill Moyer expressing her sympathy regarding the recent death of his father. In this handwritten letter, she asked, "I wonder if perhaps your father might have had ambivalent feelings about his tutor. Did he miss his parents? Did he feel exploited? And what happened to those other boys, I wonder."[428]

Mary Halter, a.k.a. Madame Berlino, 1940
Photo: Courtesy of Moyer Family Archives

Chapter XIV

Vinalhaven

Vinalhaven is a small island in Penobscot Bay fifteen miles off the coast of Rockland, Maine. The island is seven miles long and three miles wide. Kilton Vinal Smith and his wife, Cecilia, calculated the coastline to be approximately two hundred miles in length. Over a period of some years, he and his wife walked the entire shoreline including the long promontories and deep inlets.[429]

Kilton is a descendent of John Vinall for whom the island is named. He was a former tuba player for the Boston Symphony Orchestra, is a native of the island, and lives there during the summer months. As part of the Fox Islands, Vinalhaven is the largest and most populated of that island group. The islands received their name from the first recorded adventurer, Martin Pring of England, who accidentally stumbled upon them in search of food for the crews of his two ships in 1603.[430] Legend has it that he spotted many grey foxes and, therefore, gave the island group its name of "Fox."[431]

English settlers did not arrive until after the end of the French and Indian Wars in 1763.[432] Around 1785, the settlers sought legal counsel from attorney John Vinall of Boston to petition the General Court of Massachusetts to allow them to hold titles for their lands. (The independent State of Maine was established in 1820. Prior to this date the territory was governed by Massachusetts.)[433] Within this petition, the settlers promised to "build a place for public worship and to settle a minister of the gospel among them and found a public school for the education of their children."[434] These conditions were prerequisite for inclusion in the Commonwealth of Massachusetts. The citizens of Vinalhaven did not "build a place for public worship" until 1860.[435] They did, however, periodically hire a minister of the gospel for short periods of four to six months, but this practice was never consistent. Public schools were formed and maintained most of the time throughout the island.[436] Needless to say, their petition was successful, and they named their island Vinal Haven (original spelling) as a tribute to their legal representative and friend. John Vinall never visited the island, but some of his descendants have lived there for continuous generations.

In the 1760s, English settlers began to inhabit the island. The settlers employed themselves in fishing, farming, logging, boat building, and fishing. They were able to use some of the timber available without interference from the local Indians. It seems that no one, settler or Indian, immediately gave much attention to the tons of natural granite available on the island until 1826 when a man named Tuck from New Hampshire arrived on the island with a schooner, a work crew of men, tools, and supplies to extract the first sizeable quantity of granite. Tuck had been commissioned by the Commonwealth of Massachusetts to build a prison out of stone in Boston.[437] The first commercial quarry activity, however, did not take place in the Fox Islands until twenty years later when the Carlton Brothers and Joseph Kittredge began quarrying on Leadbetter's Island, west of Vinalhaven. Nevertheless, this business venture was short lived. Reading the history of the granite industry in this area, it is revealed that there were many small partnerships and dissolutions in the early years of granite mining. In 1851, Moses Webster of Pelham, New Hampshire arrived on Vinalhaven for the purpose of establishing a new quarrying business there. He purchased the East Boston quarry for three hundred dollars from Joseph Kittridge and then formed a partnership with him. They both had experience as stonecutters and had a strategic plan for developing the nonexistent granite business. It was Moses Webster who brought with him into the business the first federal government contract for making spindles for powder houses to be located at Fiddler's Ledge, a rather small sandbar among the Fox Islands.[438] The following year, another federal contract was obtained. J. R. Bodwell and S. Gilman Webster, a cousin of Moses, became additional partners in the firm. A second contract was awarded by the federal government to supply granite to Fort Richmond on Staten Island, New York.[439] Bodwell and Webster established their business and modeled it on the coal mining industry that also flourished during this period. They rented accommodation to many of the workers and established a company store where the employees bought their goods. They wielded a heavy hand over the employed residents of the island. While the quarrying business employed most of the able-bodied men on the island, the horse net enterprise employed the women. The manufacturing of horse nets was a very important domestic industry since the nets were used to keep the flies off the horses, a necessary component of the emerging granite industry. These horse nets were exported quite widely and were not produced just for local consumption. Horses were used to move the granite, once cut from the source, to locations along the shore for shipping across the United States on sloops, schooners, and barges. These nets helped to protect the horses from multiple fly bites. Granite became a much sought-after resource, especially by the federal government after the Civil War to reinforce gun platforms at various forts up and down the East Coast and the Gulf Coast. During the height of the granite period on Vinalhaven, many men and families traveled to this remote island for work from all over the United States, the British Isles, Scandinavia, and Italy.[440] It took hundreds of men to quarry, cut, carve, shape, and polish the granite required for the many projects throughout the United States, e.g., the base of the Brooklyn Bridge, the Washington Monument, the New York Customs House, the Masonic Temple in Philadelphia, various post offices, and privately owned mansions, monuments, and paving blocks for the streets of such cities as Philadelphia, Boston, and New York to name a few.[441] The building, which the islanders are most proud, is the Cathedral of St. John the Divine in New York City.

After the Civil War, major restructuring of businesses through out the country was taking place. The Bodwell and Webster Company followed suit. In 1871, the Bodwell and Webster Quarry Company became incorporated. This act of incorporation permitted the company to buy out all of the smaller quarries on Vinalhaven and Spruce Head Island, thereby increasing the workforce from three hundred men to six hundred men. The two immediate benefits were that the company could raise more money and use that money to increase the size of their operation and control any local competition. It also enabled, in the short term, the corporate owners to prevent the development of many unions forming on Vinalhaven as well. By 1874, the company needed to raise more money and the stockholders approved the goal of four hundred thousand dollars to be raised. The only way this goal could be reached was to lay off over three hundred granite workers on Vinalhaven. By 1877, the workforce consisted of only eighty men because of a lack of contracts obtained. In addition, the company was four months in arrears with payments to many of its workforce, which caused much dissention between owners and workers. Some workers requested credit from the Bodwell company store to assist them in feeding their families, but they were refused. It is no surprise then that in March 1877, a union was finally established there. [442] The company continued in spite of general economic depressions and labor issues that seemed to be recur every few years. It did become quite heavily involved in the paving block industry as well as stone blocks for buildings and decorative work, but the development and growth of railroad networks throughout New England made it possible for other quarries to fill orders at more competitive prices.[443] The lucrative quarrying that had taken place in Vinalhaven for so long eventually ceased. By the end of the 1920s, it seems that the industry was just lingering along with little future. By the early 1930s, the new products of asphalt and concrete replaced the need for granite.[444] By 1932, the gallymander that had once moved so much granite to the shore for shipping was placed on the town green and remains there today as a monument to what once was. With usual New England resiliency, the residents of Vinalhaven were not beaten by the demise of the granite industry that for so long sustained them economically. They became heavily involved in the fishing and lobstering enterprises, and this, coupled with a growing tourism trade, is what provides economic security for the stable year-round residents. Today, remnants of the great granite age still litter the landscape of the island. Scattered throughout are long-abandoned quarries now used as freshwater swimming areas, and large cracked and broken columns that, for one reason or another, never made it to the shipping vessels intact.

David first learned about Vinalhaven from his Oberlin colleague and friend Maurice Kessler. In 1933, the Moyer family journeyed to Vinalhaven for the first time and fell in love with the place. The first two summers they rented a house and the entire family, including Gee Gee Ma, her caged birds, and the dog Bootsie traveled for three days to get there and, at the end of the summer, three days to return to Oberlin. The following summer when the home of Herbert "Ambrose" Delano became available for sale, David and Jessie jumped at the opportunity to buy his property. Mr. Delano was a former lobster fisherman and had spent his entire life on Vinalhaven. It appears from census records that he was the third generation of his family to reside there. He was widowed in 1931 and, although he and his wife had one son, Freeland, who lived and worked in Bath, Maine, apparently had no interest in the property. Ambrose lived alone when he needed to sell the property.

A search of real estate records in Oberlin during the 1930s provides some insight into the difficulties of purchasing a home there. Buying a home in Oberlin must have seemed like an endless mountain to climb because the homeowners seem never to have sold their houses. If these people left the area for a while, they leased their property but still maintained their ownership.[445] The opportunity of owning a home on Vinalhaven, a somewhat isolated and insular community, was a real incentive and possibility for David and his family to realize their goal of sharing in one of the American dreams, i.e., home ownership.

The property of Mr. Delano was situated on the bay at Old Harbor and consisted of a main house and five outbuildings on three and one-half acres of land when David and Jessie first viewed it. From David's own expense records, it appears that the property was in a state of disrepair, which might explain why it was so cheap to purchase. The purchase price of $1,100.00 dollars was affordable for them. However, there was one unusual condition to buying the house: whoever bought the property would have to drive Mr. Delano to the Vinalhaven Town Farm, the poor house, where he would live until his death, which occurred nine months later.

The Town Farm was purchased by the town in 1895 for the sum of $900.00 to care for the poor of the island.[446] Prior to this acquisition, the poor of the community were supported by the town from tax revenues collected. Nevertheless, there were times when the town actually sold the care of the poor to individual citizens for a period of one or two years for an agreed price.[447]

According to David and Jessie's son, Bill, the idea of driving Mr. Delano to the Town Farm was appalling to his mother. He remembers his mother saying, "I couldn't do that," while David retorted with his wry smile that he could! There is no evidence available explaining why Mr. Delano needed to reside at the Town Farm, but it is obvious that he was impoverished and needed to sell the property, more than likely, to pay off back taxes.

David and Jessie paid the asking price and, additionally, paid to Mr. Delano the sum of $300.00 for furniture already in the main house. The furniture price was one quarter of the selling price of the property. It was either very good furniture, or it was David and Jessie's way of helping the man to have some small amount of money to preserve his own dignity.

David did, in fact, drive Mr. Delano to his new residence, and during the first year of ownership, David invested heavily in repairing the property so his family could live comfortably and safely in what he and Jessie called the Music Box. Although David certainly had the skill to do most of the work himself, his list of expenses for the first year does include some labor costs. The actual costs incurred, as recorded meticulously by him, demonstrate the poor condition of the property. All the buildings required new electrical wiring, new roof shingles, two outhouses had to be renovated for use, both the barn and the studio building required internal completion to be useable, and the pier had to be rebuilt in order to be used. Externally, land needed to be cleared, stone walls repaired, and trees removed, etc. David's costs the first years to renovate the property were in excess of $3,900.00. How the family managed to live in the property while all the work was going on that first summer of ownership demonstrates their commitment and courage to take on such a project. It must have been hard work for all of the family, but in usual style from what Bill remembers, they had a good time doing it. There is video footage (original 16 mm film transferred to video format) of Jessie and Sonia clearing one of the outhouses that was seriously unusable. "They both smoked cigars to cut the other odors. Whew!"[448]

The investment Jessie and David made in this property turned out to be a happy one for the family. Every summer, the family made the long arduous journey to Rockland, Maine, and boarded the ferry for Vinalhaven. Many summers, Jessie's mother, Gee Gee Ma would make the journey as well complete with her gilded caged, prized birds. This must have been an interesting journey because in addition to the family members, the birds, Jessie would bring her own pets including Bootsie, the cocker spaniel and one or more of her cats. Jessie was always known to care for stray animals that would appear at the Music Box as well at her own home in Oberlin. When Bud (David Jr.) married in the 1940s, he and his wife, Judy, lived year round at the Music Box for a couple of years until they were able to purchase a home of their own on Vinalhaven.

The Music Box, Vinalhaven, Maine c. 1938
Photo: Courtesy of Moyer Family Archives

The Music Box turned out to be more than simply a middle-class vacation spot for the family. For seven summers, David invited approximately seven or eight music students, some, but not all of them, from Oberlin to join his family on vacation for the purpose of extra private study. He outfitted two of the outbuildings as bunk houses (males and females lived in separate buildings), and he also provided for practice instruments on the island for the students' use. The students required several hours of practice each day. David outfitted The Music Box with about four pianos. He made arrangements with various churches and halls located on the island to rent additional pianos for the remainder of his students. (This may be similar to the way in which Mary provided practice pianos for David on the tour in 1905 and 1906,) The students paid their own costs for transportation to and from the island, for room and board, and for instruction and practice piano rental.

Again, according to Bill, there were always one or two students who simply did not have the financial means to pay the costs, so in essence, they were given a work scholarship. The work scholarship required that the student or students helped Jessie with meal preparation and other household duties. There are no records to suggest who these students were or how much they paid to David for the privilege of private tuition and expenses. According to Bill, "it probably wasn't much."[449]

However, it was not all work and no play. Bill informs us that the students had time to attend local dances, time for outdoor activities, sailing, swimming at the local abandoned quarries, and whatever other entertainment they provided for themselves. On Sundays, David would organize sailing trips to some of the nearby islands complete with picnic lunches for the students. The Moyer children joined with the students in all the fun and had treasure hunts and night games with flashlights. All enjoyed themselves! Bill said his Pa occasionally would pull one of his unannounced pranks at some daily event such as an afternoon swim, appearing fully clothed including shoes and all and, to everyone's amazement, suddenly jumped from the pier into the freezing waters of Penobscot Bay! There were other kinds of pranks, but this one seems to stand out in Bill's mind. The students were generally surprised and startled by David's prank since he was always the consummate, well-mannered, retiring professor who rarely showed his zany side to his family or his students.

Local dances were held on the green near the cemetery, Blueberry Hill. With so many musicians living on the island during the summer months, there was no lack of entertainers to supply the needed music. Once nightfall arrived, the local residents who owned automobiles would park their cars on the perimeter of the green and put on the headlights to illuminate the area for the dancers. The dancing would continue until some of the locals became intoxicated and an altercation would develop. Once this started, the headlights of the cars were extinguished and the dance ended abruptly, and all went home without fanfare.[450]

David monitored his students' diligence and progress on a regular basis while Jessie prepared food and performed other chores to keep the family and the students well fed and content. On occasion, a few of the piano students would give free concerts for the residents, and by doing this, they gained experience as solo performers.

Bill remembers that he and his brother, Bud, would spend hours sailing and rowing in the bay and shooting their BB guns in the woods while their sister, Sonia, helped their mother in the house. Bill has stated that he always felt sorry for his sister, Sonia, as she was not given the freedom to experience the pleasures of the island because she was, like so many daughters in the late 1930s and early 1940s, overprotected by her mother who relied upon her to help with the domestic needs of the home. It was the mother's responsibility to hand down the duties of domestic responsibility. It was just the way life was in those days! David continued to invite students to his summer home for approximately ten years with the exception of two years during World War II when he opted to support the war effort by staying at home in Oberlin and working in one of the local shipyards in nearby Lorain, Ohio, stringing electric cables into warships and tankers. From the end of the 1940s onwards, the Music Box became the summer retreat for the family, their friends, and an ever-expanding family.

Gayna Uransky, David and Jessie's eldest grandchild, recalls affectionately her summers spent with her grandparents, uncles, aunts, cousins, and parents on

Vinalhaven. Gayna would travel to Vinalhaven for most of the summer with one of her friends in tow. She would stay on the island until her parents arrived for their vacation, and then she and her friend would travel back home to Virginia with her parents, Sonia and Norman Uransky, at the summer's end. She has clear memories of her grandmother as being quite a hostess and outstanding for her handwork skills. Jessie was a great homemaker, knitter, and artist. She took painting lessons on the island for a number of summers and became quite proficient. "Grandpa" was in his own world of music, woodworking, puzzle, and marionette making. Gayna speaks fondly of his woodworking abilities, and among other things, he created sewing notion boxes that are still used by her and her two daughters. For her yearly visits to the island, he would always have a new wooden puzzle that he had made. He would tell her first that it was "devilishly hard." These puzzles would require a lot of time and consultation with friends and family members to solve. In addition, David would spend hours filming the family with his movie camera. Gayna's main point in her written memories of her grandparents is how much she loved them and still misses them. "They were truly kind, gentle, and salt-of-the-earth folks."[451]

The Music Box was well used by David's extended family and friends. He brought his mother from Philadelphia to Vinalhaven one summer. His oldest brother, Vincent, and his wife, Cora, also visited before they purchased an island of their own on Moosehead Lake, Maine. Numerous cousins and their families, who had more than likely heard how wonderful summer life was in Maine, actually, bought their own summer homes in Maine and paid many visits to David and his family.

David and Jessie sold the Music Box in 1961 when they bought a smaller and more manageable house that was built on pylons over the bay. Here, he would live out the majority of the rest of his life until his death in 1987.

The Moyer Family, Vinalhaven, 1938.
Photo: Courtesy of Moyer Family Archives

"Dinner time at Vinalhaven"
Jessie feeds her friends, Bootsie the cocker spaniel,
two cats and a crow called Jim, 1935.
Photo: David E. Moyer
Courtesy of Moyer Family Archives

CHAPTER XV

Later Oberlin Years: The Students

From 1932 until 1960 when David would retire, he had some of the most exciting, talented students for which any professor could wish. Complementing this array of gifted students, David fulfilled the dictum usually attributed to Einstein, "It is the supreme art of the teacher to awaken joy in creative expression and knowledge."[452]

In the summer of 1932, **Camille Nickerson** of New Orleans, Louisiana, studied piano with David as part of her master's degree program at Oberlin Conservatory. Her interest in music blossomed during her childhood under the ever-present influence of her musician parents. At age nine, she was the pianist for the Nickerson Ladies Orchestra directed by her father, William Nickerson. In her undergraduate days at the conservatory, she began to compose and publish some of her own music. Camille returned to her undergraduate alma mater (class of 1916) after spending years as a performer known as the Louisiana Lady throughout the United States and Europe, keeping alive the music tradition of the Creoles. She dressed in traditional Creole fashion wherever she performed. After receiving her master's degree in music at Oberlin, she continued her studies at both the Juilliard School and Columbia University.

Initially, Camille began her teaching career at her father's own music school, Nickerson School of Music in New Orleans. In 1926, she accepted the position of teacher of music at Howard University in Washington DC where she would remain until her retirement in 1962.[453] Camille succeeded as performer, composer, arranger, collector, and teacher of music. Her passion for keeping alive the musical traditions of a unique culture for future generations was perhaps her greatest gift. She died in 1982.

During the spring of 1937, **George Walker,** an aspiring fourteen-year-old musician of Washington DC arrived at Oberlin for his admission interview and audition and left with a full scholarship offer to attend in the autumn and begin what would be a lifelong career as a performer and composer. He was fifteen years old when he began his studies at the conservatory.

George kindly agreed to a telephone interview on December 12, 2006, to speak about his student days and his lifelong friendship with his teacher and mentor David E. Moyer. George wanted to become a concert pianist but also wanted the college life, including playing tennis, living in a dormitory, and all the social things that make up the college life experience. George never considered himself a child prodigy. However, he does admit to being considered academically precocious. George chose David for his teacher because David had studied with Busoni while in Berlin. George was impressed with Busoni as a performing musician. George, like most of the former students of David's, never knew that David himself was once considered a child prodigy. Probably, the subject never came up during the teaching or social sessions. "I really didn't know until years later, after his death, his son Bill and I spoke about it and I learned a little bit about his training and study. Amazing isn't it!"[454] George does give us some insight into the pedagogy that David used with his students:

> Professor Moyer was always genial and unassuming as a person. Unlike his serious colleagues, he enjoyed a good laugh in every conversation. He recognized my potential as a pianist and gave me the opportunity to perform on student concerts when he felt that I was capable of making a strong impression. He obviously believed in my talent. I was delighted to be invited by him to hear Rachmaninoff play in Cleveland, Ohio, with the Cleveland Orchestra.[455]

What George has stated here does describe the majority opinion represented by David's former students. He was dedicated to assisting his students in developing their talent as much as possible. Through his own genuine concern, coupled with his unique gift of always seeing the humorous side of things, David was able to encourage and stimulate his students to develop not only the requisite skills to perform but also to believe in their own talents and, therefore, themselves. After graduation from Oberlin, George continued his musical education at the Curtis Institute of Music in Philadelphia where he studied with pianist, Rudolf Serkin. George further pursued his studies at the Eastman School of Music where he earned a doctoral degree in 1955.[456] He was then awarded a Fulbright Fellowship and spent the next two years studying in France with Nadia Boulanger, world-renowned teacher and composer. In 1983, he was recalled to Oberlin Conservatory to receive an honorary doctorate in music.

In addition to a fulfilling concert career and the publication of over ninety compositions, he has taught at Smith College, Dillard University, the Delacroze School of Music, and the School for Social Research, the University of Colorado at Boulder, Peabody Conservatory of Music, the University of Delaware, and Rutgers University in Newark, New Jersey. In 1996, George was the first black American composer to be awarded the Pulitzer Prize in music. George still works on his compositions and recordings and, when possible, fits an occasional tennis match into his rigorous schedule.

Natalie Henderson was another young student to study with David. A former child prodigy, Natalie was a native of Oberlin. Her mother was a piano instructor at the Cleveland Institute of Music. At age eight, Natalie performed her first full public recital and, afterwards, was accepted as a pupil of David Moyer in the Oberlin Conservatory Special School (no longer in existence). She graduated from Oberlin Conservatory in 1945, only two years after her official graduation from Oberlin High School in 1943. She was two months shy of her eighteenth birthday when she graduated from Oberlin Conservatory with the highest possible honors.[457]

She is credited with being the most prominent graduate from the conservatory at that time.[458] After Oberlin, Natalie studied for a graduate degree at Juilliard School of Music under the renowned critic and teacher, Olga Samaroff, until Samaroff's death in 1948. She was encouraged to adopt a more ethnic name and from then on used the stage name of Natalie Hinderas. Her name now often appears as Natalie Henderson Hinderas.

Natalie continued her studies with Edward Steuermann at the Philadelphia Conservatory of Music. During the 1950s, Natalie performed under contract with NBC-TV. These concerts were broadcast around the nation. What also made her contract with NBC unusual was that she was the first black classical musician to receive this exposure. In spite of two world tours, Natalie had never played with what was considered a world-class orchestra. "Orchestras simply wouldn't hire a black woman—this was in the days when there weren't even black players in the Orchestras. People used to say to me; you're the only black musician around. And I think I was until Andre Watts—he broke the barrier. Before that I felt like a freak; it was a terrible sense of responsibility."[459]

In 1966, Natalie accepted a teaching position at Temple University's College of Music in Philadelphia and began lecturing and performing at various colleges around the United States. One of her goals was to reconcile the chasm between the black community and classical music. In her opinion, the black community saw classical music as white man's music and could not relate to the genre because of what they perceived as a lack of representation in their own community. Natalie helped to close that chasm by making a recording featuring the works of nine black American composers, one of whom was George Walker who studied at Oberlin Conservatory with her.

In the autumn of 1971, Eugene Ormandy, conductor of the Philadelphia Orchestra, invited Natalie to perform Piano Concerto No. 1 by Argentine composer Alberto Ginastera. Almost instantly after this performance, she was engaged to perform with world-class orchestras in New York, Cleveland, Atlanta, Chicago, San Francisco, Pittsburgh, and in Los Angeles with the L.A. Philharmonic Orchestra at the Hollywood Bowl. After her performance at the Hollywood Bowl, in a side comment to a reporter from the *New York Times*, Natalie recalled a statement by one of her former managers: "You know, Natalie, a little colored girl like you, can't play in the Hollywood Bowl."[460]

Natalie's alliance with the major TV networks, she believed, would help to promote the cause of classical music and demonstrate that classical music was for everyone regardless of race. To these ends, she spent the rest of her life until her untimely death in 1987.

"David adored Natalie's talent,"[461] says Judy Moyer Shreiner, widow of Bud Moyer, the Moyers' oldest son. Judy was around the family a good deal and clearly remembers David speaking of Natalie with such fondness.

Joyce Arnold in 1953 was sixteen years old and traveled alone by train from Austin, Texas, to Oberlin to begin her conservatory studies. Joyce was "ecstatic" knowing that she was "independent and responsible for herself."[462]

> Mr. Moyer was assigned to me as my teacher. From the first lesson, I felt his warmth and concern for me as his student. He was always encouraging, no matter how I played. As I recall, I had one one-hour lesson per week. There were two grand pianos in his studio in Warner Hall. I sat and performed at one, he at the other. He would illustrate phrases for me. I was always impressed with his hands and his facility.
>
> I did know that he was a child prodigy, but he never boasted. I don't remember how I knew that. Several times during the year, Mr. and Mrs. Moyer invited his students to their home on Sunday afternoons. Mrs. Moyer would make a delicious dessert and Mr. Moyer would play for us, and we'd all talk and have a grand time. I studied with Mr. Moyer all four years at Oberlin. He was great! At no time was he temperamental or judgmental. He always encouraged me and always said positive things. If something needed work, he would illustrate that at his piano, without making me feel badly.[463]

Joyce graduated from Oberlin Conservatory in 1957 and immediately began graduate studies at the University of Iowa where she received a master's degree in music in 1959. She tried her hand at public school teaching and, after three and a half years, learned that she was not a teacher. She sang with the Robert

Shaw Chorale, lived, and sang opera in Europe for three years. Joyce later married and had children but always retained an appreciation of her time as a student of David Moyer's at Oberlin.

Not all graduates of Oberlin Conservatory of Music or former students of David's concentrated on working as pure performance artists. It is a very difficult way to make a living, said David. There are no guarantees of regular salaries, health benefits, or pensions for the long run. David, as already stated, had great difficulty himself launching a performance career in the United States once he returned in 1914 from Berlin. So he knew first-hand the difficulties and uncertainties involved.

William Cundiff was born in a small town in Southeastern Ohio. He mentions that the town was so small that there was not even a qualified piano teacher in it. Somehow, he did learn to play the piano and sight-read music, which enabled him to participate as an accompanist for the local school choir and chorus. While Bill was a sophomore in high school, his family moved to Lorain, Ohio, not far from Oberlin, and he was able to enroll in the special school of the conservatory. Although little information is available about the special school, it is understood that students who were too young or too inexperienced to attend the conservatory were able to take courses taught on a part-time basis by conservatory faculty. For Bill, this was a real opportunity, in effect, "to catch up" where he had had so little formal training.

Bill's first semester at the special school was not so satisfying and productive as he had hoped. He was appointed a young teacher; they just did not "gibe." He was then assigned to David. One of the reasons why David was chosen to teach him was that David had a son about Bill's age, and the administration thought that this relationship might work out better, and it did. Every Saturday morning, Bill would attend a thirty-minute lesson with David in his studio. This relationship was short lived because before the beginning of the following academic year, Oberlin closed the special school. Bill was left to his own devices, which proved a good thing for him. He studied and learned Rachmaninoff's Prelude in G Minor for a music contest. When he showed up to perform, David Moyer was the judge. Bill did well, won the contest, and then was able to compete in the state contest where he played a selection by Debussy and again succeeded. The following fall, he was accepted to study full-time at Oberlin Conservatory where he remained a student until the completion of his master's degree in piano.

Bill had David as a teacher for only one semester after enrolling in the conservatory; he had to change from David to Arthur Dann because David took a six-month sabbatical. Rather than make another change, Bill found his progress with Mr. Dann to be good, so he stayed on with him.

In 1952, Bill accepted a teaching post at Miyagi College for Women in Sendai, Japan, where he would spend the next forty-three years of his professional career. He did take a break from Japan for study at Juilliard in New York City during one of his sabbaticals.

Bill commented that his life has been music![464] He credits David with introducing him to Beethoven, Bach's inventions, and Schumann pieces. "So he opened the doors that were never shut again! I adored him"![465] In 1995, Bill retired to Claremont, California, and still continues to do a bit of traveling and performing in the United States and Japan.

James J. Edmonds originally from Pittsfield, Massachusetts, arrived at Oberlin Conservatory in the fall of 1949 and was assigned David Moyer as his teacher. He remained David's student until his graduation in 1953. James, like so many other graduates of Oberlin Conservatory, combined professional performance and university teaching into a lifelong career. He received his master's degree and doctorate from the University of Michigan. He performed as a soloist and chamber musician throughout the United States, Europe, and Australia and coupled these appearances with a full teaching schedule on both the undergraduate and graduate level at Eastern Washington University where he taught piano and music theory. He became professor emeritus in music in 1987 and, shortly thereafter, was tragically killed in an auto accident. From the listing of awards and honors that James received in his lifetime, it is easy to draw the conclusion that he was a very successful pianist and a well-respected teacher.

Henry Janiec was born to Polish immigrant parents in Passaic, New Jersey, a few miles from New York City. During his early life, Henry had piano lessons and considered himself to be a fairly good pianist prior to his admission to Oberlin Conservatory. While growing up, Henry had many opportunities to listen to good music and good performers and to perform himself in various local venues. He commented that he was very fortunate to have an excellent piano teacher who contributed greatly to his craft even before deciding which conservatory he would attend.

Very early on, Henry decided that he wanted to be a conductor and not just an instrumental performer. Fortunately, he was accepted to both the Eastman School of Music and Oberlin Conservatory. He chose Oberlin as it offered him some tuition assistance, and that was important for his family circumstances. He majored in music education (a program that prepared future school music teachers) and also studied conducting, and he was able to work toward his chosen career in this way.

> When I got to Oberlin, piano was my principal instrument and I was assigned to study with a teacher other than Mr. Moyer. My lessons with that first teacher really did not go well during that first semester, so I requested a change of teachers and was then assigned to Mr. Moyer's studio. I did not know him at all at that time but soon saw how fortunate that assignment was. [466]

Henry studied with David for the remainder of his time at Oberlin. His lessons were one hour each week for three and one-half years. When he first began his lessons, David simply asked him what he planned to do in music. Henry's forthcoming answer was not a problem for David. His answer was simply, conducting and accompanying. According to Henry, David just smiled and nodded, and the work began.

There were times when Henry admittedly wasn't fully prepared for his once-a-week lesson but, in usual student style, did the best he could. Of course, David was always well aware that the student had not, perhaps, studied the assigned piece properly, and he simply would suggest that he would like to hear the same selection at the next lesson.[467] When a difficult passage was reached and Henry really didn't understand how to play it during the lesson and appeared "stumped," David would "just lean over and play it perfectly with his left hand!"[468]

Henry recalls a little embarrassing moment one night at the Moyer household. As often happened, David and Jessie had a group of David's students to the house for dinner. Henry had the unpleasant experience of accidentally spilling a glass of milk on the carpet. According to his telling of the story, he was devastated with embarrassment. David and Jessie just laughed and grabbed more paper napkins and sopped up the spill, and the party continued as if nothing had happened.

During this time, it seems that only a few of the conservatory teachers performed regularly on the campus at Oberlin. Henry recalled David's playing the Shostakovich Piano Concerto No. 1 with the Oberlin Symphony. "The performance was superb, of course, and such a lesson for all of us students."[469]

After graduating from Oberlin Conservatory with both bachelor's and master's degrees, Henry taught at the School of Music at Converse College in Spartanburg, South Carolina. He conducted the Spartanburg Symphony, directed the newly established opera company at the college, and also was guest conductor for the Charlotte Symphony orchestra. Later in Henry's career, he would be promoted to dean of the School of Music at Converse College and would serve as vice president until 1995 when he retired.

Henry served as the artistic director and principal conductor of the Brevard Music Center for thirty-two years. Brevard is located in the beautiful Blue Ridge Mountains of western North Carolina. The opera company associated with the center is now called the Janiec Opera Company as an honor to Henry, its founder. In closing, Henry wrote:

> David Moyer was a wonderful pianist, a patient teacher, and a warm, kind person. He was always cheerful and seemed to sincerely love his work in teaching. My relationship with Mr. Moyer was a truly happy and fruitful one. We exchanged some letters in the early years, then Christmas notes when he retired and moved to Massachusetts.

I do remember a letter I got from him when he was celebrating a birthday and he wrote about some of the concerts he'd heard there. He was a man, who never criticized other musicians, but in this one instance he lamented that so much music he was hearing was too fast, too loud, and so much of the piano playing was "banging!" Years after having Mr. Moyer for my teacher he asked me to address him as David but I respectfully declined. He would always be that special "Mr." in my life.[470]

Jacqueline Stark Wood from Great Neck, Long Island, New York, studied with David from 1949 until she graduated in 1953. Jacqueline married a local artist, Paul Wood, and together they had four sons who are all professional musicians or artists. On March 14, 2006, Jacqueline wrote a lovely letter about her life at Oberlin and her great respect for her teacher, David. At the time of the writing of this letter, Jacqueline was seventy-five years old and in declining health. Nine months after the writing of this letter sadly she passed away.

> I am very happy to write about my beloved teacher, David Moyer who has been such an influential and inspiring person in my life! Because of him, his encouragement and special teaching, I have been a successful pianist, teacher of piano and contributor musically and personally in my town of Port Washington for fifty years. This is what he advised me to do after my graduation from the Conservatory in 1953. I will never forget his patience and love just before my Senior Recital, when I was so nervous and couldn't remember a note! My fiancée and my mother were in the audience March 16, 1953. David came back stage, smiled and laughed and said, "You just go out there and show them what you can do!" And I did. At a lovely reception at his home with his wife having cooked an entire meal for me and my guests, I felt I was indeed in heaven! His wife would call me at my dormitory many times and say, "Do you know how happy you made David today at your piano lesson?"

> David taught me to really love music and let my musicality and musical instincts lead me. He said, "Always play with style!"

The above-quoted letter and the other testimonial comments by some of David's former students, still living, create a full-color picture of the professional teacher and person that was David Moyer. David and Jessie made a real impact on the lives of his students at Oberlin Conservatory. Many times, David and Jessie invited students, especially those from far away, to come to their home for dessert, to celebrate special occasions, and sometimes, to enjoy full family meals. Their own children—Sonia, Bud, and Bill—were all growing up in this environment of good music, good company, and one of nondiscrimination toward people who appeared different from themselves. Just as David had a totally color-blind attitude to his students, so did and still do his children. All David saw in his students was their talent, coupled with their intense desire to succeed, and this he related to so naturally.

Sonia, Bud, and Bill Moyer all grew to maturity during these special years. Sonia would graduate from Oberlin College and work for the CIA for years alongside her husband, Norman Uranksy. Bud, the boy with the wonderful hands, did not choose music for his career, but served his time during World War II in the United States Navy as a communications specialist in the Pacific. Upon his return home, he moved with his wife, Judy Loskamp Moyer, to Vinalhaven where they had their four children and where for several years he ran the island power plant. Bill, the youngest, who had fallen in love with the trombone at age eight, attended Oberlin Conservatory of Music and married his college sweetheart, Betsy Green. Shortly after their marriage in 1952, Bill's Vinalhaven friend Kilton Vinal Smith, tubist with the Boston Symphony Orchestra, suggested that Bill auditioned for the second trombone position that was at the time vacant. Bill won the audition, and he and his wife and trombones moved to Boston to begin a thirty-five year career first as a player and then as personnel manager of the Boston Symphony Orchestra.

Bill Moyer with Maestro Arthur Fiedler, Berlin, Germany, 1971
Photo: Courtesy of Moyer Family Archives

Once the children were married and all lived away from Oberlin, David and Jessie moved to a smaller house, and in 1960, David retired from Oberlin Conservatory after thirty-five years of continuous service. Their plans were to eventually move to Vinalhaven, Maine, to live out their retirement near son Bud and his family.

Chapter XVI

Return to Europe

David retired in June 1960 from Oberlin Conservatory of Music. As a way of celebrating this important milestone in David and Jessie's life, Bill and Betsy gave David and Jessie on Easter Sunday that year a round-trip passage on an ocean liner for a three-month tour of Europe. This was an unexpected dream come true for both of them! After the usual summer stint at Vinalhaven, they started their journey on August 31 to Europe from New York City where they boarded the ship for the cruise that would end at Cuxhaven, Germany. For David, especially, this must have brought back so many memories from his childhood and the numerous crossings he made back and forth on the same route. Leaving New York harbor, the journey began in intense, heavy fog that lasted for the entire ten-day crossing. Jessie kept a daily diary of this trip from start to finish, and some of her comments are priceless. This diary is a valuable source although she did not always write in complete sentences, but on many days, simply in sound bites. Jessie had never traveled to the continent before, but for David, it must have been somewhat of a homecoming. He hadn't seen Germany since 1914 when he had hurriedly left to avoid being caught up in the First World War on the side of the Germans. There is no hard evidence to suggest that he would have been conscripted into the German army or, perhaps, imprisoned if he had stayed, but the possibility of it would be enough to send just about anyone packing toward the safe ground of home.

According to Jessie's first entry on the night of the actual departure, they stood on the deck of the ship until after 1:00 a.m. with many of the other passengers and observed passing the Statue of Liberty adorned with many lights. Even through the fog, Jessie thought it was a thrilling sight.[471] Jessie was impressed by the volume of flowers and all the messages of goodwill they found in their cabin. Although Jessie, because of her propensity to claustrophobia, was not impressed with the location of their cabin, an inside cabin with no windows, she did make the best of the situation and spent most days seeing movies that were on offer and enjoying the ever-present meal times. Cruise ships are known for having a never-ending array of food available to passengers twenty-four hours a day. Jessie said that she ate too much too often. Most ocean liner passengers all share this complaint. It appears from her comments that they met some very interesting people and played a good deal of bridge. They had their turn sitting at the Captain's Table for a meal after which they were invited to the first class deck for an evening of recitations and singing. In spite of horrible weather and eating too much, the diary reveals that it was a pleasant crossing.

One of the high points of this trip was the time they were able to spend with their only daughter and her family. Sonia, Norman, and Gayna were living in Frankfurt, Germany, since 1957 when Norman was assigned there by the DIA (Defense Intelligence Agency) the precursor of the CIA. Norman Uransky, according to his daughter Gayna was from the Polish ghetto of Cleveland, Ohio. "His family was on the breadlines due to his father's alcoholism. Norman was a brilliant man. He must have decided quite early that he wanted a different life and went about making it happen."[472] Norman, like so many other young men of this time, joined the armed forces so he could eventually use the newly created Servicemen's Readjustment Act of 1944 or more commonly known as the G.I. Bill to obtain funding for higher education that would have been beyond his reach without help.[473] Norman enlisted in the navy and was trained as a code breaker at Harvard University, Oberlin College, and Notre Dame. It was during Norman's time at Oberlin that he met Sonia and actually told a friend of his that "she would be the woman he would marry" regardless of the fact that she was already engaged to someone else.[474] Sonia's engagement had already been published in the local Oberlin newspaper, so any change would have caused a bit of embarrassment for her parents.

Jessie and David should have been used to a bit of embarrassment from Sonia. In her senior year at Oberlin High School in 1941, Sonia attended her senior prom on the arm of a classmate who was black. "Jessie was horrified."[475] People of African-American descent were very welcome in Oberlin, and in some cases, their ancestors were assisted by Oberlin people through the Underground Railroad system of escape for slaves during the American Civil War, but obviously the code of everyday life was a bit different. As Gayna states, "The town of Oberlin had been liberal for many years—just not liberal enough for Sonia."[476]

Norman studied at Harvard University in Cambridge, Massachusetts, both before and after studying at Oberlin College. Sonia was still in Oberlin. He and Sonia must have missed each other so intensely that one weekend, Norman, with the help of his navy buddies, simply left Cambridge and traveled to Oberlin where he and Sonia were married June 3, 1945. This was not an elopement. They were married in the local church in Oberlin with all the family and many guests in attendance. Technically, Norman was AWOL, but the navy officially never knew that. After Norman and Sonia were married, he was hired by the DIA. It had been three years since David, Jessie, Sonia, and her family had been together, so this trip was especially important for all of them.

While on board, Jessie received a message from Sonia that she and her family would meet them at the Port of Cuxhaven upon arrival. After a few days with Sonia's family, Jessie and David purchased a secondhand purple Volvo car for the rest of their time in Europe. In the diary, a notation was made by Jessie that it took David an entire day of waiting around police stations to get the necessary paperwork filed to he could drive the car legally. Once they were settled into life in Frankfurt, Sonia and Norman took a week's vacation to Switzerland, and Gayna stayed behind with her grandparents. Jessie wrote two entries into her travel diary for September 18, 1960: "Sept 18—word ghma died 2:30 p.m." and ". . . we start our teen age sitting—short trip to the zoo settled us—we were afraid to return to apt."[477] Gee Gee Ma had resided at a local nursing home in Oberlin for a few years due to failing health and old age. Receiving the information via a telegram that her mother had died must have been a terrible shock for both Jessie and David. It was not feasible for them to return to Ohio for any funeral or burial services at the time. The price alone of making a return journey from Frankfurt, Germany to Ohio and back to continue their trip would have been prohibitive and even though they received their passage as a gift from their son and daughter-in-law, they had still invested heavily in this long awaited for tour of Europe. So they grieved in their own way and when Sonia and Norman returned from Switzerland, they continued their tour. There are no entries in their travel diary until September 21, 1960.

Throughout their tour, it rained more often than not according to Jessie's daily diary. They had intermittent trouble with the car, and although David tried to do some of the repairs himself, they usually ended up spending an extra day or two in some town waiting for the local garage to fix the problem. None of this, however, spoiled their enthusiasm or good time.

Wherever they went, they visited local cathedrals, museums, and took extra time seeing and hearing great organs being played. Jessie, daily in her journal, commented on the quality of the beds and the desserts in each hotel and restaurant they visited. According to her, some of the beds were absolutely horrible while others were extremely comfortable. It seems that in almost every town and city they visited, Jessie purchased items for the family at home as well as for Sonia and her family in Germany. They traveled through most of the provinces in Germany and took the time to go to Fouday in Alsace where Rev. John Frederick Oberlin had his church and community. Jessie's comment is recorded as "dead city now."[478] They decided to drive back to Frankfurt to reorganize themselves before setting out on the rest of their "adventure." On the way back to Frankfurt, they had a most unpleasant experience driving in a severe rainstorm with no working windshield wipers on the car. They arrived back at Sonia's home laughing and full of stories about their first trip around Germany.

They did visit Berlin where David had spent so many years of his youth. Jessie recorded how disappointed he was that what he remembered was no longer standing. The reality of it all must have been very difficult for David emotionally. Berlin was still struggling to rise from the ashes and from the division of city and country. Nineteen-sixty was a painful time in Berlin because of the horrible conditions that remained after World War II. The city was not a very nice place to visit. Even though the Hochschule für Musik was still standing, it seems that David just stopped looking for other places out of obvious disappointment. Seeing the rubble that marked the building where he once lived, the places he enjoyed visiting, so many of the homes, and other venues where he once performed would have made anyone want to abandon this trip down memory lane! He may have felt that a very important part of his earlier life had been simply bombed into oblivion. Even though David's old haunts were in the western zone of Berlin, there were armed soldiers everywhere, and this sight was probably too threatening for both David and Jessie.

They wasted no time in leaving Berlin and were off again in search of more entertainment and fascinating sights. They traveled to all provinces in Germany and saw much of the country. Jessie records in her diary the trouble they seemed to have dealing with the European bedding. On the continent during this time and even still today, many hotels still use the eiderdown quilts inside a changeable cover. These quilts are very heavy and made with eider duck feathers for warmth. Many hotels used these on guest beds because they more than likely did not have central heating. David and Jessie became frustrated with the quilts and asked for blankets instead. Jessie never comments as to whether they were given blankets, but once they reached Italy, the eiderdown quilts become a faded memory.

They arrived in Italy in the last week of October. It appears they had slightly better weather. They drove through the Umbrian Mountains to Assisi, the birthplace of St. Francis. While walking around this walled city, David and Jessie met a newly wedded couple that in Jessie's own words, "adopted us!"[479] There is no notation regarding the nationality of the couple, but they took Jessie and David into the church where there was a wedding taking place. They heard a lovely soloist sing during the ceremony. This must have been very special for Jessie as she was a soloist at many weddings and funerals in Oberlin. After the wedding, they walked around the church, and David took many photos. They visited the tomb of St. Francis and quietly left for their hotel accommodation in Rome that night. It seems they were trying to see so many places and travel so many miles that they didn't seem, at this stage, to spend more than a few hours in each place.

The next day, they were up early, the sun was shining, and they were off to the city of Naples. While in Naples, Jessie found the poor living conditions of the residents there almost too much to bear. They were headed to the American Express Office hopefully to pick up some mail, but the office wasn't open until 3:30 p.m., so they spent their time walking around the town. "The squalor and poverty of the sad people in the slums, so much filth" was Jessie's comment regarding Naples.[480] Once they had found a place for lunch and had finished their business at the American Express, they were off and on their way to the Amalfi Coast of Italy.

Positano is often referred to as the pearl of the Amalfi Coast. The small quaint town sits nestled in the side of the Lattari Mountains. The very small houses cling in tiers to the rock face and are built one on top of the other.[481] Although Positano is one of the most photographed places by visitors, Jessie wrote that it was a village for midgets! Whether the village was for midgets or not, they stayed there for ten days and took many day trips but always returning for the night.

On Halloween Day, October 31, David went off with a man he had met in the village of Montepertuso. Montepertuso is a sleepy village nestled on the top of a mountain and, as the guides say, "lost in the olive groves."[482] It was quite a hike from Jessie and David's pension/hotel to this area, so Jessie decided to stay behind as her legs were very sore from the walking and hill climbing the previous days. Also, one of Jessie's legs was never the same after she had the bout with phlebitis in 1924 while pregnant with her first child, Sonia. David was gone for twelve hours that day, and Jessie's only comment about it was that she did not like being alone. Jessie would not have known Italian, so her interactions with locals and other guests in the hotel would have been very limited. She did take a walk on the beach, and as luck would have it, it rained once she got into her stride. When David arrived back at the hotel, he had a beautiful collection of wildflowers from his walking excursion for Jessie.

The following day, they hired a guide, Salvatore, to take them to see Mt. Vesuvius. Salvatore being their guide was ridiculous as he informed David in the middle of the journey that he had never actually been to the volcano before in his life. Although it seems this fact annoyed Jessie to some extent, but in the end, she was glad they paid him to go along. Once at the volcano, they paid the entry fees, and those that sold the tickets "made it very clear that a guide would have to go along. A good thing he did, he pulled me up with his belt tied around a stick up and down the volcano for about eight hours."[483] Jessie then reported the following day in her diary how badly her knees ached. No wonder!

Other trips to Naples and the American Express office followed to collect mail; Jessie reveals that there was a ton of it for them to read. Jessie loved getting the letters and cards from home and gladly spent many evenings sending notes and letters to friends and relations back home. On their way back to Positano from the Sorrento region, they got seriously lost several times because of a missed left turn. In usual Moyer spirit, they simply laughed at these errors and continued on their journey toward Rome on November 7. Two full days of touring were spent in Rome, and from the list of places visited, it is hard to imagine that they missed anything in the Eternal City.

They journeyed on to Florence and Pisa and spent a good deal of time in both places touring museums, churches, and other places of interest, and of course, shopping. After leaving Pisa they traveled in the car along the coast toward the village of Viareggio "where we got a nice pension along the coast—walked on beach in sand before dark—saw sunset over Mediterranean—very lovely."

On the November 15, David and Jessie arrived in Nice. They booked into the pension, Scandinavia, and settled in for approximately ten days until they would travel northward to the area where David spent his time during World War I. They took a day trip to Monte Carlo for lunch and, afterwards, to the Casino and "watched many old hags try to win." [484] Evidently, gambling casinos and the people who frequented them were not high on Jessie's priority list.

On another day, they again traveled to Monaco. They parked the car in front of the Royal Palace. They were there for lunch and made their way back to their parked car so David could change the film in his camera. Jessie observed a huge car coming from the Palace grounds, and in the car were Princess Grace and Prince Rainier. Jessie was overjoyed! For any American to see Princess Grace, the former Hollywood actress, Grace Kelly, was a treat! Unfortunately, David did not succeed in changing his film quickly enough because there is no photo of the royal couple in his collection.

Jessie and David were in Nice for American Thanksgiving Day and, like so many Americans who find themselves abroad on this special holiday, did their best to celebrate the day. David went out to bakeries and shops in the morning and came back at noon with goodies for a picnic on the beach along the southeast coast of France. He had purchased canned turkey, onion pie, pickle relish, French bread and butter, and what Jessie described as a wonderful bottle of wine. An interesting pile of rocks on the beach was found that they used as a makeshift table, and there, they had their own Thanksgiving meal. [485]

David and Jessie stayed in Nice until November 28, and once again, they did a tremendous amount of sightseeing all over the area. Their travels took them east and west of Nice. During the last few days of their stay along the French Riviera, they journeyed northward over one hundred miles to visit some of the battle areas where David had spent time as a soldier in 1918.

They stopped at Orange and visited the ancient Roman Theatre that was built in the first century AD. From comments in Jessie's diary, they enjoyed seeing all that was to be seen while in Orange. The next day, they set out for Beaune (the location of the AEF University where the offer for David to teach never materialized), and David decided to stop to find out information concerning signs he had seen regarding local wine cellars. After purchases at the wine cellar, David and Jessie went to a restaurant for what Jessie described as "the best meal in France." This meal was accompanied by "sparkling burgundy," something new for David and Jessie. Jessie's comment after this lovely dinner was that they "took a short, slow walk and then immediately to bed after a very nice day."[486]

They continued on to many abandoned battlefields where David had old memories. Per usual, they visited churches and cathedrals in almost every small town. It seems, according to Jessie, that David didn't think the places had changed all that much since he had been there almost fifty years before.

A stop at Damvillers was made, and according to David, time had simply stood still. It looked to him as if nothing had changed here as well. While viewing the battlefields, they saw certain areas where access was restricted for visitors. These areas were bounded by barbed wire and signs that suggested the enclosed lands still contained buried war mines. They also saw some trenches that appeared to be intact and also saw some pillboxes scattered here and there.[487]

Their journey continued on toward Frankfurt with a stop at Worms. They had a hard time finding the church where Martin Luther preached his epochal sermon in his own defense, but after what seems to be considerable diligence, they finally stood in the chancel. Both Jessie and David seemed duly impressed. In the nearby park, there is a beautiful statue of Luther and the remains of a Reformation-era church where the actual sentencing of Luther took place. Although it had been bombed severely during the last war, there now stands a more modern building housing the famous mosaic containing fourteen thousand stones.[488] Then it was onward to Frankfurt to begin the ordeal of packing more gifts and sending them on to the States for family and friends and getting their own personal packing organized for their departure on December 14. They had a few social engagements to attend with Sonia's friends, and they had their traditional Christmas Sunday gathering with poems and other entertainments. "It was much fun," recorded Jessie.[489] Also, David had to resell his secondhand car before leaving Germany. Jessie's only comment about this is that it was sold at a minus of what they paid for it, but such was the lot of the American tourist in Europe in the early '60s. International auto rental was in its infancy and not as available as it is today.

December 14 arrived, and the farewells at the Port of Cuxhaven must have been emotional for all of them. For David, it was just another farewell. He had been doing these farewells since he was almost six years of age. It is doubtful that these events ever became routine for him. It just involved another two generations of family to leave. Jesse and David sailed from Cuxhaven to London for their final voyage across the Atlantic.

David and Jessie Moyer, 1960
Photo: Courtesy of Moyer Family Archives

Chapter XVII

Coda

Once back on familiar American soil, Jessie and David had the chore of getting around visiting their sons and their families to tell them all about their marvelous trip. They also had many gifts to distribute that had been mailed from Europe to their home. Some boxes of gifts that had been shipped from Frankfurt never arrived in Oberlin. They had to spend days going back and forth to the local airport, visited shipping companies, and finally they found their belongings at the Railroad Express office in Cleveland.[490] From what Jessie wrote in this letter dated January 6, 1961, this was one exhausting ordeal. Once the missing boxes were back in their possession, they rested a bit easier. Jessie also mentions that the Christmas of 1960 was the only Christmas she and David had spent with their sons since they married and moved far from Ohio.[491]

Jessie gave talks, accompanied by David's slides, to several of the local women's clubs about their European excursion. The retired life seemed to be perfect for David and Jessie! They had their normal social involvements in Oberlin and always looked forward to their summer retreat at the Music Box on Vinalhaven when the extended family would gather for a few weeks. Both David and Jessie had more time to work on their own interests. For Jessie, these included knitting, other handiwork, and she took up oil painting studies. For several summers in Maine, she was able to fit in art classes, and now that she was retired, she had more time to devote to this new pastime. She continued to sing for funerals and other events whenever requested. David had more time for his woodworking projects, studying music scores, and was usually active playing his instruments—piano or the clavichord that he built from a kit and, basically, living in his own world that he treasured. According to their granddaughter, Gayna Uransky, "David almost did not live in this world. His vocation—teaching music—was fairly ethereal. The most grounding thing he did was his woodworking. His demeanor was always extraordinarily pleasant and kind"[492]

Jessie and David had begun to discuss with the family their thoughts about selling the Music Box and perhaps buying a smaller place on Vinalhaven. From what Jessie states in some of her letters to both her sons, it seems the Music Box is just too large a property for them, in their later years, to manage.

In April 1961, Jessie was called away from Oberlin to help her aging Aunt Jane Magee, one of her mother's sisters who lived with her sister, Florie, in the family home on Lippincott Street in Ardmore, Pennsylvania. Aunt Florie was taken ill with pneumonia, and when Jessie arrived in Ardmore, the ambulance was taking her out of the family home to the hospital. The visiting doctor told Jessie that it would only be a matter of hours before she passed away.[493] Aunt Jane was in a bad way on her own. Jessie went to Ardmore to help and realized at that point just how ill her Aunt Jane really was. The poor woman was terribly crippled with arthritis and could no longer walk on her own or get out of bed. Jessie had her work cut out for her it seems. The first order of business was to rid the house of six cats, three adults and three very young kittens. "I can't sleep thinking of sending pets to the gas chamber—it has to be done." One of the adult cats was apparently quite vicious. Jessie tried to gather the cats herself but had to call on the SPCA to come and take them all away.[494] All her life, Jessie was an A1 lover of animals and had a reputation for taking in many strays. Her real concern was the welfare of her sickly aunt. Jessie was raised in the house on Lippincott Street as a child. She had fond memories there and how it became a bit of a struggle for her to reconcile herself to the realities. Aunt Jane was the last of the older generation of her mother's family, and it seems the reality of all this was difficult for Jessie. "Honestly, one could become a mental depressive staying too long in this gloomy house."[495] Jessie had every intention of moving Aunt Jane to Oberlin, Ohio, and placing her in the same rest home where her mother, Gee Gee Ma, had lived until her death in 1960. Aunt Jane was not at all interested in going to any rest home, especially, one so far from where she was born and raised. In addition to having to take care of the physical needs of her aunt, Jessie had the task of selling the family homestead. It was impossible for her aunt to remain in this house on her own. Jessie contacted David who was still in Oberlin, and he drove with the two dogs to Ardmore, Pennsylvania to help Jessie with her tasks. From the tone of Jessie's letters during this period, both she and David were getting stressed rummaging through all the collected items of a house that at one time had three generations living in it. Jessie's solution was to divide all the worthwhile belongings of the Magee family among her three children. Jessie was the only descendant of the Magee family. David did his part and found a real estate man to handle the sale of the house and worked on packing all the things that Jessie wanted to give to her three children as, well as, all the things she wanted to take back to Oberlin. It was a good thing that David had the presence of mind to bring the trailer on the back of the car. He knew Jessie so well that he expected there would be things to take home. In her April 1961 letters, Jessie is adamant that she wants to get to Vinalhaven for a good vacation before "it gets too cold to enjoy it." Once back in Oberlin, a friend came to visit Jessie and tried to talk Jessie out of selling the Music Box. Jessie wrote, "She thinks we'd enjoy living there all year round. I question that—there is no stimulus in island life especially, at Vh. [Vinalhaven]. But we'll see."[496]

In July 1961, Jessie and David sold the Music Box property on Vinalhaven Island. The new buyers said they could stay there until the middle of August, and then they would take possession of it. This plan seemed to fit nicely into place for all involved. Jessie and David had looked at a cottage-type building practically in son Bud's backyard and decided to purchase it for a very low price. The locals referred to it as a fish house, and son Bud said it had been used as a dance hall at one time, and also, it served as a bait shop, and at another time, it was used as a boat builder's shed. The building is twenty-three feet by thirty feet, has a new forty-foot pier out into the channel, and they decided instead of having a staircase to the second floor, they would put in an elevator. Their son Bud would do all the carpentry work on the building to make it livable for them. Jessie toyed with the idea of calling the property Finn-an-Haddie because when the building was used as a dance hall, it was called Finn Hall.[497]

By this time, Jessie's Aunt Jane was safely in a rest home in Media, Pennsylvania, and Jessie was convinced that Aunt Jane had enough money to pay for her own care for many years to come if she should live that long. Even though Jessie's instinct was correct, the State of Pennsylvania had something to say about it. None of Jane's maiden sisters had ever written a will, so when they died, their financial interests were simply absorbed by the others still living in the family home. To these elderly women, this was normal practice. The tax department of Pennsylvania had other ideas. Aunt Jane's finances were audited, and the state removed from her control thousands of dollars that no inheritance tax had ever been paid. This was devastating to Aunt Jane. Jessie hired a lawyer, and Aunt Jane lost her plea and most of her money. Now, the situation existed that Aunt Jane didn't have enough money to cover all her expected expenses at the nursing home, so the same state that took her money away had to pay her support in the nursing home until she died. Ah, sweet justice!

Back in Oberlin for the winter of 1962, Jessie and David received a letter from their daughter Sonia still in Germany, telling them that they will be returning to the United States sometime during the summer. In reality, it was the rising tensions of the Cuban Missile Crisis that brought Norman and others who worked for the CIA abroad back to the States.[498] No more ocean liner trips to visit with their only daughter and her family.

When the Uransky family moved to Germany in 1957, Sonia was offered a secretarial job as a contract wife for the agency or the company, Gayna's euphemism for the CIA. Gayna continues:

> I . . . was quite clueless as to their work until I took a job as a clerk with the Covert Operations Office in Miami, Florida—where we moved. My job was limited to filing—and no kidding—I truly never knew they worked for the C.I.A. They always told me they worked for The Department of the Army—Civilian. So for the first days of work, as we drove to the location we always drove to, they casually said, 'Oh, by the way we don't really work for the Dept. of the Army, we work for the CIA.'[499]

The only real information regarding the return of Sonia and family was the date of June 13, 1962. This was when school ended for the year for Gayna, and Sonia informed her parents that they would be leaving sometime after that date. There is no mention of where they would live. Both Jessie and David spent hours trying to figure out which part of the country their daughter would reside. It was all top secret. Sonia didn't know where they would live either. The word had not come forth from the powers that be. This was part and parcel for working for either the DIA or CIA.

Jessie spent most of the winter making more plans for the fish house in Vinalhaven and devoted a tremendous amount of time taking care of friends' plants while they were away on vacation. David developed a work project for men who were living in a rest home in Oberlin. The project involved having the men assemble birdhouses and bird feeders that he designed. He would cut out the pieces for assembly in his home workshop and would take the sets to the men in the rest home on a daily basis. The feeders and houses were sold at the annual hospital bizarre. "Dr. Jim Stephens is head of the rest home and he thinks Pa has accomplished almost the impossible with the interest the men are displaying. At least the workshop angle is keeping them less like inactive vegetables."[500] David's involvement with these men provided them with something worthwhile to do, and his work was a success. The concept and practice of occupational therapy had been known about for years, but one of the problems for many rest homes or nursing homes was finding people with the skills and the desire to be involved with these patients productively. David was always so willing to share whatever skills he had with anyone who was interested, and whether people were in a rest home environment or simply neighbors to be helped, he was always at the ready.

After a quick trip to Vinalhaven for a week or so, the end of March, life returned to normal for them. They went to watch the raising of the roof on the fish house. The roof needed to be raised in order to extend the second floor so the room would be larger and Dormer windows were put in because the elevator needing more height in the roof space to accommodate it. Jessie said it was fascinating to watch this operation, and David took many photos as well. They both realized that son Bud had so much ability doing what seemed to be almost impossible tasks. On the way to Oberlin from Vinalhaven, they took a different route to visit Jessie's Aunt Jane in the nursing home in suburban Philadelphia. Jessie felt very badly that they had not been able to visit her for over a year. Although Aunt Jane told Jessie she felt much weaker than a year ago, Jessie brushed this comment of hers aside and said that she looked and acted much better than she had the year before.[501] Jessie did offer to return for more visiting with Aunt Jane the following morning, but Jane insisted that she was talked out and they would be better off continuing their journey to Oberlin. In April, Jessie again heard from Sonia, but there was no more information as to exactly where they would be stationed once back in the U.S. She did make a remark, however, that they would not be in the Washington DC area but probably quite far from there. Well, now Jessie and David's minds worked overtime to try and figure out exactly where Sonia and her family would be living. David came up with the idea that perhaps it would be in the Miami area of Florida since Norman spoke fluent Spanish, and Jessie thought this is as good an idea as any because Miami was going through a problem with Cuban refugees.[502] In mid-June, Jessie heard again from Sonia, and in this letter Sonia told her mother that they were putting into storage all of their woolen items and heavy clothes because where they were gong to settle in the U.S., they won't be needing such clothing.[503] Sonia still did not tell her parents where they would be living. It is entirely possible that Sonia herself didn't know either. Jessie had made plans that if Sonia and family were going to be in Florida, then she and David would cut all ties with Oberlin, Ohio, and live at Vinalhaven eight months of the year and spend the four coldest months in Florida, either with Sonia or somewhere nearby.

Sonia and her family did arrive at Vinalhaven and spent a week with Jessie and David. It was then that they were told that the Uransky family would reside in Florida, Miami area. Everyone seemed very happy about this news. One theme seems to be constant in all Jessie's letters during the summer of 1962 to her son Bill and family. She was really pushing quite hard to get them to come to Vinalhaven for vacation. Bill and his family spent most of their summer at Tanglewood, the summer home of the Boston Symphony Orchestra, practicing and performing regularly throughout the summer. It was very difficult for the Bill Moyer family to get any time away from the Berkshires during the summer months. Jessie was not pleased about this, but this had been the way Bill's family had spent every summer since he joined the orchestra in 1951. It was simply a matter of his contract with the BSO. Bill was scheduled to leave Boston in mid-September for a concert tour in Germany with the BSO. There really was no available time for them to go to

Vinalhaven. Jessie continued to write to them and kept everyone posted on their doings at Vinalhaven. She and David were having a wonderful time getting all of the work done on the fish house that they could while also keeping up a very busy social life visiting friends and having many visitors to their new abode. By mid-October Jessie and David were back in Oberlin. In October 1962, Jessie wrote that the new dial telephone system was in place, and it made it so much easier and cheaper for her to telephone her three children, all living at a distance. No more need to go through an operator as before. In today's world, we sometimes forget how awkward telephone communication was at one time.

In what was to be Jessie's final letter to her son Bill and his family dated December 2, 1962, she requested that if he and his family could possibly come to Oberlin for Christmas, they would postpone their trip to Florida to Sonia's home. Even though Jessie and David's house was in some disarray because of the fact that they had moved the best beds, etc. to the fish house at Vinalhaven. They were now left with one bed in which David slept while Jessie slept on a rollaway cot that she didn't enjoy because it hurt her back. In spite of this, she practically pleaded with her son's family to make the journey where someone could sleep on a sofa and the others in sleeping bags. Bill and Betsy obviously declined the invitation so Jessie and David proceeded to plan their tedious trip to Florida for Christmas. In the early 1960s, the trip from Oberlin was arduous! Very few turnpikes or interstates were available at this time, but they could get to the outskirts of Philadelphia because the Pennsylvania Turnpike was almost completed. Jessie hadn't seen her Aunt Jane in the nursing home for at least a year, and she wanted to make sure she brightened the old woman's Christmas with a personal visit.

David and Jessie left Oberlin early on the morning of December 20 and headed to the home of Cora, David's widowed sister-in-law (my grandmother), in suburban Philadelphia. They arrived at a reasonable hour in the evening after their compulsory visit with Aunt Jane, and Cora made them a nice supper; the three of them had a nice visit. Cora had previously phoned her son Skinny and had invited his family to come after supper to visit with David and Jessie. It had been quite a few years since they had all seen each other. I, the author, remember this well. I was just sixteen years old, and of course, I had to play the piano for Uncle Earl and Aunt Jessie. They were polite and very good natured and insisted I play a couple more selections for them. After I finished playing, I was given encouragement and some praise for my efforts. The men had gone into the dining room for conversation while the ladies sat in the living room talking about things that happened in years gone by with a good deal of laughter. Uncle Earl and my father did their usual chuckling and talking about the falling snow and the type of car that Uncle Earl was driving all the way to Florida. It was all in good fun. When it was time, we said our good-byes and wished David and Jessie safe journey to Florida since they were departing early the next morning.

The falling snow was of little real concern to anyone, it seemed. The following evening, December 21, we received a late night phone call telling us that Uncle Earl and Aunt Jessie had been in a terrible auto accident in Maryland and that Jessie was dead. It was pure shock for all of us! We knew very few details at the time just that it had happened. I remember, especially since Christmas was just a few days away, how gloomy that holiday was for all of us.

According to the press reports, which we didn't read until later, David was driving along US Route 301 in a southerly direction and a Mr. Albert Seustel with his son Robert, a midshipman at the United States Naval Academy, were traveling in a northerly direction. They collided on a snow-filled two-lane highway near Centerville, Maryland. Mr. Seustel and his son as well as Jessie were fatally injured in the accident.

After the accident, David and Jessie were both taken to Easton Memorial Hospital in Easton, Maryland, where David was diagnosed with severe chest and hand injuries and possible head injuries. Jessie was pronounced dead at the scene and taken to the hospital morgue. Sonia, in Florida, was notified by her brother Bud, in Vinalhaven. As soon as was possible, she boarded the first plane to either Baltimore or Washington DC and traveled then by car to her father's bedside. Gayna, Sonia's daughter, informs us that when David saw Sonia in his hospital room, "he looked at her and said, 'Sonia, so this isn't a dream.' And she sadly told him it wasn't a dream."[504] Jessie's remains were cremated at the crematory of the Silverbrook Cemetery in Silverbrook, Delaware, on Christmas Eve, December 24, 1962, without any family member in attendance. David still required ongoing medical attention before he could even begin to consider his options for his future without his beloved Jessie by his side.

When he was finally released from the hospital in Maryland, David went directly to Sonia's home in Florida for recuperation. However, he seemed to stay on longer than his recuperation required. Although David grieved very hard and very deeply, for the most part, his grief was a very private matter. Sometimes, he would retire to his room for hours at a time, and when he felt he had himself emotionally together again, he would reemerge into the public space with the rest of Sonia's family.[505] There were other times when Sonia would find him sitting in a chair alone, doing nothing, and she would witness the tears just rolling down his face.[506]

> Mail time is grimmer than hell—he no longer can read these, so I read the stuff to him in bits and pieces. The pip was 's [name withheld] in which she said she's bought up as many copies of papers with accident

article as she could. Has 19 in all—would Pa like them? Poor guy didn't know whether to laugh or cry at that one.[507]

Gayna remembers these days very clearly. She was a high school student during this period. David stayed quite a while in Florida during his recuperation. "He did get involved with a bit of his woodworking, and Sonia and Norman got a piano from somewhere for him to use."[508] David, without a piano and without something creative to do with his hands, would have never recovered. According to Gayna, there was very little conversation between her mother and grandfather regarding Jessie's death. These people kept their emotional feelings to themselves for the most part. This was not such an unusual attitude for people of these two generations. America was not the "hugs and love you" expressive society that it appears to be today. A very different culture existed in those days. One of Gayna's fondest memories of her grandfather's time in her home is when her father, Norman, wanted David to hear a recording by jazz musician and pianist Dave Brubeck:

> Norman never showed Grandpa the jacket of the album. The recording was made at Oberlin Conservatory. The music began. Jazz. Very cool. Grandpa got a strange, quizzical expression on his face as the piano played on. After about a minute—finally—Grandpa said, "That's my piano!" Totally mystified—he looked at my father . . . and again stated, even more forcefully, "That's my piano!" It was then that Norman told him it was a recording that had been made at Oberlin! Grandpa then thought a minute, and told us he remembered leaving his piano for a concert which he had never attended for some jazz musician. We were duly impressed with his rather refined piano identification ability, to say the least.[509]

As David grew stronger and more independent both physically and emotionally, he traveled to Oberlin to clear up personal matters that needed to be completed since Jessie's untimely death such as making arrangements to turn their rented house there back into the hands of the owners and also to clear out all of their belongings. David left us no information on this process, but it must have been excruciating for him. He also returned to Vinalhaven, Maine, and began to spend some of his time at his home overlooking the sea, next door to son, Bud, and his family, and more time with youngest son, Bill, and his family, especially for the eight weeks during the summer when the Boston Symphony Orchestra was ensconced or in residence at Tanglewood in the Berkshire Hills of Massachusetts. David loved the concerts as well as the rehearsals. He was in his element, that's for sure. One summer while David was attending a rehearsal of a German operatic work, when just as he was taking his seat, the basso, pointed to the empty audience seats and sang sternly, "Setzen Sie sich!" David then rose in a huff and walked out, later complaining to Bill, that the singer had rudely told him to sit down.

In 1963, about a year after Jessie's death, David had the scare of his life. Although he really didn't remember very many of the details himself, he heavily relied on the account of his daughter-in-law Judy to fill in the blanks for him. David had had his Sunday lunch with his son's family next door in Vinalhaven. Afterwards, as was David's habit, he walked the short distance to his own house and had intended to take his usual afternoon nap, just as he had done for most of his life ever since he was eleven living in Germany. Almost instantly, he felt terribly ill and phoned his daughter-in-law Judy next door to tell her how badly he felt. Judy rushed over to his house to see what was the matter and found David on the floor. She immediately phoned the local and only doctor on the island, Dr. Ralph Earle. Dr. Earle arrived with what David describes as "his new heart attack kit" that he had never used before.

> Ralph told me that about five minutes after my heart attack, he was in my house. He opened his new kit and had to read the directions about what to do. He injected some thing in the heart to stimulate it. Then he jumped on top of me, so he said, to pump me to get some air in my lungs. He put me to bed right away and stayed with me for 24 hours. When I woke up, it was about 2:00 in the morning. (I had had my heart attack at noon). I saw him sitting at the foot of my bed and I said to him, "Well, Ralph. What are you doing down there." And he said, "You're quitting on me all the time. I have to keep watching you; I have to crawl in bed with you." You know Ralph; this is the way he talks. And he said, "It's terrible, he says. "I have to keep pumping you all the time. Your heart's quitting, and I have to keep it stimulated."

> The next time I woke up, I was in the hospital over in Rockland. That was the next day in the middle of the afternoon. The nurses said, "We never expected to see you alive, because when they brought you over you were absolutely out." Bud was there holding up bottles, intravenous feeding and all sorts of things. It was quite an affair they said. Even in the hospital I passed out a few times. Once I rolled out of bed and didn't know it. I was there for over a month.[510]

As David says, "I got through it." None of David's brothers or his father ever saw age sixty-three. They all died prior to that age from unknown heart conditions, and in the cases of his brothers Townsend and Wilmer, both died prior to age fifty, and his eldest brother, Vincent, died at age sixty-one. He never had any other heart trouble for the rest of his life and remained basically a healthy man until old age crept up on him just the same way it does on everybody. He did visit with each of his children every year, but he loved the independence and solitude that Vinalhaven offered him. David had been used to spending so much time on his own since his childhood that for him, this solitude and distance was a pleasure. There are notes recording his time alone, and he seemed to have thoroughly enjoyed doing his projects in his own way. He, on several occasions, rebuilt his clavichord and refurbished his piano. He could tune his own piano using a strobotuner and seemed to have enjoyed doing these tasks that perhaps to the rest of us would have been burdensome. He never mentioned, in any of his notes and small letters to his friends that he was lonely. He does, on occasion, mention to several of his letter recipients how much he missed them and how he looked forward to seeing them again. In one such letter to his friend Trudy Paddock, he talked about his "thankfulness for my many friends, my family, (nine grandchildren and one great-grandchild), my music and my good health—well, I am just happy with life." In the same letter, dated Thanksgiving 1976, he tells his friend Trudy that he traveled to the mainland and drove his car to Bangor, Maine, and looked in the stacks of the printed music department of a music store for new music he could sight-read, one of his favorite pastimes. He was disappointed in what he found in Bangor and simply says to his friend that "he has as much music on hand as they do."[511] He ended this letter in the same style as other letters by informing the reader what he has on the piano that he intends to play. "This is about all the news, and now back to the piano with Galuppi, Wagenseil, Martini, Mëhul Paradisi, Bach, Friedemann [Wilhelm Friedemann Bach], G. Benda, Bach, Ph. E. [Carl Philipp Emanuel Bach], Bach, Johann C. [Johann Christian], J. Häfsler and many more Baroque & Rococo. Love, Dave."

David lived at his Vinalhaven fish house almost until his death. Sadly, Jessie's wish of calling the property Finn-an-Haddie never materialized. Long before Jessie had died, all of David's own family had also passed away. Without Jessie or his brothers, he had only his own children and grandchildren to keep an eye on him and his eye on them. He would go to Florida periodically for the severe winter months, and sometimes, he would go to Bill's family home in Wayland, Massachusetts, until the season was right for returning to Vinalhaven. At other times, he spent most of the year on Vinalhaven where he would busy himself with his music and looking after the homes of his friends who only lived there in the summer months. Many of these friends were females, some were older than David and some were younger, so for them to be able to return to their winter homes with the knowledge that David was weekly checking on their summer place and making sure all was well must have brought a great sense of relief to them. Bill recalls that his father's friends would phone each other in the mornings at nine o'clock to make sure they were all still living.[512]

David at his Steinway at the Fish house, 1970.
Photo: Courtesy of Moyer Family Archives

He loved to be useful as much as he loved his music. One of his friends Trudy Paddock, originally from the suburbs of Philadelphia, was approximately thirty years younger than David, but she shared a deep understanding and feeling for classical music. She was one of David's prime admirers. They spent hours together just chatting, taking walks, and sharing bits or pieces of life, music, and sometimes, particular compositions. She did reveal in 2005 that David spoke of his young life with Madame Berlino and the two adopted boys but never in much detail. On one particular occasion, Trudy remembered a particular reference to Jessie. Trudy would go to David's home and stretch out on a rather uncomfortable couch near David's piano. David was playing a piece by Schumann about faraway lands. Trudy would allow herself to become carried away and experienced a great sense of inner peace listening to David's interpretive playing. On this one occasion, David softly and quietly said that the piece sadly reminded him of his wife, Jessie.[513] On another occasion, Trudy was having a problem with mice at her artist studio. She sought David's advice to set a few mousetraps that, of course, she did. To her distress one morning, she found a mouse partially in the trap but was still alive. She didn't know what to do. She telephoned David who came immediately to her studio and "with one stomp of his heel" put the poor creature out of its misery. Years later, when Trudy was telling this story, she was still perplexed as to how someone with David's great sensitivities could do such a thing. The reality is he did the only thing he could do.

In 2005, in preparation for this book, I had a golden opportunity to visit Vinalhaven for the first time. Luckily, one of David's former neighbors who lived very near the "fish house" granted me an interview. Mrs. Bertha L. Winslow, age 97, was a warm, engaging, and informative person. She reminisced at length about her own life and, how much she treasured those lazy island afternoons when David's music would permeate the sound waves to her enclosed porch. She said a number of times what a good and thoughtful neighbor he was. "If Mr. Moyer was going to town or to Rockland he would always come over and see if I needed anything so he could bring it back to me. He was a very caring gentleman. Now, it's his grandsons, David and Jeff, who do the same for me. I'd be lost without them.[514]

Three generations of Moyer male musicians: l to r: Bill, David and Fred.
Photo: Courtesy of Moyer Family Archives

During visits to his son's home in Massachusetts, Bill and Betsy's youngest son, Fred, developed a beautiful friendship with his grandpa. Fred was a blossoming young pianist and wanted to become a concert pianist. He and David shared many hours of stories, laughter, and David's insights into music and the technique of playing the piano to help prepare Fred for his eventual career. David always wanted the life of a concert pianist, but because of circumstances already mentioned earlier, that never happened for him. Through no ambition of his own, he entered the teaching profession. David must have thought this was wonderful to have a grandson who was going to, in some sense, fulfill his unrealized dream although he never said as much. At times, they spoke about some mutually satisfying topic, and Fred's eyes dance with delight at the memory of this. Fred would go to Vinalhaven to spend time with his grandpa, and David would share his performance experiences with Fred. David was as special to Fred as Fred was to David. Fred still is appreciative of every memory of time spent with his grandpa. "I learned so much from him about composers and pianists that he knew personally, and that I could only read about."[515] David had a wonderful knowledge of the pianists' equipment—hands, wrists, arms, elbows, etc.—and knew how to get all those parts to work together so one could play the most difficult passages "with the greatest of ease." For Fred, his sessions with Granpa were time well spent!

Some brief letters and notes between David and his children and some between David and a few of his Vinalhaven friends survive in the Moyer Family Archives. One difficulty with these glimpses into David's ordinary life was that he rarely included the year his letters were written. Month and day are stated, but not the year. Even without this accurate information, these afford insights into the man and his daily life.

David and Jessie's many summer years on Vinalhaven had provided them with some longstanding friends and acquaintances. These friendships continued when David returned to live year-round on the island, and he made many additional friends among the other retired artists and local people. They loved his music, and he loved their company. David and his friends would gather a couple of times a week for a meal together or even just a quick sail around the island. Once, a storm came up very quickly, and David had to be rescued by his two grandsons, David and Jeffrey, before his little sailboat was tossed too far. He loved to sail, and it seems this is something he learned as an adult once he had purchased the Music Box on Vinalhaven.

In a letter written in 1974 from David to Trudy Paddock of Katonah, New York, David expressed a bit of sadness about living in Florida. He loved the warm weather in Florida but missed the beauty of Maine. In the same note, he talked quite openly about the arthritis in his hands that seemed to create a problem for him playing the piano. "I'm afraid I will be able to play only light things. I am taking aspirin like mad, 20-24 a day! Kill or Cure!" David's sense of humor always seemed to prevail whenever possible. It must have been very difficult for a man who played the piano every day from age five to face such a hindrance. According to his daughter-in-law Betsy, this may have been one of the reasons he built the clavichord. "Certainly he didn't need such an instrument because neighbors, etc. never complained about the sound of his music. A clavichord would require a much lighter touch than the piano, and it may be the arthritis that inspired him to build it. He loved that instrument and played it by the hour during the time he lived with us."[516]

The winter of 1983 would once again bring deep sorrow to David. His oldest son, David E., Jr., or Bud, as he was known in the family, died suddenly. This unexpected event was yet another shock with which David would have to deal. At the time, David was still spending the winters with his daughter in Florida. The sad news came to Sonia's house, and David simply retired to his room for several hours to deal with his immediate grief and loss. Bud was a good son, loving husband, and father to four beautiful children. He spent his adult life working as a power plant engineer and building both sailing and lobster boats on Vinalhaven. According to Bud's brother Bill, Bud always excelled at model making when they were kids in their father's workshop in the basement of the Oberlin house where they were raised. Bud would build models of boats while younger brother Bill struggled with model airplanes. David was always proud of Bud's creative work. One such model of Bud's, an oil tanker, was sold to Higbee's Department Store in Cleveland for a window display. He had learned to play the flute and played in the Oberlin High School Band. Bud was not academically minded and did not attend college. Both his mother and father admired his creative and mechanical ability; although they were obviously disappointed that he did not attend college. Instead, he attended a trade school and learned the fine points of diesel engine mechanics that gave him the necessary background and experience to become a power plant engineer.[517] The details of Bud's death are not clearly known. Bud's remains were cremated, and in a private ceremony, his ashes were sprinkled in the waters near his home on Vinalhaven.

When the winter of 1985 came to an end, David left Vinalhaven for good. From some of the correspondence to his friend Trudy, it seems he just felt it was too much for him physically to make this journey every year. Instead, he moved in with Bill and Betsy in Wayland, Massachusetts, and would make only an occasional visit to Vinalhaven. David did take a short trip back to Oberlin with Bill and Betsy and renewed some old acquaintances with friends and faculty members he had known. It had been twenty-five years since David had been in Oberlin, and according to Betsy Moyer, he thoroughly enjoyed his weekend there. At home in Wayland, his daily routine consisted of walking the dog at 11:00 a.m. and 4:00 p.m., rain or shine and feeding the cat twice each day, riding his stationary exercycle, reading, playing his clavichord for several hours each day as well as his beloved piano. Bill and Betsy took him to as many public concerts in and around Boston as he could manage. They also made sure he attended as many of grandson Fred's concerts as possible.

David loved music regardless of whether it was live, made by himself, or on the radio. Betsy became his scribe since he could no longer write clearly enough for others to read, and according to a letter sent to his friends and some former students, she wrote, "I've abandoned this hearing aid because the damn thing doesn't work."[518]

David continued to enjoy his life up until two weeks before he died in September 1987. When he required constant medical care that could not be provided at his son's home, his doctor recommended he be placed in a nursing home. Although both Bill and Betsy found this decision difficult, they concurred that it was in "Pa's" best interest. David did not object at all but simply complied quietly with the arrangements. Surely, he knew that at age ninety-two, this would not be a long-term residence for him. Bill and Betsy visited him almost every day and, one time, even took his best friend, Schroeder, their part shepherd, part beagle dog to lie on his bed with him. Both David and Schroeder rested quietly together just as they so often did.

On September 8, 1987, David simply slipped away quietly and peacefully at the nursing home. His cause of death was listed as "infirmity of old age." David was cremated shortly after his death just as his dear wife, Jessie, had been. Jessie's ashes had remained in a container in Bill and Betsy's closet in their home until David died, and then both remains were intermingled together in a small coffin made by their grandson, Jeffrey, and buried at the cemetery on City Point, across the reach from the Music Box on Vinalhaven.

This spot brought back many memories for Bill. For many years, it was called Blueberry Hill, and when they were children, Jesse sent Bill and Bud with cream-colored berry boxes in hand to fill them with blueberries probably for the evening's pie. As children, the boys did not like this assignment as it was a wet one because the berries grew very close to the water's edge, and they couldn't help getting shirts, shoes, and trousers wet in their endeavor to collect the berries. Now, many years later, Bill and Betsy visit this spot whenever they go to the island, which is almost every summer. Of course, it is revered as hallowed ground by the entire Moyer family.

David's life was unusual—his younger years were beyond remarkable! In many ways, so were the lives of those unusual people who brought forth in him his amazing talent at such a tender age and created the circumstances and atmosphere for his continued growth as a first class musician and teacher. He expressed only two regrets in his life—one, that he never knew his own father very well and, second, that perchance he should have been more accepting and understanding of Bud's desire not to follow the paths to which higher education can lead. Ironically, although David himself taught at two conservatories in his life, he himself never had a formal education beyond the early elementary level. Maybe Bud was marching to the same independent drummer just as his father had marched.

David appreciated the value of friendships and lived his life as a true friend to many, sharing his beautiful language of music, the substance of his soul, and the ballast of his identity and the bond of his relationships. The poet W. B. Yeats in the last stanza of his poem, "The Stolen Child," characterizes, rather poignantly, a central thread running through David's unusual life and career.

> Away with us he's going,
> The solemn-eyed:
> He'll hear no more the lowing
> Of the calves on the warm hillside
> Or the kettle on the hob
> Sing peace into his breast,
> Or see the brown mice bob
> Round and round the oatmeal-chest.
> For he comes, the human child,
> To the waters and the wild
> With a faery hand in hand,
> From a world more full of weeping than he can understand.

David, Vinalhaven, Maine, 1980
Photo: Courtesy of Moyer Family Archives

ENDNOTES

Introduction

1   Feldman, D.H. with Goldsmith, L.T. *Nature's Gambit: Child prodigies and the development of human potential*, New York: Teachers College Press

2   Lorin Maazel, *Lorin Maazel, The official website for the Music Director of the New York Philharmonic.* http://www.maestromaazel.com./janos_starker.html

3   Winner, Ellen, *Gifted Children: Gifts and Realities.* New York: Basic Books, 1996, p. 4-5

4   Winner, Ellen, *Gifted Children: Gifts and Realities.* New York: Basic Books, 1996, p. 4-5

5   Philadelphia Government, Department of Records, City Archives, April, 2003.

6   Hucho, Christine, Female Writers, Women's Networks, and the Preservation of Culture: *The Schwenkfelder Women of Eighteenth-Century Pennsylvania in Pennsylvania History,* Vol 68, January, 2001, pp 101-130.

7   Sachs, Harvey, *Rubinstein: A Life.* New York: Grove Press, 1999, p. 24

Chapter I

8   Daniel Kolb Cassel, *A Genealogical History of the Cassel Family in America* (Norristown: Morgan R. Wills, 1896), 14.

9   Daniel Kolb Cassel, *A Genealogical History of the Cassel Family in America* (Norristown: Morgan R. Wills, 1896), 13.

10 Daniel Kolb Cassel, *A Genealogical History of the Cassel Family in America* (Norristown: Morgan R. Wills, 1896), 13.

11 William J. Whalen, "The Quakers, or Our Neighbors," *FGC Friends General Conference of the Religious Society of Friends*, General Conference of the Religious Society of Friends, http://http://www.fgcquaker.org.

12   Daniel Kolb Cassel, *A Genealogical History of the Cassel Family in America* (Norristown: Morgan R. Wills, 1896), 13.

13   Daniel Kolb Cassel, *A Genealogical History of the Cassel Family in America* (Norristown: Morgan R. Wills, 1896), 14.

14   Daniel Kolb Cassel, *A Genealogical History of the Cassel Family in America* (Norristown: Morgan R. Wills, 1896), 29.

15   Daniel Kolb Cassel, *A Genealogical History of the Cassel Family in America* (Norristown: Morgan R. Wills, 1896), 29.

16   *Some Reminiscences from Taped Family Conversations with David Moyer, unpublished manuscript*, Moyer Family Archives, Wayland: 1975, p. 1,

17   Daniel Kolb Cassel, *A Genealogical History of the Cassel Family in America* (Norristown: Morgan R. Wills, 1896), p. 29 and Tsh@harborside.com

18   *Towamencin Township*, http://http://townamencin.org/history.htm

19   *Towamencin Township*, http://www.townamencin.org/history.htm

20   *Towamencin Township*, http://www.townamencin.org/history.htm

21   Douglas Wiegner, "*Schwenkfelders: Who Are They?*" Douglas Wiegner, http://http://pages.prodigy.com/JPBC05A/schwenk1.htm.

22   Douglas Wiegner, "*Schwenkfelders: Who Are They?*" *Douglas Wiegner*, Douglas Wiegner, http://http://pages.prodigy.com/JPBC05A/schwenk1.htm.

23   Douglas Wiegner, "*Schwenkfelders: Who Are They?*" *Douglas Wiegner*, Douglas Wiegner, http://http://pages.prodigy.com/JPBC05A/schwenk1.htm.

24   Douglas Wiegner, "*Schwenkfelders: Who Are They?*" *Douglas Wiegner*, Douglas Wiegner, http://http://pages.prodigy.com/JPBC05A/schwenk1.htm.

25   Douglas Wiegner, "*Schwenkfelders: Who Are They?*" *Douglas Wiegner*, Douglas Wiegner, http://http://pages.prodigy.com/JPBC05A/schwenk1.htm.

26   Douglas Wiegner, "*Schwenkfelders: Who Are They?*" *Douglas Wiegner*, Douglas Wiegner, http://http://pages.prodigy.com/JPBC05A/schwenk1.htm.

27   Douglas Wiegner, "*Schwenkfelders: Who Are They?*" *Douglas Wiegner*, Douglas Wiegner, http://http://pages.prodigy.com/JPBC05A/schwenk1.htm.

28   Douglas Wiegner, "*Schwenkfelders: Who Are They?*" *Douglas Wiegner*, Douglas Wiegner, http://http://pages.prodigy.com/JPBC05A/schwenk1.htm.

29   *Genealogical Record of the Descendants of the Schwenkfelders, Who Arrived in Pennsylvania in 1733, 1734, 1736, 1737,* From the German of the Rev. Balthasar Heebner, and from other sources, By the Rev. Reuben Kriebel with an historical sketch by C. Heydrick. Manayunk: Josephus Yeakel, Printer, 4402 Cresson St., 1879.

30   USWEBGEN Archives Project, "Pennsylvania," *USWEBGEN Archives Project: Pennsylvania*, Roots Web, http://http://demos.iarchives.com/anc_04//search.jsp?toc=74n1exlmc73. Vol I, Series 1, p. 214

31   Linda Gudgel Finnell. Posting to Stauffer Genealogical Database, April 9, 2002, http://http://www.gentree.com/cgi-bin/igmget/n=Stauffer?ID6859

[32] Linda Gudgel Finnell. Posting to Stauffer Genealogical Database, April 9, 2002, http://http://www.gentree.com/cgi=bin/igmget/n=Stauffer?ID6859

[33] Linda Gudgel Finnell. Posting to Stauffer Genealogical Database, April 9, 2002, http://http://www.gentree.com/cgi=bin/igmget/n=Stauffer?ID6859

[34] Linda Gudgel Finnell. Posting to Stauffer Genealogical Database, April 9, 2002,http://http://www.gentree.com/cgi=bin/igmget/n=Stauffer?ID6859

[35] Rev. A. J. Fretz, *A Genealogical Record of the Descendants of Christian and Hans Meyer and Other Pioneers* (Harleysville: News Printing House, 1896), 521

[36] Rev. A. J. Fretz, *A Genealogical Record of the Descendants of Christian and Hans Meyer and Other Pioneers* (Harleysville: News Printing House, 1896), 520

[37] Rev. A. J. Fretz, *A Genealogical Record of the Descendants of Christian and Hans Meyer and Other Pioneers* (Harleysville: News Printing House, 1896), p, 520

[38] Rev. A. J. Fretz, *A Genealogical Record of the Descendants of Christian and Hans Meyer and Other Pioneers* (Harleysville: News Printing House, 1896), 520

[39] Rev. A. J. Fretz, *A Genealogical Record of the Descendants of Christian and Hans Meyer and Other Pioneers* (Harleysville: News Printing House, 1896), 521

[40] Rev. A. J. Fretz, *A Genealogical Record of the Descendants of Christian and Hans Meyer and Other Pioneers* (Harleysville: News Printing House, 1896), 521

[41] Rev. A. J. Fretz, *A Genealogical Record of the Descendants of Christian and Hans Meyer and Other Pioneers* (Harleysville: News Printing House, 1896), 521

[42] Rev. A. J. Fretz, *A Genealogical Record of the Descendants of Christian and Hans Meyer and Other Pioneers* (Harleysville: News Printing House, 1896), 521

[43] Rev. A. J. Fretz, *A Genealogical Record of the Descendants of Christian and Hans Meyer and Other Pioneers* (Harleysville: News Printing House, 1896), 521

[44] Rev. A. J. Fretz, *A Genealogical Record of the Descendants of Christian and Hans Meyer and Other Pioneers* (Harleysville: News Printing House, 1896), 521

[45] Rev. A. J. Fretz, *A Genealogical Record of the Descendants of Christian and Hans Meyer and Other Pioneers* (Harleysville: News Printing House, 1896), 521

[46] Jim Powell. *The Freeman: Ideas on Liberty,* October 1995, Vo. 45, No. 10, New York

Chapter II

[47] *Some Reminiscences from Taped Family Conversations with David Moyer, unpublished manuscript,* Moyer Family Archives, Wayland: 1975, p. 1

[48] Rev. A. J. Fretz, *A Genealogical Record of the Descendants of Christian and Hans Meyer and Other Pioneers* (Harleysville: News Printing House, 1896), 521

[49] Federal Census of the United States, 1900, Philadelphia, Pennsylvania, National Archives and Records Administration, Washington, D.C,

[50] Lawrence J. Biond, "Powelton Village," *Powelton Village, Philadelphia,* The Powelton Village Civic Association,http://www.swarthmore.edu/Humanities/langlab/powelton/pvca.html

51   Leon S. Rosenthal, Esq., *A History of Philadelphia's University City* (Philadelphia: The West Philadelphia Corporation, 1963), p. 18

52   Leon S. Rosenthal, Esq., *A History of Philadelphia's University City* (Philadelphia: The West Philadelphia Corporation, 1963), p. 18

53   Lawrence J. Biond, "Powelton Village," *Powelton Village, Philadelphia,* The Powelton Village Civic Association,http://www.swarthmore.edu/Humanities/langlab/powelton/pvca.html

54   Leon S. Rosenthal, Esq., *A History of Philadelphia's University City* (Philadelphia: The West Philadelphia Corporation, 1963), 18.

55   Leon S. Rosenthal, Esq., *A History of Philadelphia's University City* (Philadelphia: The West Philadelphia Corporation, 1963), 18.

56   Leon S. Rosenthal, Esq., *A History of Philadelphia's University City* (Philadelphia: The West Philadelphia Corporation, 1963), 18.

57   Leon S. Rosenthal, Esq., *A History of Philadelphia's University City* (Philadelphia: The West Philadelphia Corporation, 1963), 19.

58   Leon S. Rosenthal, Esq., *A History of Philadelphia's University City* (Philadelphia: The West Philadelphia Corporation, 1963), 18.U.S Census, 1890

59   Federal Census of the United States, 1890, Philadelphia, Pennsylvania, National Archives and Records Administration, Washington, D.C

60   *Some Reminiscences from Taped Family Conversations with David Moyer, unpublished manuscript,* Moyer Family Archives, Wayland: 1975, p. 2

61   Letter from Edward Reber, to David Earl Moyer, May 13, 1974, Personal Papers, David Earl Moyer, Moyer Family Archives, Wayland

Chapter III

62   *Some Reminiscences from Taped Family Conversations with David Moyer, unpublished manuscript.,* Moyer Family Archives, Wayland: 1975, p. 2

63   *Some Reminiscences from Taped Family Conversations with David Moyer, unpublished manuscript,* Moyer Family Archives, Wayland: 1975, p. 2

64   *Some Reminiscences from Taped Family Conversations with David Moyer, unpublished manuscript,* Moyer Family Archives, Wayland: 1975, p. 2

65   *Some Reminiscences from Taped Family Conversations with David Moyer, unpublished manuscript,* Moyer Family Archives, Wayland: 1975, p. 2

66   *Some Reminiscences from Taped Family Conversations with David Moyer, unpublished manuscript,* Moyer Family Archives, Wayland: 1975, p. 2

67   *Some Reminiscences from Taped Family Conversations with David Moyer, unpublished manuscript,* Moyer Family Archives, Wayland: 1975, p. 2

68   Hucho, Christine, Female Writers, Women's Networks, and the Preservation of Culture: *The Schwenkfelder Women of Eighteenth-Century Pennsylvania in Pennsylvania History,* Vol 68, January, 2001, pp 101-130.

[69] *Some Reminiscences from Taped Family Conversations with David Moyer, unpublished manuscript,* Moyer Family Archives, Wayland: 1975, p.4

[70] *Federal Census of the United States,* 1850, Southampton, Cumberland County, Pennsylvania., National Archives and Records Administration. Washington, D.C.

[71] *Federal Census of the United States,* 1850, Southampton, Cumberland County, Pennsylvania, National Archives and Records Administration, Washington, D.C.

[72] Richland Co., Ohio, "Mortality Schedules, 1860—City of Mansfield, 3rd Ward," *Census: Mortality Schedules/Death Records,*

[73] Mary Belle Linnell, "Virtue Amelia Halter Davis," Allen County Historical Museum, Lima, unpublished manuscript, c. 1900, p. 96

[74] *Federal Census of the United States,* 1860, Southampton, Cumberland County, Pennsylvania, National Archives and Records Administration, Washington, D.C

[75] *Records of the Orphans Court* 1873, Allen County Courthouse, Lima, Ohio Court Records, Allen County Courthouse, Lima, Ohio

[76] John J. McCusker, "Comparing the Purchasing Power of Money in the United States (or Colonies) from 1665-2005" Economic History Services, 2006, URL: http://www.eh.net/hmit/ppowerusd/

[77] http://college.hmco.com/history/readerscom/rcah/html/an_073400_railroads.htm

[78] *Federal Census of the United States,* Lima, Ohio, 1870 and, Recorder of Deeds, Allen County, Ohio, December 17, 1879.

[79] *Federal Census of the United States,* 1870, Lima, Ohio, National Archives and Records Administration, Washington, D.C.

[80] Lee, E.S., A theory of Migration. *Demography* 3 (1), 47-57, 1966

[81] Mary Belle Linnell, "Virtue Amelia Halter Davis,", Allen County Historical Museum, Lima, pg. 96

[82] *Federal Census of the United States,* 1870, Lima, Ohio, National Archives and Records Administration, Washington, DC

[83] *Lima Times Democrat,* November 11, 1880, Lima, Ohio

[84] *Lima Times Democrat,* November 11, 1880, Lima, Ohio

[85] *Lima Times Democrat,* November 11, 1880, Lima, Ohio

[86] *Lima Times Democrat,* November 11, 1880, Lima, Ohio

[87] *A Portrait and Biographical Record of Allen and Putnam Counties, Ohio, (Chicago: A. W. Bowen & Co., (1896) p. 298*

[88] Court of Common Pleas of Putnam County, Ohio, Putnam Common Please, Book 38, page 381, Judgement, November, 1885.

[89] Passport Number, 3512 for Marie Berlino, National Archives and Records Administration, Washington, DC

[90] Jeanne Porecca, private researcher, Lima, Ohio, email correspondence, Mary 16, 2006.

[91] Application for probate Will of the Estate of Mary Baker Halter (deceased) March 18, 1912, Probate Court, Allen County, Ohio, march 28, 1912.

[92] *Lima News*, February 7, 1900, Lima, Ohio

[93] *Federal Census of the United States, 1900*, Akron, Ohio, National Archives and Records Administration, Washington, D.C.

[94] *Some Reminiscences from Taped Family Conversations with David Moyer, unpublished manuscript*, Moyer Family Archives, Wayland: 1975, p.4

[95] *Some Reminiscences from Taped Family Conversations with David Moyer, unpublished manuscript*, Moyer Family Archives, Wayland: 1975, p. 4

Chapter IV

[96] *Some Reminiscences from Taped Family Conversations with David Moyer, unpublished manuscript*, Moyer Family Archives, Wayland: 1975, p.5

[97] Bloom Lefferts Mansion, Historic Homesteads of Kings County, Book No. 124, Charles Andrew Ditman, Brooklyn, N.Y.

[98] Historic Homesteads of Kings County, Book No. 124, Charles Andrew Ditman, Brooklyn, N.Y.

[99] *Some Reminiscences from Taped Family Conversations with David Moyer, unpublished manuscript*, Moyer Family Archives, Wayland: 1975, p. 5

[100] *Some Reminiscences from Taped Family Conversations with David Moyer, unpublished manuscript*, Moyer Family Archives, Wayland: 1975, p. 6

[101] *Some Reminiscences from Taped Family Conversations with David Moyer, unpublished manuscript*, Moyer Family Archives, Wayland: 1975, p. 5

[102] *Some Reminiscences from Taped Family Conversations with David Moyer, unpublished manuscript*, Moyer Family Archives, Wayland: 1975, p. 16

[103] *Some Reminiscences from Taped Family Conversations with David Moyer, unpublished manuscript*, Moyer Family Archives, Wayland: 1975, p. 28

[104] *Some Reminiscences from Taped Family Conversations with David Moyer, unpublished manuscript*, Moyer Family Archives, Wayland: 1975, p. 16

[105] *Some Reminiscences from Taped Family Conversations with David Moyer, unpublished manuscript*, Moyer Family Archives, Wayland: 1975, p. 28

[106] Oberlin College, Letter in file of David E. Moyer, July 19, 1935 from Paul Haggerty, TERA Supervisor of Music, State of New York, Temporary Emergency Relief Administration, Welfare and Education Office

[107] Steve Zeitlin and Marci Reaven, "On the Bowery," *Voices: The Journal of New York Folklore*, no.29 (2003): 2.http://www.ny folklore.org/pubs/voic29-3-4/dnstate.html

[108] Steve Zeitlin and Marci Reaven, "On the Bowery," *Voices: The Journal of New York Folklore*, no.29 (2003): 2.http://www.ny folklore.org/pubs/voic29-3-4/dnstate.html

[109] Mary Ellen Johnson, "A History of the Orphan Trains Era in American History," *Orphan Train Movement*, OTHSA, Inc, http://www.orphantrainriders.com/otm11.htm

[110] Mary Ellen Johnson, "A History of the Orphan Trains Era in American History," *Orphan Train Movement*, OTHSA, Inc, http://www.orphantrainriders.com/otm11.htm

[111] Mary Ellen Johnson, "A history of the Orphan Trains Era in American History," *Orpan Traiin Movement*, OTHSA, Inc, http://www.orphantrainriders.com/otm11.htm

[112] Mary Ellen Johnson, "A history of the Orphan Trains Era in American History," *Orpan Traiin Movement*, OTHSA, Inc, http://www.orphantrainriders.com/otm11.htm

[113] Paul Farrell Haggerty, U. S. Social Security Application, May 19, 1937

[114] N/A, *Laws of New York* (Albany: by the author, 1873), 1243-1245

[115] N/A, *Laws of New York* (Albany: by the author, 1873), 1243-1245

[116] N/A, *Laws of New York* (Albany: by the author, 1873), 1243-1245

[117] *Some Reminiscences from Taped Family Conversations with David Moyer, unpublished manuscript*, Moyer Family Archives, Wayland: 1975, p. 12.

[118] *Some Reminiscences from Taped Family Conversations with David Moyer, unpublished manuscript*, Moyer Family Archives, Wayland: 1975, p. 5

[119] Unidentified newspaper article, pre 1903, David Earl Moyer

[120] *Some Reminiscences from Taped Family Conversations with David Moyer, unpublished manuscript*, Moyer Family Archives, Wayland: 1975, p. 5.

[121] *Strabismus*, Alan Greene, M.D. http://www,drgreene.com/21_1194.html, pg. 1

[122] Cromie, William J., "Was Rembrandt's World Flat". *University Gazette*, April 28, 2005, Cambridge, Mass: pgs. 1-4

[123] Cromie, William J., "Was Rembrandt's World Flat". *University Gazette*, April 28, 2005, Cambridge, Mass: pgs. 1-4

[124] Cromie, William J., "Was Rembrandt's World Flat". *University Gazette*, April 28, 2005, Cambridge, Mass: pgs. 1-4

[125] Cromie, William J., "Was Rembrandt's World Flat". *University Gazette*, April 28, 2005, Cambridge, Mass: pgs. 1-4

[126] Betsy Green Moyer, interview, December, 2004.

[127] William C. Moyer, conversation, December, 2004

[128] *Historical Boys Clothing*, http://members.tripod.com/~histclo

[129] *Personal Scrapbook of David Earl Moyer*, Moyer Family Archives, Wayland

[130] *Personal Scrapbook of David Earl Moyer*, Moyer Family Archives, Wayland

[131] *Some Reminiscences from Taped Family Conversations with David Moyer, unpublished* manuscript, Moyer Family Archives, Wayland: 1975, p 8

[132] *Personal Scrapbook of David Earl Moyer*, Moyer Family Archives, Wayland

[133] Mary B. Halter, August 28, 1903, arrival in Port of New York from Port of Cuxhaven, Germany http://www.ellisisland.org/search/passRecord.asp?MID=1824213261000 196960&F

[134] Anastasia Power Moyer-Lampe, telephone interview, January, 2006

[135] *Some Reminiscences from Taped Family Conversations with David Moyer, unpublished manuscript*, Moyer Family Archives, Wayland: 1975, p.5

[136] Letter from Ferrucio Busoni to Egon Petre from America, Chicago: 29.3.1915 pg. 8

[137] Program Bills, New York: September 7, 1904, Ct.; Nov 25, 1904 Elizabeth, N.J.; December 22nd and 24th, 1904 Brooklyn, N.Y. *Personal Scrapbook of David Earl Moyer*, Moyer Family Archives, Wayland

[138] Harold C. Schonberg, *The Great Pianists from Mozart to the Present*, Second Edition, Simon & Schuster, 1987: New York, p 384

[139] Harold C. Schonberg, *The Great Pianists from Mozart to the Present*, Second Edition, Simon & Schuster, 1987:New York, p. 385

[140] Harold C. Schonberg, The Great Pianists from Mozart to the Present, Second Edition, Simon & Schuster, 1987: New York, p. 386

[141] Harold C. Schonberg, The Great Pianists from Mozart to the Present, Second Edition, Simon & Schuster, 1987: New York, p. 386

[142] Ronald D. Patkus, Musical Migrations:" A Case Study of the Teresa Carreño Papers," *Musical Migrations*, Project Muse, http://www.ala.org/ala/acri/acripubs/rbm/backisuesvol6no1/Patkus06.pdf

[143] Gail Smith, "Mothers Who Were Composers and Concert Pianists," *Creative Keyboard*, Mel Bay, http://www.melbay.com/creativekeyboard/may03 carreño/.html

[144] Gail Smith, "Mothers Who Were Composers and Concert Pianists," *Creative Keyboard*, Mel Bay, http://www.melbay.com/creativekeyboard/may03/carreño.html.

[145] Marta Milinowski, *Teresa Carreño: by the grace of God* (New Haven: Yale University Press, 1940), 395.

[146] Marta Milinowski, *Teresa Carreño: by the grace of God* (New Haven: Yale University Press, 1940), 396,7

[147] Email, Betsy Green Moyer, to Ruthann D. Moyer, April 17, 2006, David Earl Moyer, Research Archives of R. D. Moyer, n/a, Greysteel.

[148] *Some Reminiscences from Taped Family Conversations with David Moyer, unpublished manuscript,.* Moyer Family Archives, Wayland: 1975, p. 4

[149] Personal Scrapbook of David Earl Moyer, Moyer Family Archives, Wayland

[150] Program, Rubinstein Club, Reception Rehearsal, Mendelssohn Hall, Wednesday, February 24th, 1904: *Personal Scrapbook of David Earl Moyer*, Moyer Family Archives, Wayland

[151] Frederic Dean. "Boy Choristers." *St. Nicholas Magazine, Vol. XXIX, No. 6*, April, 1902, 6

[152] David E. Moyer, Original transcript taped conversation, unedited. Interview by author, January, 1975, *Some Reminiscences from Taped Family Conversations with David Moyer, unpublished manuscript.* Moyer Family Archives, Wayland: 1975, p.19

[153] Program KIA Mandolin Club, April 22, 1904: Brooklyn. *Personal Scrapbook of David Earl Moyer*, Moyer Family Archives, Wayland

[154] *The Mandolin Page*, http://www.banjolin.supanet.com

[155] *A Brief History of the Mandolin*, http://www.mandolincafe.com/archives/briefhistory.html

[156] *Announcement, Personal Scrapbook of David Earl Moyer*, Moyer Family Archives, Wayland

[157] Anastasia Power Moyer-Lampe, interview, March, 2004.

[158] *New York Herald, Brooklyn Supplement* June 26, 1904, pp. 1—*Personal Scrapbook of David Earl Moyer*, Moyer Family Archives, Wayland

[159] Brian Kovach, "Preserving an American Musical Heritage" in *Creative Keyboard Publications*, Pacific Mo., 2000

[160] J. J. Fisher, "The Girl I Loved in Sunny Tennessee" *Audio Archive*, Internet Archive, http://www.archive.org/about/about.php

[161] *New York Herald*, program notes, Chandler & Held Piano Warerooms, November 28, 1904, Elizabeth, N.J.

[162] Email, Betsy Green Moyer, to Ruthann D. Moyer, April 17, 2006, David Earl Moyer, Research Archives of R. D. Moyer, n/a, Greysteel

[163] *New York World*, program notes, Chandler & Held Piano Warerooms, November 28, 1904, Elizabeth, N.J., *Personal Scrapbook of David Earl Moyer*, Moyer Family Archives, Wayland

[164] *The North American*, Philadelphia, Friday, November 11, 1904

[165] *Washington Post*, Washington, D.C. January 9, 1905

Chapter V

[166] *Washington Post*, Washington, D. C. January 9, 1905

[167] *Washington Post*, Washington, D. C. January 9, 1905

[168] *Washington Post*, Washington, D.C. January 28, 1905, p. 12

[169] Gilder, "d'Albert, Eugene Francis Charles," *Gilder-Music Web Dictionary of composers*, Classpedia, http://www.musicweb-international.com/Classpedia/Albert.htm

[170] *D'Albert Next Friday, Washington Post*, Washington, D.C., 01/08/1905, http://www.newspaperarchive.com/Search.aspx?Search=eugened'albert

[171] Personal Scrapbook of David Earl Moyer, Moyer Family Archives, Wayland

[172] *Personal Scrapbook of David Earl Moyer*, Moyer Family Archives, Wayland January 19, 1905

[173] *Some Reminiscences from Taped Family Conversations with David Moyer*, unpublished manuscript, Moyer Family Archives, Wayland: 1975 p.5

[174] *Anderson & Co. Recital Hall*, 370 Fulton Street, Brooklyn, NY, 01/26/1905. *Personal Scrapbook of David Earl Moyer*, Moyer Family Archives, Wayland

[175] John Kenrick. *A History of The Musical Vaudeville*, 1996. pg 4

[176] *With the Men and Women of the Twice-a-Day, The New York Times.* May 6, 1906: New York, p. 3

[177] *Some Reminiscences from Taped Family Conversations with David Moyer*, unpublished manuscript, Moyer Family Archives, Wayland: 1975 p.6

[178] Concert Program, March 21, 1905, David E. Moyer, pianist, Grace Lutheran Church, Philadelphia, Pennsylvania, *Personal Scrapbook of David Earl Moyer*, Moyer Family Archives, Wayland

[179] "Railroad Surveyors," *National Railroad Museum*, National Railroad Museum, http://www.nationalmuseum.org/index/php80

[180] n/a, "Railroad Surveyors," *National Railroad Museum*, National Railroad Museum, http://www.nationalmuseum.org/index/php

[181] *The Times Democrat*, Lima, Ohio, Monday, April 24, 1905

[182] Anonymous Informant from Lima, Ohio, May 2, 2006

[183] *The Time-Democrat*, Lima, Ohio, April 24, 1905

[184] Interview with no by line available, "No Idle Talk." *The Times-Democrat*, Lima, Ohio, April 28, 1905

[185] Interview with None, "At The Congregational Church, *The Times-Democrat*, 5 May, 1905

[186] "The Berlino Children" *Lima Daily News* May 9, 1905

[187] *Some Reminiscences from Taped Family Conversations with David Moyer*, unpublished manuscript. Moyer Family Archives, Wayland: 1975, p.7

[188] Wikipedia, "History of Colorado," *History of Colorado*, http://en.wikipedia.org/wiki/History of Colorado

[189] Charles Ralph, "Opera in Old Colorado," *Opera in Old Colorado*, Opera Pronto, http://operapronto.home,comcast.net/index.html

[190] n/a, "The Social World Inside and Out" *Newspaper Archive.com* http://www.newspaperarchive.com 15465382

[191] n/a, "Louis Persinger," *Musical Times*, Musical Times, http://www.musicaltimes.co.uk/archive/0104/stern.html

[192] n/a, "Louis Persinger," *Musical Times*, Musical Times, http://www.musicaltimes.co.uk/archive/0104/stern.html

[193] n/a, "The Social World Inside and Out," *Newspaper Archive.com*, Newspaper Archive.com, http://www.newspaperarchive.com 15465382

[194] *Some Reminiscences from Taped Family Conversations with David Moyer*, unpublished manuscript. Moyer Family Archives, Wayland: 1975, p.6.

[195] "Alberto Jonas, Questia," *Questia.com*, http://htttp://www.questia.com/PM.qst?a=o&d=2602782.

[196] J. P. Schneider, *Alberto Jonas: The Beloved Spanish Pianist*, Canada, Hamilton, Ontario, December 13, 1891.

[197] "Master School of Modern Piano Playing and Virtuosity," *Find in a Library*, World Cat, http://www.worldcatlibraries.org/wcpa/top3mset/76ba9f212b359f06.html

[198] *Advertisement*, Unitarian Church, Colorado Springs, Colorado, Sept. 1 and 2, 1905

[199] John S. McCormick, "Salt Lake City," *Utah History Encyclopedia*, University of Utah, http://www.media.utah.edu/UHEs/SALTLAKECITY.html

[200] John S. McCormick, "Salt Lake City," *Utah History Encyclopedia*, University of Utah, http://www.media.utah.edu/UHEs/SALTLAKECITY.html

[201] Ronald W. Walker, "Salt Lake Theatre," *Theatre in Utah*, Utah, http://historytogo.utah.gov/utah_chapters/utah_today/saltlaketheatre.html

202 Ronald W. Walker, "Salt Lake Theatre," *Theatre in Utah*, Utah, http://historytogo. utah.gov/utah_chapters/utah_today/saltlaketheatre.html

203 Ronald W. Walker, "Salt Lake Theatre," *Theatre in Utah*, Utah, http://historytogo. utah.gov/utah_chapters/utah_today/saltlaketheatre.html

204 Ronald W. Walker, "Salt Lake Theatre," *Theatre in Utah*, Utah, http://historytogo. utah.gov/utah_chapters/utah_today/saltlaketheatre.html

205 Ronald W. Walker, "Salt Lake Theatre," *Theatre in Utah*, Utah, http://historytogo. utah.gov/utah_chapters/utah_today/saltlaketheatre.html

206 Betsy Green Moyer, former piano teacher and daughter-in-law of David E. Moyer, conversation, October, 2005

207 "Butte, Montana" *Wikipedia*, the free encyclopedia, http://en.wikipedia.oarg/wik/ Butte,_Montana.

208 "Butte, Montana," *Wikipedia*, the free encyclopedia, http://en.wikipedia.oarg/wik/ Butte,_Montana

209 *Free Concerts Daily*, Orton Bros, Butte, Montana, Oct. 10-15, 1905. *Personal Scrapbook of David Earl Moyer*, Moyer Family Archives, Wayland

210 George Everett, "When Toil Meant Trouble: Butte's Labor Heritage," *Butte America*, http://www.butteamerica.com/labor.htm.

211 J. L. Paine, Secretary, To Whom It May Concern, 21/10/1905, *Personal Scrapbook of David Earl Moyer*, Moyer Family Archives, Wayland

212 *Some Reminiscences from Taped Family Conversations with David Moyer*, unpublished manuscript Moyer Family Archives, Wayland: 1975. p.7

213 "Railroad Surveyors, "*National Railroad Museum*, http://www.nationalmuseum. org/index/php

214 Syndicate Buys Costly Parcel. *Los Angeles Times*, Los Angeles, California, August 21, 1927

215 N/a. Interview with Ethel Dolson, *Tots With Adult Brains Do Mental Acrobatics*. *Los Angeles Herald*, Los Angeles, California: February 28, 1906

216 N/a. Interview with Ethel Dolson *Tots With Adult Brains Do Mental Acrobatics*. *Los Angeles Herald*, Los Angeles, California: February 28, 1906

217 Conversation with Bill and Betsy Moyer, October, 2005, Wayland

218 Ethel Dolson. *Tots With Adult Brains Do Mental Acrobatics*. *Los Angeles Herald*, Los Angeles, California, February 28, 1906

219 Ethel Dolson. *Tots With Adult Brains Do Mental Acrobatics*. *Los Angeles Herald*, Los Angles, California. February 28, 1906

220 Encarta Dictionary, English, North America

221 Program, March 17, 1906, Synagogue, El Paso, Texas, *Personal Scrapbook of David Earl Moyer*, Moyer Family Archives, Wayland

222 Ray Burns and Steve Grande, *Train Web*. http://www.google.com/ custom?domains=trainweb.com

[223] Ray Burns and Steve Grande, *Train Web* http://www.google.com/custom?domains=trainweb.com

[224] Ray Burns and Steve Grande, *Train Web* http://www.google.com/custom?domains=trainweb.com

[225] Ray Burns and Steve Grande, *Train Web* http://www.google.com/custom?domains=trainweb.com

[226] Ray Burns and Steve Grande, *Train Web* http://www.google.com/custom?domains=trainweb.com

[227] Ray Burns and Steve Grande., *Train Web* http://www.google.com/custom?domains=trainweb.com

[228] John H. Baron, "Mozart in 19th Century New Orleans," p. 13, *Satchmo meets Amadeus,* Howard Tilton, Tulane University, New Orleans

[229] *The Evening Bulletin,* Front Page, Wednesday, April 18, 1906, Philadelphia

[230] *The Philadelphia Inquirer,* Thursday Morning, Aril 19, 1906, Philadelphia

[231] Unknown, In the World of Music, *Atlanta Constitution,* April 22, 1906

[232] Unknown, In the World of Music, *Atlanta Constitution,* April 22, 1906

[233] James Francis Cooke, *Great Pianists on Piano Playing.* Philadelphia: Theodore Presser Co., 1917; Dover Publications, Inc., 1999, 80

[234] James Francis Cooke, ed., *Great Pianists on Piano Playing* (Philadelphia: Theodore Presser, 1917), 79.

Chapter VI

[235] unknown, The Hamburg-America Line, http://www.norwayheritage.com/p_shiplist.asp?co=haam1

[236] Elam Douglas Bomberger, *The German Musical Training of American Students, 1850-1900* (Ph.D. diss., University of Maryland, 1991), 32

[237] Elam Douglas Bomberger, *The German Musical Training of American Students, 1850-1900* (Ph.D. diss., University of Maryland, 1991) p. 32.

[238] *Some Reminiscences from Taped Family Conversations with David Moyer,* unpublished manuscript. Moyer Family Archives, Wayland: 1975, p. 6,

[239] Elam Douglas Bomberger, *The German Musical Training of American Students, 1850-1900* (Ph.D. diss., University of Maryland, 1991), p, 2

[240] Elam Douglas Bomberger, *The German Musical Training of American Students, 1850-1900* (Ph.D. diss., University of Maryland, 1991), p.4

[241] *Some Reminiscences from Taped Family Conversations with David Moyer,* unpublished manuscript. Moyer Family Archives, Wayland: 1975, p. 7

[242] *Some Reminiscences from Taped Family Conversations with David Moyer,* unpublished manuscript. Moyer Family Archives, Wayland: 1975, p. 20

[243] *Some Reminiscences from Taped Family Conversations with David Moyer,* unpublished manuscript. Moyer Family Archives, Wayland: 1975, p. 9

[244] Geoff Layton, *From Bismarck to Hitler: Germany 1890-1933* (London: Sempringham, 1995), 32.

[245] *Some Reminiscences from Taped Family Conversations with David Moyer*, unpublished manuscript. Moyer Family Archives, Wayland: 1975, p. 7

[246] *Some Reminiscences from Taped Family Conversations with David Moyer*, unpublished manuscript. Moyer Family Archives, Wayland: 1975, p. 8

[247] *Some Reminiscences from Taped Family Conversations with David Moyer*, unpublished manuscript. Moyer Family Archives, Wayland: 1975, p. 18

[248] Census Records, 1906-1914, No. 19 Steigerlitzerstrasse, Berlin, Germany, Landis Archive, 2006.

[249] Elam Douglas Bomberger, *The German Musical Training of American Students, 1850-1900* (Ph.D. diss., University of Maryland, 1991)

[250] Richard Kitson, *Dwight's Journal of Music*, Retrospective Index to Music Periodicals, National Information Services Corporation, http://www.nise.com/ripm/volume_description/DJM.htm

[251] Alexander Wheelock Thayer, Musical Correspondence: *Dwight's Journal of Music* *XIV/5* (October, 1858): Boston

[252] Alexander Wheelock Thayer, Musical Correspondence: *Dwight's Journal of Music* *XIV/5* (October, 1858): Boston

[253] Alexander Wheelock Thayer, Musical Correspondence: *Dwight's Journal of Music* *XIV/5* (October, 1858): Boston

[254] Alexander Wheelock Thayer, Musical Correspondence. *Dwight's Journal of Music* *XIV/5* (October, 1858): Boston

[255] Alexander Wheelock Thayer, Musical Correspondence. *Dwight's Journal of Music* *XIV/5* (October, 1858): Boston

[256] Alexander Wheelock Thayer, Musical Correspondence. *Dwight's Journal of Music* *XIV/5* (October 1858): Boston

[257] Expenses, 1858, Alexander Wheelock Thayer, Musical Correspondence, *Dwight's Journal of Music* XIV/5 (October 1858).n/a; Calculations for 1906 and 2005, Purchasing Power of Money in the United States from 1774 to 2005, http://www.measuringworth.com/calculators/ppowerus/

[258] Elam Douglas Bomberger, *The German Musical Training of American Students, 1850-1900* (Ph.D. diss., University of Maryland, 1991), 36

[259] Elam Douglas Bomberger, *The German Musical Training of American Students, 1850-1900* (Ph.D. diss., University of Maryland, 1991), 36

[260] House of Ibach, http://www.historische-datn.de/projeckte/museum/sterne/namen.shtml

[261] Königliche Akademische Hochschule für Musik in Berlin, n/a, *Jahresbericht, über die mit der* Königlichen Akademie der Künste zu Berlin *verbunden Hochschule für Musik 1901-1918 Für deh Zeitraum Vom 1. October 1911 bis zum 30. September 1912 p.26*

262 Albert Spalding, Record Corporation of America, http://http://www.4music. net/spalding.html

263 Albert Spalding, Record Corporation of America, http://http://www.4music. net/spalding.html

264 Albert Spalding, Record Corporation of America, http://http://www.4music. net/spalding.html

265 Albert Spalding, Record Corporation of America, http://http://www.4music. net/spalding.html

266 *Some Reminiscences from Taped Family Conversations with David Moyer*, unpublished manuscript. Moyer Family Archives, Wayland: 1975, p. 10

267 Marie Sloss, "Marie Sloss Writes from Berlin," *Sunday State Journal*, October 25, 1908, http://www.newspaper archive.com.

268 Marie Sloss, "Marie Sloss Writes From Berlin," *Sunday State Journal*, October 25, 1908, http://www.newspaper archive.com

269 Alexander Wheelock Thayer, "Musical Correspondence," Dwight's Journal of Music *XIV/5* (October 1858): pg. 245.

270 *Some Reminiscences from Taped Family Conversations with David Moyer*, unpublished manuscript. Moyer Family Archives, Wayland: 1975, p. 7

271 *Some Reminiscences from Taped Family Conversations with David Moyer*, unpublished manuscript. Moyer Family Archives, Wayland: 1975, p. 8,

272 *ome Reminiscences from Taped Family Conversations with David Moyer*, unpublished manuscript. Moyer Family Archives, Wayland: 1975, p.8,

273 *Programme zum Sonnabend, Den 14. März 1908: Personal Scrapbook of David Earl Moyer*, Moyer Family Archives, Wayland

274 *Some Reminiscences from Taped Family Conversations with David Moyer*, unpublished manuscript. Moyer Family Archives, Wayland: 1975 p.8

275 Ellis Island: free Port of New York Passenger Records: arrival, November 22, 1908, Marie Berlino, age 41 and Clarence Berlino (child) age 3 http://www.ellisisland. org/search/passRecord.asp?MID=1824213261000196960&F

276 *Some Reminiscences from Taped Family Conversations with David Moyer*, unpublished manuscript. Moyer Family Archives, Wayland p.8

277 *Some Reminiscences from Taped Family Conversations with David Moyer*, unpublished manuscript. Moyer Family Archives, Wayland p.10

278 *Some Reminiscences from Taped Family Conversations with David Moyer*, unpublished manuscript. Moyer Family Archives, Wayland p.10

279 *Some Reminiscences from Taped Family Conversations with David Moyer*, unpublished manuscript. Moyer Family Archives, Wayland p.11

280 *Some Reminiscences from Taped Family Conversations with David Moyer*, unpublished manuscript. Moyer Family Archives, Wayland p.11

281 S. Swiggum and M. Kohli, *The Ships List*, http://www.theshipslist.com/ships/lines/ hamburg.html.

282 *Some Reminiscences from Taped Family Conversations with David Moyer*, unpublished manuscript. Moyer Family Archives, Wayland p.11

283 *Some Reminiscences from Taped Family Conversations with David Moyer*, unpublished manuscript. Moyer Family Archives, Wayland p.11

284 *Some Reminiscences from Taped Family Conversations with David Moyer*, unpublished manuscript. Moyer Family Archives, Wayland p.11

285 *Some Reminiscences from Taped Family Conversations with David Moyer*, unpublished manuscript. Moyer Family Archives, Wayland p.12

286 *Wikipedia*, unknown ed., s.v. "Kaliningrad"

287 *Some Reminiscences from Taped Family Conversations with David Moyer*, unpublished manuscript. Moyer Family Archives, Wayland p.11

288 Girard College Invitation, *Personal Scrapbook of David Earl Moyer*, Moyer Family Archives, Wayland

289 Girard College, Wikipedia, the Free Encyclopaedia, *http://en.wikipedia.org/wiki/Girard*

290 *Some Reminiscences from Taped Family Conversations with David Moyer*, unpublished manuscript. Moyer Family Archives, Wayland: 1975 p.2

291 Genealogical Record of the Schwenkfelder Families, pg 267

292 *Lima Daily News*, Lima, Ohio, October 7, 1910, death announcement, John D. Halter

293 Jeanne Porreca, email, dated March 16, 2006

294 *Some Reminiscences from Taped Family Conversations with David Moyer*, unpublished manuscript. Moyer Family Archives, Wayland: 1975 p.9

295 *Leipsiger Zeitung*, Leipzig, DE. January 14, 1911, *Personal Scrapbook of David Earl Moyer*, Moyer Family Archives, Wayland

296 Press reviews, David Moyer Berlino, 1911, *Personal Scrapbook of David Earl Moyer*, Moyer Family Archives, Wayland

297 *Some Reminiscences from Taped Family Conversations with David Moyer*, unpublished manuscript. Moyer Family Archives, Wayland: 1975 p.9

298 *Some Reminiscences from Taped Family Conversations with David Moyer*, unpublished manuscript. Moyer Family Archives, Wayland: 1975 p.10

299 *Some Reminiscences from Taped Family Conversations with David Moyer*, unpublished manuscript. Moyer Family Archives, Wayland: 1975 p.10

300 William Weber. From the Self-Managing Musician to the Independent Concert Agent in *The Musician As Entrepreneur, 1700-1914*. Bloomington: 2004, p 105

301 William Weber. From the Self-Managing Musician to the Independent Concert Agent in *The Musician As Entrepreneur, 1700-1914*. Bloomington: 2004, p 122

302 William Weber. From the Self-Managing Musician to the Independent Concert Agent in *The Musician As Entrepreneur, 1700-1914*. Bloomington: 2004, p 122

303 William Weber. From the Self-Managing Musician to the Independent Concert Agent in The Musician As Entrepreneur, 1700-1914. Bloomington: 2004, p 124

304 Murray Mclachlan Concert Pianist, Article 10, http://www.murraymclachlan.com/articles/ignace.htm

Chapter VII

305 Siegfried Borris, "Hochschule Für Musik," in *Berlin Gestalt and Geist*, Eine Sachbuchreihe Herausegegeben von Irmgard Wirth, 1963-1965:Berlin

306 Elam Douglas Bomberger, *The German Musical Training of American Students, 1850-1900* (Ph.D. diss., University of Maryland, 1991)

307 Hugo Riemann, Unsere Konservatorien, in *Präludien und Stuidien* I. Leipzig, 1895; Hildesheim: Georg Olms, 1968, 22-23, translation by Elam Douglas Bomberger.

308 Elam Douglas Bomberger, *The German Musical Training of American Students, 1850-1900* (Ph.D. Diss., University of Maryland, 1991), p 2

309 Elam Douglas Bomberger, *The German Musical Training of American Students, 1850-1900* (Ph.D. Diss., University of Maryland, 1991), p 10

310 Hugo Riemann, "Unsere Konservatorien," in *Präludien und Stuidien I*. Leipzig, 1895; Hildesheim: Georg Olms, 1968, 29, translation by Elam Douglas Bomberger

311 Winner, Ellen, "*Uncommon Talents: Gifted Children, Prodigies and Savants*," Scientific American, Inc., 1998

312 Elam Douglas Bomberger, *The German Musical Training of American Students, 1850-1900* (Ph.D., Diss., University of Maryland, 1991), p 11

313 Harold T. Betteridge, Cassell's German Dictionary: German-English, English-German, 2006: Boston

314 Harold T. Betteridge, Cassell's German Dictionary: German-English, English-German, 2006: Boston

315 *Some Reminiscences from Taped Family Conversations with David Moyer*, unpublished manuscript. Moyer Family Archives, Wayland: 1975, p.20

316 *Engelbert Humperdinck*, DSO Kids, Dallas Symphony Orchestra, http://www.doskids.com/2001/dso.asp?PageID=531

317 *Some Reminiscences from Taped Family Conversations with David Moyer*, unpublished manuscript Moyer Family Archives, Wayland: 1975 p.20

318 *Some Reminiscences from Taped Family Conversations with David Moyer*, Unpublished manuscript, Moyer Family Archives, Wayland: 1975,p.20

319 *Jahresbericht* (Charlottenburg: Königliche Akademische Hochschule Für Musik in Berlin, [1912]), 4

320 Musical Biographies, *Music Encyclopedia, Everything about the history of music*, Tribal Smile, http://www.tribalsmile.com/music/article_141_.shtml

321 Hugh Allen, Granville Bantock, Edward J. Dent, *A Dictionary of Modern Music and Musicians* (Hull: J. M. Dent & sons, Ltd., 1924),

322 n/a, "Errno Dohnanyi," *Wikipedia, the free encyclopedia*, Wilipedia, http://en.wikipedia.org/wiki/Ern%C5%91_Dohn%C3%A1nyi.

323 *Some Reminiscences from Taped Family Conversations with David Moyer*, unpublished manuscript. Moyer Family Archives, Wayland: 1975, p.19

[324] *Some Reminiscences from Taped Family Conversations with David Moyer*, unpublished manuscript, Moyer Family Archives, Wayland: 1975,p.19

[325] *Some Reminiscences from Taped Family Conversations with David Moyer*, unpublished manuscript, Moyer Family Archives, Wayland: 1975, p.19

[326] *Some Reminiscences from Taped Family Conversations with David Moyer* Unpublished manuscript, Moyer Family Archives, Wayland: 1975, p.19

[327] Lillian Tan, Franco-American Virtuosa: Aline van Barentzen," *Clavier*, Feb. 1981, 29-33

[328] *Some Reminiscences from Taped Family Conversations with David Moyer* Unpublished manuscript, Moyer Family Archives, Wayland: 1975, p.19

[329] Rose Eide-Altman, Aline van Barentzen, *Women at the Piano*, unknown, http://www.pianowomen.com/Barentzen.html

[330] *Some Reminiscences from Taped Family Conversations with David Moyer*, unpublished manuscript. Moyer Family Archives, Wayland: 1975, p.19

[331] *Some Reminiscences from Taped Family Conversations with David Moyer*, unpublished manuscript. Moyer Family Archives, Wayland: 1975, p.19

[332] *Some Reminiscences from Taped Family Conversations with David Moyer*, unpublished manuscript. Moyer Family Archives, Wayland: 1975, p.19

[333] "Ferruccio Busoni," *Wikipedia*, Wikipedia, http://en.wikipedia.org/wiki/Ferruccio_Busoni.

[334] K. Robert Schwarz, Busoni; The Contradictions Persist, *The New York Times*, http://query.nytimes.com/gst/fullpage.html?res=9F00E6D7173BF932A3575AC OA963848260

[335] George Walker, interview, 2005

[336] *Some Reminiscences from Taped Family Conversations with David Moyer*, unpublished manuscript. Moyer Family Archives, Wayland: 1975, p.13

[337] *Some Reminiscences from Taped Family Conversations with David Moyer*, unpublished manuscript. Moyer Family Archives, Wayland: 1975, p.13

[338] *Some Reminiscences from Taped Family Conversations with David Moyer*, unpublished manuscript. Moyer Family Archives, Wayland: 1975, p.13

[339] Michael Duffy, The Causes of World War One *First World War: The war to end all wars*, Michael Duffy, http://www.firstworldwar.com/origins/causes.htm.

[340] *Some Reminiscences from Taped Family Conversations with David Moyer*, unpublished manuscript, Moyer Family Archives, Wayland: 1975, p.14

[341] NationalArchives, *HooverOnline*, http://www.ecommcode.com/hoover/hooveronline/hoover_bio/wwi.htm

Chapter VIII

[342] Marriage Records, City of Philadelphia, Feb. 1912, Vincent Cassel Moyer and Ellcora Aldred.

[343] *Some Reminiscences from Taped Family Conversations with David Moyer*, unpublished manuscript. Moyer Family Archives, Wayland: 1975, p.14

[344] *Some Reminiscences from Taped Family Conversations with David Moyer*, unpublished manuscript. Moyer Family Archives, Wayland: 1975, p.14

[345] *Some Reminiscences from Taped Family Conversations with David Moyer*, unpublished manuscript. Moyer Family Archives, Wayland: 1975, p.14

[346] J. Fenner Douglas, correspondence, March 15, 2007.

[347] J. Fenner Douglas, correspondence, March 15, 2007.

Chapter IX

[348] N/A, "The History of Bucknell," *Bucknell University*, Bucknell University, http://www.bucknell.edu/x1177.xml

[349] N/A, "The History of Bucknell," *Bucknell University*, Bucknell University, http://www.bucknell.edu/x1177.xml

[350] Mary Ann Williard, To Ruthann D. Moyer, 01/14/2005, Bucknell University Catalogue, Bucknell University, College of Music, Lewisburg, PA

Chapter X

[351] William Cassel Moyer, to Ruthann D. Moyer, 2/13/2005

[352] Betsy Green-Moyer, conversation, October, 2005

[353] N/A, "Expo Camera Watch," *Scott's Photographica Collection*, Scott, http://www.vintagephoto.tv/expowatch.shtml.

[354] N/A, "Expo Camera Watch," *Scott's Photographica Collection*, Scott, http://www.vintagephoto.tv/expowatch.shtml

[355] *WWI Daily Diary*, DEM, August 8, 1918, Moyer Family Archives, Wayland

[356] *WWI Daily Diary*, DEM, August 18, 1918, Moyer Family Archives, Wayland

[357] *WWI Daily Diary, DEM*, September 2, 1918, Moyer Family Archives, Wayland

[358] *WWI Daily Diary*, DEM, September 13, 1918, Moyer Family Archives, Wayland

[359] *WWI Daily Diary*, DEM, September 16, 1918, Moyer Family Archives, Wayland

[360] *War Pigeon*s, http://en.wikipdeia.org/wiki/War_pigeon

[361] Conversations with Betsy Green Moyer, August, 2007

[362] *WWI Daily Diary*, DEM, September 24, 1918, Moyer Family Archives, Wayland

[363] *WWI Daily Diary*, DEM, September 30, 1918, Moyer Family Archives, Wayland

[364] *WI Daily Diary*, DEM, October 30, 1918, Moyer Family Archives, Wayland

[365] *WWI Daily Diary*, DEM, November 3, 1918, Moyer Family Archives, Wayland

[366] *WWI Daily Diary*, DEM, November 3, 1918, Moyer Family Archives, Wayland

[367] *WWI Daily Diary*, DEM, November 3, 1918, Moyer Family Archives, Wayland

[368] *WWI Daily Diary*, DEM, November 8, 1918, Moyer Family Archives, Wayland

[369] WWI Daily Diary, DEM, November 8, 1918, Moyer Family Archives, Wayland

[370] *WWI Daily Diary, DEM*, December 20, 1918, Moyer Family Archives, Wayland

[371] *WWI Daily Diary*, DEM, December 22, 1918, Moyer Family Archives, Wayland

[372] *WWI Daily Diary*, DEM, December 25, 1918, Moyer Family Archives, Wayland

[373] *WWI Daily Diary*, DEM, March 8, 1919, Moyer Family Archives, Wayland

[374] *WWI Daily Diary*, DEM, March 12,-June 13, 1919, Moyer Family Archives, Wayland

[375] *WWI Daily Diary*, DEM, March 12,-June 13, 1919, Moyer Family Archives, Wayland

[376] *WWI Daily Diary*, DEM, March 12,-June 13, 1919, Moyer Family Archives, Wayland

[377] *WWI Daily Diary*, DEM, March 12,-June 13, 1919, Moyer Family Archives, Wayland

[378] *WWI Daily Diary*, DEM, March 12,-June 13, 1919, Moyer Family Archives, Wayland

[379] *WWI Daily Diary*, DEM, June 20, 1919, Moyer Family Archives, Wayland

Chapter XI

[380] Passport of Madame Marie Berlino, U.S. National Archives and Records Administration, Washington, DC

[381] American Family Immigration Center, ed., *American Family Immigration Center* (Ellis Island, New York; New York: Statue of Liberty-Ellis Island Foundation, Inc., 2001), text-fiche, p. 58, 11.

[382] Hugh R. Wilson, 2nd Secretary of Embassy, Berlin, Germany, to Robert Haggerty, July 5, 1916, Passport, National Archives of the United States of America, n/a, Berlin, Germany.

[383] Hugh R. Wilson, 2nd Secretary of Embassy, Berlin, Germany, to Arthur Haggerty, July 5, 1916, Passport, National Archives of the United States of America, n/a, Berlin, Germany.

[384] Statement of Appeal, Philadelphia, Pa., September 13, 1916, National Archives of the United States of America, College Park, Maryland

[385] United States Supreme Court "Zemel v Rusk, 381 U.S. 1 (1965)," *Find Law*, Find Law, http://case law.lp.findlaw.com/cgi-bin/getcase.pl?court=US&vol381&invol=1

[386] *Republican-Gazette*, Lima, Ohio, April 1, 1917

[387] Interview, Margaret Fry, January 17, 2006

[388] *Lima News*, Lima, Ohio, Mary 17, 1937, Death Notice for Ellen Halter

[389] *Lima News*, Lima, Ohio, May 18, 1937, obituary, Ellen Halter

[390] hospital records, Arthur Haggerty, New York

Chapter XII

[391] *Some Reminiscences from Taped Family Conversations with David Moyer*, unpublished manuscript. Moyer Family Archives, Wayland: 1975, p.22

[392] Louise Benner, "A New Woman Emerges," *North Carolina Museum of History*, North Carolina Department of Resources, http://www.ncmuseumofhistory. org/collateral/articles/s04/.newwoman.emerges.pdf.

---

393 *Some Reminiscences from Taped Family Conversations with David Moyer*, unpublished manuscript. Moyer Family Archives, Wayland: 1975, 23

394 *Lewisburg Journal*. Lewisburg, Pennsylvania, April 15, 1921. Arts and Entertainment

395 Adelina Patti and Craig-y-Nos Castle, http://www.opera-singer.co.uk, pg 1

396 *Some Reminiscences from Taped Family Conversations with David Moyer*, unpublished manuscript. Moyer Family Archives, Wayland: 1975, p.21

Chapter XIII

397 Oberlin Review, Oberlin, Ohio Aug. 16, 1925.

398 Oberlin Review, Oberlin, Ohio Friday, October 29, 1926.

399 Answers.com, http://www.answers.com/topic/oberlin-college?cat=travel, pg 1

400 G. Frederick Wright, *Charles Grandison Finney*, http://truthinheart.com/EarlyOberlincd/cd/Finney/Briograph/finneybi.htm., pg 60

401 Richard D. Skyrm, *Oberlin Conservatory: A Century of Musical Growth and Influence*, Doctoral dissertation, January 1962, USC

402 G. Frederick Wright, *Charles Grandison Finney*, http://truthinheart.com/EarlyOberlincd/cd/Finney/Briograph/finneybi.htm., pg 61

403 Answers.com, http://www.answers.com/topic/oberlin-college?cat=travel, pg 1

404 1867-1967: Con Marks 100th Year, The Oberlin Review, Oberlin, Ohio, May 12, 1967

405 Fairchild, James H. *Oberlin: The Colony and the College.* Oberlin: E.J. Goodrich, 1883, pg. 196

406 *Bulletins of Oberlin Conservatory of Music*, Oberlin, Ohio 1865-66, pg. 51

407 *Teaching Registers*, David E. Moyer, 1925-1960, Oberlin Conservatory of Music, Moyer Family Archives

408 Richard D. Skyrm, *Oberlin Conservatory: A Century of Musical Growth and Influence.* Doctoral dissertation, January, 1962, USC, pg.78

409 Richard D. Skyrm, *Oberlin Conservatory: A Century of Musical Growth and Influence*, Doctoral dissertation, January, 1962, USC, pg.79

410 Richard D. Skyrm., *Oberlin Conservatory: A Century of Musical Growth and Influence*, Doctoral dissertation, January, 1962, USC, pg.157-160

411 Richard D. Skyrm. *Oberlin Conservatory: A Century of Musical Growth and Influence*, Doctoral dissertation, January, 1962, USC, pg. 188-189

412 Teaching Registers, David E. Moyer, 1925-1960. Moyer Family Archives, Wayland

413 *Delightful Piano Recital on Tuesday*, W.T. Upton, Oberlin Review, Sept. 1925, Oberlin, Ohio

414 *The Chronicle-Telegram*, Oberlin, Ohio, December 19, 1928

415 *Chronicle-Telegram*, Oberlin, Ohio, 1928-1961

416 *Chronicle-Telegram*, Oberlin, Ohio, June 23, 1931

[417] William C. Moyer, March, 2008

[418] Conversation with Bill and Betsy Moyer, December, 2007

[419] Richard D. Skyrm. *Oberlin Conservatory: A Century of Musical Growth and Influence*, Doctoral dissertation, January, 1962, USC, pg 27

[420] William C. Moyer, April, 2008.

[421] Margaret (Maggie) Fry is a fictious name for a real informant who wishes to remain anonymous.

[422] Margaret Fry Telephone interview, January 18, 2006.

[423] Tele Margaret Fry Telephone interview, January 18, 2006.

[424] Margaret Fry Telephone interview, January 18, 2006.

[425] *Paul's Case* by Willa Cather. Kessinger Publishing, 2005: Whitefish

[426] *Paul's Case* by Willa Cather. Kessinger Publishing, 2005: Whitefish

[427] Conversation with William Cassel Moyer, January, 2005

[428] Letter from Margaret Fry to William C. Moyer, June 2, 1988.

Chapter XIV

[429] Conversation with Bill and Betsy Moyer, August, 2007, Vinalhaven, Maine

[430] *The Voyage of Martin Pring* 1603 http://www.americanjourneys.org/aj-040

[431] *A Brief Historical Sketch of the Town Of Vinalhaven*, Vinalhaven Historical Society, 1900, Rockland, pg. 6

[432] *A brief history of Vinalhaven* http://www.midcoast.com/~vhhissoc/vhistory.htm

[433] Merriam-Webster Atlas Online, *State of Maine, 2001*, New York Times On the Web

[434] *A Brief Historical Sketch of the Town Of Vinalhaven*, Vinalhaven Historical Society, 1900, Rockland, pg. 8

[435] *A Brief* Historical Sketch of the Town Of Vinalhaven, Vinalhaven Historical Society, 1900, Rockland, pg. 59

[436] *A Brief Historical Sketch of the Town Of Vinalhaven*, Vinalhaven Historical Society, 1900, Rockland, pgs 14-34

[437] *Tombstones and Paving Blocks* by Roger L. Grindle, Courier-Gazette. Inc/ Rockland, Maine, 1979, pp 37-39

[438] *Joseph Robinson Bodwell*. New England Magazine, Vol 5, 1886.

[439] *Joseph Robinson Bodwell*. New England Magazine, Vol 5, 1886.

[440] *Maritime Communities: Nineteenth Century Coastal Maine*. http://www.penobscotbayhistory.org/section/show.page/35.

[441] *A brief history of Vinalhaven*, http://www.midcoast.com/~vhhissoc/vhistory.htm

[442] *Bodwell: King of the Granite Ring, 1852-1922*. Aaron A. Dumont, 2004, unpublished manuscript

[443] *Tombstones and Paving Blocks* by Roger L. Grindle, *Courier-Gazette Inc/* Rockland, Maine, 1979, pp 101-110

[444] *Granite by the Sea*, video presentation, Vinalhaven Historical Society. 2002: http://www.midcoast.com/~vhhissoc

[445] Homes of Ohio, http://www.oberlinheritage.org/inventory/

[446] *A Brief Historical Sketch of the Town of Vinalhaven*, Rockland, Free Press publication, 1889, p. 83

[447] *A Brief Historical Sketch of the Town of Vinalhaven*, Rockland, Free Press publication, 1889, p. 30-31

[448] Gayna Uransky, Written memories of Vinalhaven, unpublished letter. April 14, 2007

[449] Conversation with Bill and Betsy Moyer, August, 2007, Vinalhaven, Maine

[450] Conversations with Bill and Betsy Moyer, August, 2006, Vinalhaven, Maine

[451] Gayna Uransky, Written memories of Vinalhaven, unpublished letter, April 14, 2006

Chapter XV

[452] Kevin Harris. Quotes by Einstein. 1995 http://www.rescomp.stanford.edu/~cheshire/EinsteinQuotes.html

[453] Perkins, Holly, Ellistine. *Biographies of Black Composers and Songwriters; A Supplementary Textbook*. Iowa: Wm C. Brown Publishers, 1990.

[454] George Walker. Telephone Interview, December 12, 2006.

[455] George Walker. Telephone Interview, December 12, 2006.

[456] Tamima Friedman. *Looking Past the Pulitzer*, Oberlin Alumni Magazine, summer, 2002, Vol 98, No. 1

[457] Rob Nagel. Natalie Hinderas, *Biography*, in *Index of Musician Biographies*. p.1 http://www.musicaianguide.com/biographies/1608001131/Natalie-Hinderas.html

[458] Rob Nagel. Natalie Hinderas, Biography, in *Index of Musician Biographies*. p.2 http://www.musicaianguide.com/biographies/1608001131/Natalie-Hinderas.html

[459] Natalie Henderson Hinderas Interview, *New York Times*, November 14, 1954. New York

[460] *New York Times*, November 10, 1972. New York

[461] Judy Loskamp Moyer Shreiner, telephone interview, April 5, 2007

[462] Joyce Arnold, Written email interview response, March 23, 2006.

[463] Joyce Arnold, Written email interview response, March 23, 2006.

[464] William Cundiff, Written letter response, October 15, 2007.

[465] William Cundiff, Written letter response, October 15, 2007.

[466] Henry Janiec, Written letter response, March 12, 2006.

[467] Henry Janiec, Written letter response, March 12, 2006.

[468] Henry Janiec, Written letter response, March 12, 2006.

[469] Henry Janiec, Written letter response, March 12, 2006.

[470] Henry Janiec, Written letter response, March 12, 2006.

Chapter XVI

[471] *European Tour Diary*, David and Jessie Moyer, August 31, 1960-Dec. 1960, entry, September 1, 1960, Moyer Family Archives, Wayland

[472] Letter from Gayna Uransky, April 14, 2007, p.3

[473] Milton Greenberg, *The G.I. Bill: The Law That Changed America (New York: Lickle Publishing, 1997*

[474] Letter from Gayna Uransky, April 14, 2007, p.3

[475] Letter from Gayna Uransky, April 14, 2007, p. 5

[476] Letter from Gayna Uransky, April 14, 2007, p. 4

[477] *European Tour Diary*, David and Jessie Moyer, August 31, 1960-Dec., 1960, entry, September 18, 1960, Moyer Family Archives, Wayland

[478] *European Tour Diary*, David and Jessie Moyer, August 31, 1960-Dec., 1960, entry, October 8, 1960, Moyer Family Archives, Wayland

[479] *European Tour Diary*, David and Jessie Moyer, August 31, 1960-Dec., 1960, entry, October 27, 1960, Moyer Family Archives, Wayland

[480] *European Tour Diary*, David and Jessie Moyer, August 31, 1960-Dec., 1960, entry, October 28, 1960, Moyer Family Archives, Wayland

[481] Positano, Hotel, Travel and Tourist Guide http://www.italyheaven.co.uk/positano.html

[481] Positano, Hotel, Travel and Tourist Guide http://www.italyheaven.co.uk/positano.html

[483] *European Tour* Diary, David and Jessie Moyer, August 31, 1960-Dec., 1960, entry, November 1, 1960, Moyer Family Archives, Wayland

[484] *European Tour Diary*, David and Jessie Moyer, August 31, 1960-Dec., 1960, entry, November 19, 1960, Moyer Family Archives, Wayland

[485] *European Tour Diary*, David and Jessie Moyer, August 31, 1960-Dec., 1960, entry, November 24, 1960, Moyer Family Archives, Wayland

[486] *European Tour Diary*, David and Jessie Moyer, August 31, 1960-Dec., 1960, entry, December 1, 1960, Moyer Family Archives, Wayland

[487] *European* Tour Diary, David and Jessie Moyer, August 31, 1960-Dec., 1960, entry, December 3, 1960, Moyer Family Archives, Wayland

[488] *European Tour Diary*, David and Jessie Moyer, August 31, 1960-Dec., 1960, entry, December 5, 1960, Moyer Family Archives, Wayland

[489] *European Tour Diary*, David and Jessie Moyer, August 31, 1960-Dec., 1960, entry, December 11, 1960, Moyer Family Archives, Wayland

Chapter XVII

[490] Letter from Jessie Moyer to William C. Moyer, January 6, 1961,

[491] Letter from Jessie Moyer to William C. Moyer, January 6, 1961,

[492] Letter from Gayna Uransky, April 14, 2007, p.1

[493] Letter, Jessie C. Moyer to William C. Moyer, Easter Sunday, April 16, 1961.

[494] Letter, Jessie C. Moyer to William C. Moyer, Easter Sunday, April 8, 1961

[495] Letter, Jessie C. Moyer to William C. Moyer, Easter Sunday, April 8, 1961

[496] Letter, Jessie C. Moyer to William C. Moyer, Easter Sunday, April 8, 1961

[497] Letter, Jessie C. Moyer to William C. Moyer, Easter Sunday, July 23, 1961

[498] Letter from Gayna Uransky to Ruthann Moyer, April 14, 2007, p.6

[499] Letter from Gayna Uransky to Ruthann Moyer April 14, 2007, p.6

[500] Letter, Jessie C. Moyer to William C. Moyer, Easter Sunday, February 26, 1962

[501] Letter, Jessie C. Moyer to William C. Moyer, Easter Sunday, April 15, 1962

[502] Jessie C. Moyer to William C. Moyer, Easter Sunday, March 15, 1962

[503] Jessie C. Moyer to William C. Moyer, Easter Sunday, June 10, 1962

[504] Letter from Gayna Uransky to Ruthann Moyer April 14, 2007, p.7

[505] William Cassel Moyer, to Ruthann D. Moyer, 2/13/2005, Moyer, n/a, n/a, Derry

[506] Letter from Sonia Uransky to Bud Moyer, January 10, 1963

[507] Letter from Sonia Uransky to Bud Moyer, January 10, 1963

[508] Letter from Gayna Uransky to Ruthann Moyer April 14, 2007, p.8

[509] Letter from Gayna Uransky to Ruthann Moyer April 14, 2007, p.8

[510] *Some Reminiscences from Taped Family Conversations with David Moyer*, unpublished manuscript. Moyer Family Archives, Wayland: 1975, p.2

[511] Letter from David Moyer to Trudy Paddock, Thanksgiving, 1976

[512] Responses to written questions from William C. Moyer to Trudy Paddock, August 29, 2005, Vinalhaven

[513] Responses to written questions from William C. Moyer to Trudy Paddock, August 29, 2005, Vinalhaven

[514] Interview with Bertha L. Winslow, October 24, 2005, Vinalhaven, Maine.

[515] Conversation with W. Frederick Moyer, August 13, 2007, Vinalhaven, Maine

[516] Betsy G. Moyer to Ruthann Moyer, December, 1007

[517] William C. Moyer. Email to Ruthann Moyer, February 13, 2005.

[518] Letter for Friends of Dave Moyer, May 8 1986, written by Betsy G. Moyer, Wayland, Mass.

BIBLIOGRAPHY

Bean, Theodore W., *History of Montgomery County, Pennsylvania, Illustrated.* Philadelphia: Everts & Peck, 1884

Bomberger, Elam Douglas, *The German Musical Training of American Students, 1850-1900* (unpublished doctoral dissertation, University of Maryland 1991)

Cassel, Daniel Kolb, *A Genealogical History of the Cassel Family in America,* 1896 (reprinted by Selby Publications, Kokomo, Indiana, 1989)

Conroy, Frank, *Body and Soul, a Novel.* New York: Dell Publishing, 1993

Cooke, James Francis, *Great Pianists on Piano Playing.* Mineola, New York: Dover Publications, 1999

Duchen, Jessica, *Erich Wolfgang Korngold.* London: Phaidon Press, 1996

Dumont, Aaron A. *Bodwell: King of the Granite Ring,* 1852-1922, 2004, (unpublished manuscript)

Edwards, Albert, *Cassel Genealogical History: An Every-Name Index.* Lancaster Mennonite Historical Society, 1993

Feldman, David Henry, *Nature's Gambit, Child Prodigies and the Development of Human Potential.* New York: Basic Books, 1986

Frevert, Ute, *A Nation in Barracks: Modern Germany, Military Conscription and Civil Society,* (tr.) Boreham, A and Brüchenhaus, Oxford: Berg, 2004

Haroutounian, Joanne, *Kindling the Spark: Recognizing and Developing Musical Talent*. Oxford University Press, 2002

Humphrey, George Norwood, *Becoming A Musician*. Philadelphia: Xlibris Corporation, 2007

Johnson, Doyle Paul, *Sociological Theory*. New York: John Wiley and Sons, 1981

Kenneson, Claude, *Musical Prodigies: Perilous Journeys, Remarkable Lives*. Portland, Oregon: Amadeus Press, 1998

Kriebel, Rev. Reuben, *Genealogical Record of the Descendants of the Schwenkfelders 1733-1737, from the German of the Rev. Balthasar Heebner*. Manayunk, PA: Joseph Yeakel, Printer, 1879

Milinowski, Marta, *Teresa Carreño*. New Haven: Yale University Press, 1940

Moyer, David Earl, *World War I Diary*, (unpublished diary, Moyer Archives)

Moyer, Jessie, *European Tour Diary, Aug. 31, 1960-Dec. 31, 1960*, (unpublished manuscript, Moyer Archives)

Moyers, The, Wayland, *Some Reminiscences from Taped Family Conversations with David Moyer*, January, 1975, Prepared for the Occasion of his 80th Birthday (unpublished manuscript from Moyer Archives)

Nathans, Eli, *The Politics of Citizenship in Germany: Ethnicity, Utility and Nationalism*. Oxford, Berg, 2004

Osborne, William, *Music in Ohio*. Kent State University Press, 2004

Reiss, Marcia, *Brooklyn Then and Now*. San Diego: Thunder Bay Press, 2002

Rubenstein, Arthur, *My Young Years*. New York: Alfred A. Knopf, 1973

Sachs, Harvey, *Rubenstein: A Life*. New York: Grove Press, 1995

Sadie, Stanley (Gen. Ed.) *The Billboard Encyclopedia of Classical Music*. New York: Billboard Books, 2004

Skyrm, Richard Dean, *Oberlin Conservatory: A Century of Musical Growth and Influences*, (Unpublished Ph.D. dissertation in Music Art, University of Southern California, Jan., 1962

Seashore, Carl E., *Psychology of Music*. New York: Dover Publications, 1967 (reprint of original, McGraw-Hill Book Co., 1938)

Weber, William (Ed.) *The Musician as Entrepreneur, 1700-1914*. University of Indiana Press, 2004

Wright, G. Frederick, *Charles Grandison Finney*. *http://truthinheart.com/* earlyoberlin Cd/cd/Finney/Biography/finneylib.htm

Winner, Ellen, *Gifted Children: Myths and Realities*. New York: Basic Books, Perseus Book Groups, 1996

Younger William Lee, *Old Brooklyn in Early Photographs, 1865-1929*. New York: Dover Publications, 1978

Articles and Pamphlets

Aurand, A. Monroe, "Those Odd Folk Called 'Amish,'" *Little Known Facts About the Amish and Mennonites*, 1938

Bloom, B., "The Role of Gifts and Markers in the Development of Talent," *Council of Exceptional Children*, Vol. 48, No. 6

Borris, Siegfried, "The Virtuoso High School of the Joachim Era," Academy of Music Publishing House, Berlin

Burns, Deborah B., Jackson, Anita, and Sturm, Arrau, "Unsung Heroines: Contributions of Selected Early Twentieth-Century Women to American Piano Pedagogy," *American Music Teacher*, Dec., 2002

Chelminski, Rudolf, "Teenage Superstar of the Piano," *Reader's Digest*, Feb., 1986, pp. 75-78

Chertok, Paula, Reviewer of, "Heifetz as I knew Him," by Ayke Agus, http.//www.soundpostline.com/archivespring2001

Curtis, A.K., Ph.D., (Ed.) "Casper Schwenckfeld Von Ossig, 1489-1561, Confessor of the Glory of Christ," *Christian History*, Vol. I, No. I, issue 21, 1989

De Pillis, Mario S., "Trends in American Social History and the Possibilities of Behavioral Approaches," *Journal of Social History*, Vol 1, No. 1 (Autumn, 1967) pp. 37-60

Ericsson, K. Anders and Charness, Neil, *Expert Performance: Its Structure and Acquisition*, Departments of Psychology, Florida State University and University of Waterloo

"Expo Watch Camera Company," *Scotts PhOotographica Collection, http://www. vintagephoto.tv/expowatch.shtml*

Feldman, D., "Child Prodigies: A Distinctive Form of Giftedness," *Gifted Child Quarterly*, Fall, 1993, Vo. 37, No. 4, pp. 188-193

Freeman, Joan, "Children's Talent in Fine-Art and Music," *Roeper Review*, 22, pp 98-101

Gauss, C., "Kaiser Wilhelm II: A Place in the Sun," *The German Kaiser as Shown in His Public Utterances*", 1915, pp. 181-183

Giftedness and the Gifted: What's It About,"? *Eric Clearinghouse on Handicapped and Gifted Children*, Reston: VA., Eric Identifier ED321481, 1990

Grugh, George, "The Vintage Catalogue," *Frets Magazine*, March, 1983

"Guess What My Li'l Chopin Played Today," *Smithsonian Magazine*, Oct., 1996

Hamburg-American Packet Company: Hamburg-American Line, http://www. thshipslist.com/ships/lines/hamburg/.html

Hanlon, Michael E. (website ed.) "The Mission of the AEF," *The Great War Society, http://www.worldwarI.com/dbc/mission.htm*

Herrera, J.E., "Bedroom Habits of the PA Dutch: Better Known as Bundling," *Night Life of the Pennsylvania Dutch*, Gettysburg, Pa: Dutchcraft Company

Heylbut, Rose, "The Basic Purpose of Music Teaching: A conference with Maryla Joan, Sensational Polish Virtuoso," *The Etude*, Feb., 1947, p. 67

Hucho, Christine, "Female Writers, Women's Networks and the Preservation of Culture: The Schwenkfelder Women of Eighteenth Century Pennsylvania," *Philadelphia Center for Early American Studies*, p.h. 68, Jan., 2001, pp 101-130

Hulbert, Ann, "The Prodigy Puzzle," *New York Times*, Nov. 20, 2005

Howe, Michael, J.A., Davidson, J.W., and Sloboda, J.A., "Innate Talents: Reality or Myth," *Behavioural and Brain Sciences*, No. 21, pp. 399-442

In Praise of Pianos and Artists Who Play Them," *Smithsonian Magazine*, March, 2000

Kolb, Robert, "The Formula of Concord and Contemporary Anabaptists, Spiritualists, and Anti-Trinitarians," *Lutheran Quarterly*, Vol. 15, 2001, pp. 450-481

Lee, E. S., "A Theory of Migration," *Demography 3* (I), 1966, pp. 47-57

Light, Nathan, "Overview of Ethnographic Research," *Field Research Project*, 2002, *http://homepages.utoledo.edu/nlight/english/fieldworkprog.htm*

Maazel, Lorin, "Transcript of Conversation Between Loren Maazel and Janos Starker, Parts I and II," *Loren Maazel Website*, Oct and Nov, 2002

McFarlane, Alan, "What Does Descent Mean? What is the Distinction Between Social and Biological Descent,?" *History of the Family: An International Quarterly*

Moulton-Gertig, Suzanne, "The Berlin Hochschule Composers During the Twilight Years of the Weimar Republic and the Advent of the Third Reich," *American Musicological Society Meeting*, Tucson, AZ., 1996

Mundie, James G., "Introduction to Prodigies—Congress of Oddities," *http://www.missioncreep.com/mundie/images/artist.htm*

Pessar, Patricia, "Engendering Migration Studies: The Case of new Immigrants in the United States," *American Behavioral Scientist*, 1999, 42; 577

Peterson, Christopher and Seligman, Martin, "Character Strengths and Virtues: A Handbook and Classification," *American Psychological Association*, Oxford University Press, 2004

Popp, M.D., A. John, *Music, Musicians, and the Brain: An Exploration of Musical Genius*, (2004 Presidential Address, Neurosciences Institute, Albany Medical Center, Albany, New York)

Roedder, Alexandra, "The Violoncello and the Romantic Era: 1820-1920," *Music 199 (Independent Study Program) U C Berkeley*, Fall 2002

Rosenthal, Leon S., "A History of Philadelphia's University City," *West Philadelphia Corporation*, Printing Office of the University of Pennsylvania, 1963

Shanks, David R., "Outstanding Performers: Created, Not Born,?" New Results on Nature vs. Nurture, *Science Spectra*, 1999, No. 18

Sloboda, John, "What Makes A Musician," *EGTA Guitar Journal*, 1994, No. 5, pp. 18-22

"Small Wonders," *Time Asia*, Feb. 17, 2003

"The Big Show: The Meuse-Argonne Offensive: Part I Overview," Doughboy Center, *http://www.worldwarI.com/dbc/bigshow.htm*

Thom, Brian, "Telling Stories: The Life of Chief Richard Malloway—Ethnographic Writing," *Sto':lo Tribal Council*, March, 1994.

Tolan, Stephanie, S., "Diwcoverying the Gifted Ex-Child," *www.stephaniet-olan.com/giftedex-cild.htm*

"Theater Playbills and Programs," *American Memory: Library of Congress*, *http://memory.loc.gov./ammen/vshtml/vsprge.html*

Vinalhaven Island, The Vinalhaven Historical Society, 1979

A Brief Historical Sketch of the Town of Vinalhaven, Rockland, Maine: Fress Press Office, 1889

"Who are the Mennonites," *Third Way Café*, *http://www.thirdway.com/menno/*

Winn, Steven, "For Prodigies, Harsh Reality, Like Genius, Comes Early," *San Francisco Chronicle*, Sed., April 21, 2004

Winner, Ellen, "The Origins and Ends of Giftedness," *American Psychologist*, 2000, 55, 1, pp. 159-169

Winner, Ellen, "Uncommon Talents: Gifted Children, Prodigies and Savants," *Scientific American, Inc.*, 1998

Xiang, Alan, "Opinion: Child Prodigies are People Too," *Daily Illini*, issue date: 9/24/04, Section: Opinions

INDEX